Business Meeting & Event Planning

A Wiley Brand

Business Meeting & Event Planning

by Susan Friedmann, CSP

A Wiley Brand

Business Meeting & Event Planning For Dummies®

Published by: **John Wiley & Sons, Inc.**, 111 River Street, Hoboken, NJ 07030-5774, www.wiley.com

Copyright © 2023 by John Wiley & Sons, Inc., Hoboken, New Jersey

Media and software compilation copyright © 2023 by John Wiley & Sons, Inc. All rights reserved.

Published simultaneously in Canada

For general information on our other products and services, please contact our Customer Care Department within the U.S. at 877-762-2974, outside the U.S. at 317-572-3993, or fax 317-572-4002. For technical support, please visit www.wiley.com/techsupport.

Wiley publishes in a variety of print and electronic formats and by print-on-demand. Some material included with standard print versions of this book may not be included in e-books or in print-on-demand. If this book refers to media such as a CD or DVD that is not included in the version you purchased, you may download this material at http://booksupport.wiley.com. For more information about Wiley products, visit www.wiley.com.

Library of Congress Control Number: 2022949721

ISBN: 978-1-119-98281-4 (pbk); ISBN: 978-1-119-98282-1 (ebk); ISBN: 978-1-119-98283-8 (ebk)

SKY10038932_112822

Contents at a Glance

Introduction 1

Part 1: Been to Any Good Meetings or Events Lately? 5
CHAPTER 1: Gearing Up for Meetings and Events. 7
CHAPTER 2: Strictly Business: Defining Meetings 17
CHAPTER 3: The ABCs of Meeting Preparation 25
CHAPTER 4: Mixing Business with Pleasure: Events 45
CHAPTER 5: Bringing an Event to Life 57

Part 2: It's All Show Business 79
CHAPTER 6: Get Me to the Meeting on Time 81
CHAPTER 7: Food for Thought 93
CHAPTER 8: Selecting Great Speakers. 109
CHAPTER 9: It's the Extras That Count. 123
CHAPTER 10: Lights, Camera, Action!. 129

Part 3: No Guts, No Story 145
CHAPTER 11: Nuts and Bolts: Negotiating, Contracting, and Ensuring Safety 147
CHAPTER 12: Working with Vendors 161
CHAPTER 13: Drinking Champagne on a Beer Budget 171

Part 4: Building Bridges with Technology 185
CHAPTER 14: Making Meeting Technology Work for You 187
CHAPTER 15: This Phone's for You: Conference Calling 197
CHAPTER 16: Holding Meetings Online. 207
CHAPTER 17: Expanding Your Reach with Virtual Events 223

Part 5: Exhibiting at Trade Shows 231
CHAPTER 18: Planning for Gold: Exhibiting 101 233
CHAPTER 19: Strutting Your Stuff: Exhibiting 201 251
CHAPTER 20: Presenting the Floor Show: Exhibiting 301 263

Part 6: The Part of Tens 271

CHAPTER 21: Ten Creative Ways to Meet 273

CHAPTER 22: Ten Common Meeting Mistakes to Avoid. 277

CHAPTER 23: Ten Top Negotiating Tactics 281

CHAPTER 24: Ten Strategies For Exhibiting Overseas. 285

Appendix: Checklist Heaven 291

Index 307

Table of Contents

INTRODUCTION 1
 About This Book. 1
 Foolish Assumptions. 3
 Icons Used in This Book 3
 Beyond the Book 4
 Where to Go from Here 4

**PART 1: BEEN TO ANY GOOD MEETINGS
OR EVENTS LATELY?** 5

CHAPTER 1: **Gearing Up for Meetings and Events** 7
 Being Wise About Holding Meetings 8
  Choosing to hold a meeting or event 9
  Breaking the meeting habit 10
 Focusing on Your Purpose 11
 Figuring Out Who Should Be Involved 11
  Keeping your meetings lean and mean .12
  Identifying your event audience 13
 Knowing How Long a Meeting or Event Should Last 14
 Finding the Right Setting 15
 Getting Help When You Can 15

CHAPTER 2: **Strictly Business: Defining Meetings** 17
 Holding Shareholders Meetings 17
  Inviting the shareholders 18
  Sending out meeting announcements 18
  Understanding the order of business 19
 Gathering the Board of Directors 20
 Getting Away: Corporate Retreats 21
 Setting Up Successful Sales Meetings 22
 Prepping Quickly: Impromptu Meetings 24

CHAPTER 3: **The ABCs of Meeting Preparation** 25
 Identifying the Purpose 26
 Planning the Agenda. 27
 Inviting Attendees 30
  Discovering the right number 30
  Fitting into busy schedules. 31

Assessing Your Needs...32
    Meeting location 32
    Transportation...34
    Specific material and equipment needs......................34
    Refreshments..36
Assisting Guests with Special Needs.............................36
    Accommodating deaf & hard-of-hearing participants..........37
    Accommodating visually-impaired participants 38
    Accommodating mobility-impaired participants 38
Setting the Scene..39
    Seating..39
    Heating and cooling 40
    Room noise and other distractions..........................40
    Lighting...42
    Essential details 43

CHAPTER 4: **Mixing Business with Pleasure: Events**.............45
Heading to a Destination Event..................................46
Connecting with the Media.......................................47
    Before the event 48
    During the event 49
    After the event 49
Honoring Employees..50
Launching a Product...51
    Define your launch strategy and objectives 52
    Decide on a date and location...............................52
    Develop a budget..52
    Put together your "dream team".............................52
    Verify the guest list 52
    Formulate the creative ideas 53
    Make decisions about outside vendors/suppliers 53
    Plan the program..53
    Go over program details with participants 54
    Double-check the details....................................54
    Direct the event 54
    Critique the results 55

CHAPTER 5: **Bringing an Event to Life** 57
Deciding When to Stage Your Event...............................58
Choosing Your Venue...59
    Mapping out a location......................................59
    Looking at some venue options 64
    Visiting venue possibilities 66
Scripting the Event 68

Analyzing Your Audience 70
Creating the Atmosphere. 71
  Planning the entertainment and decorations. 71
  Choosing foods and beverages. 72
Creating a Memorable Theme. 72
  Selecting a theme that fits 72
  Integrating a theme into your event. 73
Entertaining the Groups. 75
  Choosing appropriate entertainment 75
  Hiring the talent. 75

PART 2: IT'S ALL SHOW BUSINESS. 79

CHAPTER 6: Get Me to the Meeting on Time 81
Up, Up, and Away: Air Travel Made Easy 82
  Understanding ticket classes. 82
  Booking airline tickets. 83
Organizing Ground Transportation 85
  Airport shuttles 85
  Chauffeured vehicles 86
  Rental cars 87
Working with a Travel Agent 88
Timing It Right 90
  Considering the time-of-week demand 91
  Reviewing the time-of-year demand. 91

CHAPTER 7: Food for Thought 93
Considering Food and Beverage Concerns 93
  Fitting food into your meeting purpose. 94
  Keeping your budget in mind 94
  Looking over your venue 94
  Understanding your audience. 94
  Timing it right. 95
Exploring Eating Options 96
  Breakfast. 96
  Brunch. 97
  Refreshment breaks 97
  Lunch. 98
  Dinner 98
  Receptions 99
  Parties 99
  Banquets. 99
Serving Drinks at Your Event 100
Working with the Catering Manager. 102

Getting It All in Writing 105
    Guaranteeing guests. 106
    Setting up the room 106

CHAPTER 8: Selecting Great Speakers. 109
Understanding Types of Presentation 110
Selecting Good Speakers 111
    Know the program objectives 111
    Understand audience needs 112
    Check for reputation. 112
    See a demo. 113
    Watch out for celebrity speakers 114
    Be wary of grandiose claims 114
    Provide and ask for good information 115
    Ask for an outline, handouts, and promotional material 116
    Maximize opportunities 116
    Trust your instincts 117
Using Help to Find a Speaker. 117
Understanding Fees 119
Confirming Arrangements in Writing 121

CHAPTER 9: It's the Extras That Count 123
Helping Guests Get a Good Meal 123
Showing Off the Location to Your Guests 125
Putting Sports and Exercise on the Menu .126
Welcoming Spouses and Partners 127

CHAPTER 10: Lights, Camera, Action! 129
Taking Control of Your Environment 129
    Setting up the meeting room. 130
    Planning your seating arrangement. .132
    Setting up a stage 134
Handling Your Audiovisual Needs. 135
    Microphones 135
    Projection screens. 136
    Projectors 138
    Lighting. 139
Exploring Special Presentation Situations .140
    Team presentations 140
    Presentations read from a script 141
    Q & A sessions 142

PART 3: NO GUTS, NO STORY 145

**CHAPTER 11: Nuts and Bolts: Negotiating, Contracting,
and Ensuring Safety** 147

Finding the Best Supplier with RFPs 148
    Determining who gets the RFP 148
    Writing an RFP 148
Negotiating the Deal 152
    Narrowing the list 152
    Playing the negotiating game 153
    Knowing which areas to negotiate 154
    Requesting perks from hotels 155
Signing on the Dotted Line 156
Creating a Safe and Secure Event 158
Liability and Insurance Issues 159

CHAPTER 12: Working with Vendors 161

Teaming Up 162
    Searching for vendors 162
    Conducting interviews 163
    Checking references 163
    Making the relationship work 164
Working with Specific Types of Vendors 165
    Caterers 165
    Florists 167
    Destination management companies 167
    Selecting promotional items 168
    Ground transportation providers 169
    Audiovisual companies 169

CHAPTER 13: Drinking Champagne on a Beer Budget 171

Preparing a Budget 172
    What on earth do I include in the budget? 172
    Categorizing your budget 173
    Keeping costs under control 174
    Looking for help? 175
Making Money 177
Cost-Cutting Tips for the Savvy Planner 179
    Locating a cost-effective meeting site 179
    Getting the details in writing 180
    Keeping program expenses to a minimum 180
    Traveling cheap 181
    Feeding the masses on a budget 182
    Serving alcohol without breaking the bank 182

PART 4: BUILDING BRIDGES WITH TECHNOLOGY 185

CHAPTER 14: **Making Meeting Technology Work for You** 187
Why Go Virtual? 188
Exploring What's Available 188
Conference calling 188
Video conferencing 189
Online conferencing 189
Other cool stuff 190
Selecting the Right Meeting Alternative 194

CHAPTER 15: **This Phone's for You: Conference Calling** 197
Exploring Service Options 199
Dial-in 199
Dial-out 199
Operator-assisted 200
Lecture/broadcast 200
Question-and-answer 200
Subconferencing 200
Polling 201
Secured line 201
Recording/rebroadcast 201
Tips for a Successful Conference Call 202
Preparing for the call 202
Running the meeting 203
Soliciting feedback 204
Minding Your Manners: Conference Calling Etiquette 205

CHAPTER 16: **Holding Meetings Online** 207
The Pros and Cons of Meeting Online 208
Considering the positives 208
Weighing the negatives 209
Determining Your Needs 209
Choosing the Right Format 210
Staging a Successful Videoconference .212
Early planning 212
Final preparations 213
Springing into Action 214
Creating your presentation 214
Staying out of trouble 215
Connecting with speed 215
Preparing the room 216
Running the meeting 217
Planning for disaster 219
Special Considerations for Webinars 220
Running Hybrid Meetings 222

CHAPTER 17: **Expanding Your Reach with Virtual Events** 223
    Understanding Virtual Events 224
    Types of Virtual Events 225
        Video calls. 225
        Video conferences. 225
        Webinar/online conferences 225
        Hybrid conferences. 226
    Doing it Yourself or Getting it Done for You 226
    Making Your Event Run Well 227
        Understanding the features of virtual event platforms. 228
        Fine-tuning the details 228
        Enjoying the benefits 229

PART 5: EXHIBITING AT TRADE SHOWS .231

CHAPTER 18: **Planning for Gold: Exhibiting 101** 233
    Planning a Successful Exhibit. 234
        Choosing the right show. 234
        Having a proper exhibit marketing plan 235
        Reading the exhibition bible 238
        Determining your space and display needs 239
        Concerning yourself with details. 241
    Promoting Your Exhibit 242
        Defining your promotional plan 243
        Creating a memorable message 244
        Choosing your promotional tools carefully. 244
        Using giveaways effectively 248
        Selecting marketing collateral 248

CHAPTER 19: **Strutting Your Stuff: Exhibiting 201** 251
    Counting on People for Exhibit Success. 251
        Selecting the right team 252
        Preparing your team for the job 253
        Creating a strong presence at the show 254
        Keeping your exhibit staff motivated 256
    Ensuring a Productive Exhibit 258
        Making your show leads pay off 258
        Developing a follow-up system 259
    Measuring Results. 261
        Evaluating your efforts 261
        Rating your performance 261

CHAPTER 20: Presenting the Floor Show: Exhibiting 301 263

Honing in on Leads 263
Giving Visitors a Touch of Show Biz 264
Feed Them and They Will Come: Using Hospitality Suites 265
  Managing the logistics 265
  Staffing your hospitality suite 266
Getting into Uniform 267
Dealing with Snoops 267
Outfoxing the Competition 268
  Researching general information 268
  Finding product and service information.................269
  Gathering sales and marketing information 269
  Compiling customer information 270

PART 6: THE PART OF TENS................................271

CHAPTER 21: Ten Creative Ways to Meet 273

Being a Sport 273
Starting a Thread..274
Getting on the Phone 274
Making It a Game...274
Recording a Message 274
Sharing the Knowledge......................................275
Writing an E-Mail 275
Tapping Productivity Apps 275
Whiteboard Brain Storm 275
Sending out a Survey 276

CHAPTER 22: Ten Common Meeting Mistakes to Avoid 277

Forgetting to Check Dates 277
Booking a Site Before Making a Visit 278
Failing to Market Your Event 278
Signing Contracts That Lack Specifics......................278
Failing to Plan..278
Neglecting to Check References 279
Leaving Important Details to the Last Minute...............279
Letting Someone Else Do the Planning 279
Neglecting Contingencies...................................280
Trying to Save Money 280

CHAPTER 23: Ten Top Negotiating Tactics 281

Knowing What You Want 281
Doing Your Research..282
Rehearsing Your Opening 282

Asking Powerful Questions 282
Becoming an Information Monger 282
Being a Champion Listener 283
Creating a Positive Mood 283
Being Prepared to Walk Away 283
Knowing Negotiating Styles 284
Exercising Silence 284

CHAPTER 24: **Ten Strategies For Exhibiting Overseas**. 285
Doing Your Homework. 285
Starting Early 286
Budgeting Carefully. 286
Designing Your Overseas Exhibit Space. 286
Constructing Your Exhibit. 287
Dealing with Customs Issues. 287
Providing Hospitality. 288
Exhibiting Sensitivity to the Host Culture. 288
Using Native Speakers for Translations. 288
Being Patient 289

APPENDIX: CHECKLIST HEAVEN 291
INDEX. 307

Introduction

The business meetings and events industry, like so many other industries, has experienced major changes in recent times. The technology revolution has made it possible to come together virtually or in a hybrid event (with attendees present in-person and virtually), to become more inclusive, get more bang for your buck, and be more efficient with participants' time. Meeting and event planners have had to reexamine what they do and how they do it. The need to hold meetings and events remains strong, because getting together with other people continues to be an effective way to accomplish goals and exchange ideas. But the way meetings and events take place is constantly changing.

This book explores how to hold meetings and events in-person, virtually, and as a hybrid of both, to meet the needs of your audience. Let it be your guide to mastering successful strategies and tactics, as well as your source for insider secrets from the pros. Savvy meeting leaders and event planners recognize that every meeting or event they arrange will be different. They also know the importance of constantly staying abreast of new and emerging trends, in addition to fully understanding the ongoing wants and needs of their participants.

About This Book

This book is truly a how-to manual for planning and conducting all types of business meetings and events. It is a down-to-earth, step-by-step guide that takes the mystery out of the planning process. It covers all the vital ingredients needed for success. It takes you through the complex labyrinth of what seems like an endless stream of details in as simple and practical a format as possible. The book is packed full of hot tips, techniques, suggestions, and gems of wisdom for making each event a winner. My aim is to hear you say, after each chapter you read, "That's easy. I can do that!"

The key to success in business meeting and event planning is being organized and detail-oriented. During the planning process, you encounter a countless number of specifics that demand your constant attention, and this book helps you stay on top of each one. It contains tons of practical advice for getting through the challenges you might face. It also shows you how to skillfully put together a well-designed and flawlessly orchestrated program, even on a shoestring budget, that will earn glowing reviews and make your boss proud . . . even if you are the boss!

I've organized the contents into distinct parts, and the chapters within each part cover specific topic areas in detail. Here's what you'll find and where you'll find it:

>> **Part 1: Been to Any Good Meetings or Events Lately?** In this part, I explore the vital components needed to manage an effective business meeting or event, together with the essential questions to ask before getting started. You find out about many different kinds of business meetings and events, including their design format and major characteristics. I guide you through the ABCs of meeting and event preparation by outlining, in Chapter 3, the necessary components for preparing a small business meeting so that it accomplishes the planned objectives, and then devoting Chapter 5 to planning larger events.

>> **Part 2: It's All Show Business.** This part covers everything you need to know to develop a business meeting or event that will earn you rave reviews. There's a lot of nitty-gritty detail, but it's all stuff you must know. You get the essential behind-the-scenes elements for your event planning, plus I highlight various ancillary meeting considerations. You discover the ins and outs of being an astute travel organizer so that you have happy participants arriving at your meeting or event. Possibly the best part of this section is the chapter that focuses on the basics of food and beverage planning and management. (Remember that the way to a participant's heart is through their stomach.) I also address the importance of booking good speakers and presenters. It provides guidelines to avoid hiring duds, in addition to giving you information on room layouts and the technology that ensure a high-impact presentation.

>> **Part 3: No Guts, No Story.** This part comes with a "not-to-be-missed" sticker — especially the first chapter, which deals with understanding the fine points of contract negotiations. Master these successfully, and you've completed a major portion of the meetings and events formula. In addition, this part helps you grasp some essential information on safety and security concerns and liability and insurance issues. With so many details to take care of, you often want some helping hands, so I dedicate a chapter to helping you find the right vendor to get the job done. However, you won't manage anything without a realistic budget. I worked hard to make this as easy and palatable as possible, giving you detailed information on preparing a budget and loads of cost-cutting tips to help you get more for less.

>> **Part 4: Building Bridges with Technology.** The title of this part says it all. The chapters in this part explain in simple terms many of the modern meeting alternatives, including conference calling, videoconferencing, webcasting, and other cool stuff. I take the mystery out of each option and outline the major pros and cons. In addition, you discover plenty of hot success strategy tips and techniques.

>> **Part 5: Exhibiting at Trade Shows.** This part takes you into the world of exhibiting at trade shows. It's highly comprehensive, giving you the must-knows

about preshow, at-show, and postshow activities. You find out how to develop strategies that help you maximize exhibiting as a powerful marketing tool.

>> **Part 6: The Part of Tens.** This part is made up of short chapters that highlight some of the basic themes that run through meeting and event planning. The chapters in this part examine meeting alternatives, offer tips on avoiding common meeting mistakes, and help you master negotiating tactics — all essential to becoming a super-successful meeting and event planner.

Finally, because I provide specific, detailed techniques and a blueprint for organizing your meetings and events that's as easy as 1–2–3, I've created several checklists to help you remember all the necessary details; you can find them in the book's appendix.

Foolish Assumptions

I've made a few assumptions about you as a reader, based on why you might have picked this book up and started reading it. Many people within a company or organization may find themselves responsible for planning one or many meetings and events, both large and small.

Generally speaking, if you're an executive assistant, marketing communications specialist, public relations expert, solopreneur, or (of course) meeting and event planner, this book is most definitely for you. Or perhaps you are looking to use meetings and events to build your company image, bring people together to collaborate, or to educate them on new concepts, products, or services. This book will guide you through the process. Or you are already familiar with setting up live meetings and events but you want to explore the best practices for virtual and hybrid meetings, then this book is also for you! Business meetings and events are valuable tools for connecting with customers. For those looking to jump into the event planning industry, this book will help guide you to success.

Icons Used in This Book

For Dummies books use little pictures, called icons, to mark certain chunks of text that I'd like to call to your attention when you're reading through the chapters. Keep your eyes peeled for them, as this is what they mean:

REMEMBER

This icon marks the information you don't want to forget.

TIP

This icon points to the tips I share that are based on my years of meeting and event planning. This way, you can learn from my experience to make your meeting or event run smoothly — while saving money and time, too.

TECHNICAL STUFF

Occasionally, I talk about matters that are a bit technical in nature. This icon lets you know that you can skip the information if you want only the basics.

WARNING

This icon indicates an area of concern or offers a tip on how to avoid trouble.

Beyond the Book

In addition to the abundance of information and guidance related to business meetings and events planning that I provide in this book, you get access to even more help and information online at Dummies.com. Check out this book's online Cheat Sheet. Just go to www.dummies.com and search for "Business Meeting & Event Planning For Dummies Cheat Sheet."

Where to Go from Here

If you are new to this "meetings and events" thing, you may decide to start at the beginning and keep reading and flipping the pages until you reach the back cover, reading all of the chapters in the sequence presented!

If you are looking to improve the knowledge and experience you already have, you may only need a bit more insight here and there. For example, if you're interested in hybrid meetings, flick through to Chapter 16. Or if trade show success is something you've always wanted to find out more about check out Part 5. And if you're looking for an overview of business meetings and events planning, get started with Chapter 1.

If you want to digest the entire book in chronological order, go for it. If you want to dip in and out of chapters, based upon what you need to know, that works too. Each section stands alone, but I'll let you know if you are reading a section on a topic which is discussed in more detail elsewhere in the book.

1

Been to Any Good Meetings or Events Lately?

An ancient Chinese proverb states that the journey of a thousand miles begins with the first step. In this part, you take your first step into an exciting, multifaceted arena.

Right from the get-go, you find out about the vital components needed to manage an effective business meeting or event and the essential questions to ask before you even get started. You discover that there are many different kinds of business meetings and events and you see what makes one different from another.

When you're ready to get down to the business of planning, I give you the building blocks to put together a small business meeting as well as a larger event. I highlight the must-knows so that your meeting or event achieves its planned objectives and you come out smelling like a rose.

Chapter 1

Gearing Up for Meetings and Events

Business meetings and events can be a total waste of time, or they can be powerful and productive communication tools that solve problems, stimulate ideas, promote team spirit, and generate action. The end results lie totally in how they're run. People expect efficiency when they are called to a meeting or when they are participating in a multi-session event. They want to get back to their "real" work as quickly as possible, yet come away from the meeting or event feeling that they made solid connections, were heard, or learned something useful.

Having experienced the wonderful sense of satisfaction from productive sessions, as well as the frustration and anger from ineffective sessions, I believe the key to success lies in preparation and organization, as well as the actual meeting management. In this chapter, I encourage you to make thoughtful choices about when to hold meetings and events, and when to use other means to accomplish your goals. I also begin to lay the groundwork for making your business functions — from small meetings to trade fairs — productive and fun.

REMEMBER

All meetings are events, but not all events are meetings! *Meetings* are focused on a deep-dive with a very specific audience and fall into one of four categories:

>> Decision making (to collaborate and align)

>> Innovating (to collaborate and ideate)

>> Selling (to educate a customer)

>> Training (to teach and learn)

An *event* has many of these functions plus, it may also include a celebratory component to acknowledge an achievement or support a cause.

Being Wise About Holding Meetings

Are meetings really necessary? Well, sometimes they are, and sometimes they aren't. Wisdom lies in knowing the difference.

Humans need a connection with others to survive. I'm sure that, like me, you may occasionally fantasize about being alone on a desert island, far away from the trials and tribulations of everyday life. But people also need to belong, communicate, and share a common purpose with like-minded individuals. In essence, what this means is simply that meeting is a natural function of our existence. In reality, doing things alone for any length of time is counterproductive. Working in partnership with others and pooling resources can lead to getting things done more effectively and efficiently.

People need to come together to share information, make decisions, plan, discuss, argue, question, iron out differences, celebrate, gossip, chitchat, schmooze, and much more. Families, schools, clubs, businesses, and governments are key examples of groups of men, women, and children who regularly come together for specific purposes.

These days, with the plethora of entrepreneurs operating home-based businesses and employees telecommuting or working endless hours in front of computer screens, meetings are becoming even more necessary for people's survival. The need for human interaction is critical. In addition, meetings can minimize or eliminate many time-wasting activities such as playing phone tag, sending unnecessary e-mails, or exchanging volumes of paper. But, when you consider the myriad business meetings held every year, many should never (ever) take place. The $1,000,000 question is "When should you hold a meeting or organize an event (and when should you not)?"

Choosing to hold a meeting or event

Deciding to hold a meeting or event demands serious consideration because of the many costs involved. Direct costs include travel, food, facility rental, and possibly lodging. Indirect costs include people's time and lost productivity. (I cover costs in more detail in Chapter 14.)

REMEMBER

Your time and fiscal budget can be extended by opting for virtual or hybrid meetings. A virtual meeting means that you'll incur no travel, food, or lodging expenses, while a hybrid meeting allows more people to attend who may not need to participate a full three-day event, but would like to participate in special training or breakout sessions.

People today suffer from *time poverty* — they don't have enough time to do all the things they want and need to do. Based on this realization, the first thing the person responsible for holding a meeting or event has to determine is how necessary it is to meet. Use the following list to double-check your rationale for holding a business meeting or event. Good reasons for getting a group of people together include:

>> To communicate or request vital information

>> To achieve a group consensus

>> To respond to questions or concerns

>> To decide on or evaluate an issue

>> To gain acceptance or support of an idea

>> To create awareness of or to sell an idea, product, or service

>> To brainstorm ideas

>> To solve a problem, conflict, or difference of opinion

>> To generate a sense of team spirit

>> To provide training or clarification of a project

>> To provide reassurance on an issue or situation

>> To give new information about your product or company

>> To bring people together outside the normal office environment

>> To launch or introduce a new product/service

>> To offer training opportunities

>> To obtain media exposure

Breaking the meeting habit

Meetings can easily become addictive, but meeting for the sake of meeting is not a productive use of time. Prioritization is key. You must decide whether a potential meeting is a must-do, a should-do, or a nice-to-do — eeny meeny miney mo. If any of the following apply to your situation, it's time to consider an alternative to meeting (for some suggestions on alternatives, see Chapter 21):

>> Meeting for the sake of meeting — same time, same place, every week

>> Meeting when the information could be communicated another way

>> Meeting when key people are unavailable

>> Meeting when participants don't have time to prepare

>> Meeting when the costs (both direct and indirect) are greater than the benefits

>> Meeting when other issues blur the issue at hand

>> Meeting when nothing would be gained or lost by not having a meeting

Focusing on Your Purpose

The adage "if you don't know where you're going, any road will take you there" directly applies to knowing the purpose of your business meeting or event. Naturally, meetings and events can be held for myriad reasons. The key to success is to be crystal clear about your purpose, aim, and end result. Clarify in your own mind the acceptable outcomes. After you have determined acceptable outcomes, your job is to communicate them to the people you want to attend.

REMEMBER

People hate being invited to a meeting and not knowing what will be discussed — that's a sure way to start the rumor mill working overtime, cause paranoia to set in, and give people a reason to start assuming the worst. And if your target audience doesn't know the purpose of your event, you can be certain they won't be attending. To make sure that these scenarios don't occur, you must determine your justification and motivation for holding a meeting or event. Ask yourself three essential questions:

>> What do you expect to accomplish?

>> What do you want participants to do, think, or feel as a result of the meeting or event?

>> What must you do if the meeting or event doesn't accomplish your goals?

The third question is a safety net that forces you to think about a contingency plan. For example, just in case participants don't see eye to eye when resolving issues or generating new ideas to move a project along, having a prudent follow-up strategy can give you enormous peace of mind. As you know, even the best-laid plans can often go astray.

Figuring Out Who Should Be Involved

Before you decide who to invite to any meeting or event, revisit your purpose and analyze who would be the very best people to help you achieve it. Don't fall into the trap of inviting people just because you don't want to hurt their feelings or because it's the politically correct thing to do. (For more on identifying meeting participants, see Chapter 3.)

Keeping your meetings lean and mean

TIP

For the sake of efficiency and productivity, the fewer people involved in a business meeting, the better. Keeping attendance to a minimum enables you to keep the discussion as focused as a laser and get done what needs to get done. Decide on the optimum number of people necessary to give you the result you want. Research indicates that a group of ten is a recommended size for general discussion. However, for making decisions and generating ideas, five to eight is considered optimum.

As you think through your invitation list, remember that certain people must attend, such as those who can help achieve your outcome or who play an important influencing role. Add to that the people with specific expertise who could improve the decision-making process. Also consider including anyone who may be directly affected by decisions made. And finally, you can't go wrong by including a good problem solver or idea generator.

If the purpose of the meeting is simply to impart one-way information to a large group, then naturally everyone should be invited. But bear in mind that a meeting's productivity is inversely proportional to the number of people attending. According to research, when more than five people attend, the meeting's productivity goes down exponentially.

TIP

Think twice about inviting those wonderful people who have a volatile or dysfunctional personality or have a reputation for any kind of disruptive behavior at meetings. Also avoid the naysayers. You're looking for positive, constructive discussions rather than negative, destructive ones.

TIP

SUSAN'S SIMPLE THREE-STEP SYSTEM

Before you devise your invitation list, try the following three-step system for creating a lean and mean list for optimal meeting productivity:

1. List everyone and anyone you think you should invite.

2. Go through each name and ask yourself two questions: "What will/can this person contribute to the meeting?" and "What would happen if they didn't attend?"

3. Cut your list in half.

Alternatively, try this scenario: If you could invite only three people to your meeting, who would they be? Having this answer in mind would certainly streamline your planning!

PERFECT TIMING

Because the timing of your meeting or event is often the key to its success, I have developed the following ideal meeting time formula:

Meeting goals + people availability + length of meeting + facility convenience and availability = ideal meeting time

Use this simple formula, and you should get a perfect answer every time.

Here's an example: You've onboarded a new advertising client and your goal is to have key team members fully aware of the project and its deadlines. You identify the people who are involved: copywriter, graphic designer, printer, and traffic manager. You determine that you need ten minutes after your morning all-hands meeting to quickly review the project and get everyone committed:

- Goal: Committing to new project deadline

- Team lead's availability: After all-hands meeting

- Length of meeting: Ten minutes

- Facility: Conference room

- Ideal Meeting Time: After all-hands meeting

Identifying your event audience

Know your event objectives, and you'll know who belongs on the invitation list. A few guidelines to think about include the following:

» Consider who has a vested interest in the company, the product, or the event itself. Potential persons include stockholders, upper management, local dignitaries, key employees and their families, customers, and vendors.

» Think about who made the event possible, such as sponsors and community leaders.

» Whenever possible, try to build good relationships with the local media — print, radio, and TV — and include them on your invitation list.

» Take advantage of all available social media platforms before, during, and after your meeting to promote and share the outcome, if appropriate for your audience.

Knowing How Long a Meeting or Event Should Last

You may think that shorter meetings are more productive than longer ones. However, research illustrates that longer meetings (especially those that last longer than five hours) are likely to be more productive than shorter meetings.

This doesn't mean that you have to turn all your one-hour meetings into five-hour marathons, but you may want to look into having one long meeting every quarter, for example, rather than holding short weekly or monthly meetings. The end result may increase productivity dramatically.

In the meantime, for those of you who are addicted to the daily, weekly, or monthly must-have meetings, remember to keep them short, sweet, and to the point.

When it comes to events, keep in mind that no one wants to stay longer than they have to. Meticulously plan the necessary activities that make up your event. Encourage your speakers to keep their remarks short and on topic while still accomplishing the event's goals. There's nothing worse than someone in love with their own voice droning on unnecessarily.

THE LONG AND SHORT OF IT: MEETING LENGTH GAUGE

The following meeting length gauge will help determine how best to break up your meeting to maximize effectiveness.

- 30 minutes: Tolerable
- 60 minutes: Restlessness starts setting in
- 90 minutes: Intolerable danger zone (people need to get up and stretch, take a bathroom break, and have something to eat or drink)

Don't even think about going longer than 90 minutes without having a 5- to 15-minute break.

Studies have shown that the average adult can pay attention in a meeting for approximately 20 minutes before starting to daydream, doodle, or fidget. If you include any kind of presentation, change what you're doing every 8 minutes. For example, switch from an LCD projector to a flip chart or whiteboard.

Finding the Right Setting

The meeting or event location can help make or break your success. The location sets the stage and creates the right environment for the action to happen. Budget, of course, plays a major role. Using your own internal conference room saves money, but is it the right place to meet? Think about a place that minimizes disturbances, offers comfort and convenience, meets your equipment and space needs, and projects the right image. I cover large and small meeting room layouts in Chapter 10.

You also have the choice of going the social route by using breakfast, lunch, or dinner as a meeting time. If building and nurturing relationships is your goal, consider doing business over a shared meal.

For larger events, match the meeting to the facility. Consider using a corporate conference center or a secluded resort for training sessions, and many large hotels are equipped for conferences. I discuss venue options in detail in Chapter 5.

Getting Help When You Can

Meeting and event planning is like putting together a jigsaw puzzle: Hundreds of pieces need to fit together for the picture to evolve. The planner or person overseeing the project has multiple responsibilities for the planning, preparation, development, and execution of an event.

TIP

The key to success is really knowing your strengths and also knowing what someone else can do best — in other words, what should be handled internally and what should be contracted to outside experts. Recognize your limitations and seek appropriate help where you can. Depending on your budget, you can outsource many tasks, or maybe you can count on some hidden talent within the four walls of your company. Put on your Sherlock Holmes garb and investigate what gems lie in your own backyard! I give you a more comprehensive understanding of outsourcing in Chapter 12.

IN THIS CHAPTER

» Finding out how to run a
shareholder's meeting

» Bringing board members together

» Having fun with corporate retreats

» Putting together a sales meeting

» Getting together unexpectedly

Chapter 2

Strictly Business: Defining Meetings

The dictionary defines a meeting as "a coming together of persons or things." In this chapter, I add some specifics to the dictionary definition by taking a look at the characteristics of several different types of corporate business meetings. This chapter shows you what a shareholders meeting is, as well as a board meeting, corporate retreat, sales conference, and more.

This chapter is a lexicon of meeting types. It provides you with the definitions of specialized meetings that you may be asked to plan. Because the basics of meeting planning hold true for each type of meeting discussed, the tips, advice, and instructions throughout this book will help you when planning all of them. The information in later chapters is relevant to board meetings and corporate retreats, to sales meetings and shareholders meetings, and so on.

Holding Shareholders Meetings

Corporations convene a meeting of their directors and shareholders yearly to elect a board of directors for the upcoming term, to review the company's progress during the previous year, and to discuss its direction for the future. This meeting, often called an *Annual General Meeting*, also offers individual shareholders a forum to raise important questions or concerns.

Special shareholders meetings can also be called whenever the chairperson or vice-chairperson of the board of directors, a consensus of the majority of the board of directors, or a group of shareholders who together hold at least 10 percent of the total number of company shares decides that another meeting is necessary. These groups often assemble the special meetings, sometimes called *Extraordinary General Meetings*, when they need shareholder approval for a particular action or transaction to proceed.

The specifics governing shareholders meetings vary from state to state and from company to company. The following guidelines provide only a brief overview of a typical shareholders meeting and are by no means all-inclusive. For important details, consult state and federal law, as well as your corporate bylaws.

Inviting the shareholders

When making a guest list for a company's shareholders meeting, you must include all individuals shown to be holding shares in the company on a specific date. For the business conducted at a shareholders meeting to be valid, the individuals in attendance must hold a majority of the outstanding shares of stock in the company. The technical term for this minimum attendance requirement is a *quorum*.

TECHNICAL STUFF

An important exception to the quorum rule exists. Through the use of proxies, a shareholders meeting can be valid even if a quorum isn't physically present. When a shareholder attends by proxy, they fill out and sign a form that allows a designated attendee who *will* be at the meeting to act and vote in their place. Thus, a quorum can be composed of both those who are physically present at the meeting and those who have returned proxy forms instead of attending.

Proxy forms are often enclosed with the letter notifying shareholders of an upcoming meeting. Shareholders fill out the required information, sign the form, and send it back. For sample proxy forms, and for more information on proxies in general, you may want to look online. Helpful sites to check out include Rocketlawyer (https://www.rocketlawyer.com) and the U.S. Securities and Exchange Commission (https://www.sec.gov/forms).

Sending out meeting announcements

You must send a written notice announcing an impending meeting to all shareholders. Depending on the organization's bylaws, the notice may be sent by hard copy mail or digitally. The notice should contain the meeting date, time, location, and topics of discussion. (See Chapter 3 for more on developing an agenda and topics of discussion for your meeting.) Mail the announcement between ten days and two months prior to the meeting (once again, according to the bylaws), except for a special meeting that may come up at the last minute.

You should follow up to ensure your shareholders have received the announcement and to confirm their participation.

If your company publishes an annual report, be sure to include a copy along with the notice of the meeting, so that the recipients can review it before attending.

Understanding the order of business

At a typical shareholders meeting, a written agenda and description of the rules governing the meeting are distributed to attendees as they arrive. At the appointed time, the meeting is called to order. The chairperson of the meeting then introduces themselves and gives a brief welcome speech. They also verbally remind the audience of the rules to follow. (See the "Rules of Order" sidebar in this chapter for a sample of rules often used.)

Although the order of events can vary from meeting to meeting, the next order of business is often the election of a board of directors for the upcoming term. (Note: It is advisable to resolve that the terms of office for the newly elected board members begin at the *close* of the event, so that the same officers will serve throughout the meeting.)

RULES OF ORDER

To maintain order in a shareholders meeting, the meeting leaders often impose the following rules:

- Shareholders may address the meeting only during specified discussion periods.

- The chairperson must recognize a shareholder before they can address the meeting.

- The shareholder may speak for a predetermined length of time.

- Questions and comments raised by shareholders must be of concern to all shareholders — matters of individual concern can be discussed with company representatives after the meeting.

The gold standard for maintaining order in a meeting of any group is *Robert's Rules of Order* by Henry M. Robert (PublicAffairs/Hachette, 2020).

After nominees for the board are introduced and an election is held, the chairperson of the meeting or a senior officer in the company gives a state-of-the-business address, and the company's annual report is discussed. This is followed by questions and general discussion from the shareholders. When all business has been completed and the discussion period is over, the meeting is adjourned.

Gathering the Board of Directors

A company holds its annual board of directors meeting soon after the annual meeting of its shareholders. This regularly scheduled meeting allows the board members to elect officers, to form committees, and to begin considering any business they must address. Additional board meetings are scheduled at regular intervals throughout the year, and special board meetings can be held at any time the need arises.

At regularly scheduled board meetings, the agenda is relatively standard. After the meeting is called to order, the secretary reads the minutes from the previous meeting, and the board approves them. The group then hears reports from various officers and committees, and the board holds votes on any actions they propose.

Following the reports, the group discusses any old business that needs to be resolved, and members may propose new business. The board then allows a time for general announcements, a review of the actions decided on during the meeting, and adjournment.

If your directors are geographically separated and you anticipate that they will need to meet frequently, you may consider conference calls, videoconferencing, or online-conferencing as alternatives to traditional meetings. These technologies cut down on travel time and cost, and they can be used to facilitate spur-of-the-moment meetings to address hot topics or to perform crisis management. See Part 4 of this book for more information on these options.

TIP

What do you do when faced with a roomful of people milling about and talking loudly before your meeting? When this happens, restrain the impulse to yell and repeatedly bang your gavel; instead set an example by standing still and silent at the front of the room. Your audience will eventually take the hint.

Getting Away: Corporate Retreats

Some meetings take place outside the office environment because of the great team-building potential offered by this change of scenery.

Corporate retreats are often destination events, where select individuals are chosen to spend anywhere from a few hours to several days together in a location far removed from the trials and tribulations of the office. Attendees might include groups of executives, directors, managers, employees working together on a project — just about anyone who may benefit from increased communication and camaraderie.

These retreats frequently provide unique, revitalizing learning opportunities for participants to increase performance and communication and develop skills to enhance productivity and creativity. Although you can certainly plan a corporate retreat on your own, several service providers specialize in this type of event. Most often, they offer custom-designed programs that fit the specific needs of the company and/or attendees. Depending on its purpose, your retreat can address any number of different topics such as team building, conflict management, leadership development skills, effective communication training, personal growth, and much more. The formal business that needs to take place at a corporate retreat follows a similar format to that discussed in the previous section on board meetings.

Because corporate retreats often involve transporting your attendees to a removed location, take a look at Chapter 6 for more information and advice on arranging travel.

IS IT A SESSION OR A CONFERENCE? CLARIFYING TERMINOLOGY

Many different types of meetings and events exist, which can vary by function and participants. Here are some definitions of various types of gatherings:

- A *session* and *meeting* differ by definition. Whereas a *meeting* is a gathering of individuals who meet for an uninterrupted period of time, a *session* is a series of meetings that can last for days, or even months (for example, a session of Congress). A session typically requires a formal adjournment to end, but a meeting ends when participants part company.

- The *general session* or *plenary session* of a conference is one that *all* conference participants attend. A keynote speaker or other major presenter usually addresses the whole group at these main gatherings.

(continued)

(continued)

- A *concurrent session* or *breakout session* of a conference is a subsession designed to focus on the individual interests of smaller groups of participants.

- *Public meetings* are called by local governments, companies, and organizations that want to share information with the general public. These meetings usually address only one topic of concern and are publicized in community papers, on social media, and at venues where local residents congregate.

- A *conference* is a series of speeches and presentations centered around one main theme. Conferences usually involve an extremely large number of attendees, so audience participation generally isn't practical (unless it's in the form of workshops or other small group discussions).

- Smaller and more interactive than a conference, a *seminar* is designed to transmit information to attendees and to stimulate and accommodate conversation on the topic being addressed.

- A *product launch* is used to present and market a new product. To organize a successful product launch, you should first determine specific goals for the event, and then be obsessively organized in your planning. Make sure that you invite the right people and that the image of both the company and the product you present to them is polished. This point is particularly important when you include people from outside your business.

- A *workshop* provides attendees with an opportunity to practically apply knowledge they've been given. A successful workshop educates attendees and provides them an opportunity to practice and improve their skills.

- *Incentive events* possess a two-fold purpose: to reward and to motivate. Individuals who have done well in their positions are invited to these highly enjoyable events, and others who haven't earned the right to attend are inspired to work harder and do better so that they can attend the next one. Incentive events can take the form of anything from an ice-cream social to an elaborate destination event, depending on your budget.

Setting Up Successful Sales Meetings

The term "sales meeting" is a bit misleading. This single label actually refers to an assortment of meetings in different shapes and sizes, all involving a company's sales force. From massive gatherings of sales representatives from around the world, to weekly meetings of local salespeople, to one-on-one planning or brainstorming meetings between supervisors and their subordinates, sales meetings can take on many forms.

The key factor in planning a successful sales meeting is understanding its goal or purpose. A sales meeting can have any one of many different objectives. The meeting may be an opportunity for management to communicate information to its sales force or for sales representatives to share knowledge and suggestions among themselves. The meeting may be intended to motivate attendees and to increase their enthusiasm for their jobs, thus increasing their productivity. See Chapter 3 for more on using the purpose of your meeting to guide your planning.

Different types of sales meetings will have a unique impact on your work as a planner. Although a motivational meeting may be full of entertainment and energy, calling for ingenuity and creativity in its planning, other meetings may be more somber, formal, and traditional. Work with the individuals who initiate the meeting to gain an understanding of what they hope to accomplish with it. This understanding of purpose will give you a better handle on the type of meeting you're expected to plan.

REMEMBER

Because sales meetings often have a direct impact on revenue, they are extremely important to a company's health!

VOTES AND ELECTIONS

When the time comes to hold a vote or an election, you can choose from the following methods:

- *Show of hands.* In small meetings, votes are often held by a show of hands. The chair of the meeting first asks for those in favor of the proposal to raise their hands, then those opposed. The chair counts and records the votes.

- *Viva voce,* or "by the voice." Participants indicate their votes by vocally stating *"yea"* or *"nay"* when their names are called from a roster. The chair repeats each vote out loud, and it is recorded. This is the type of vote held in the U.S. Congress and most other legislative bodies.

- *Balloting.* This type of vote is the most private and secretive and is often used to ensure that participants who might be intimidated by public scrutiny vote in line with their true sentiments. Tellers distribute small slips of paper, and voters write either *yes* or *no* on these ballots and return them to the teller, often by depositing them in a box or other receptacle the teller is holding. When everyone appears to have voted, the chair asks if everyone who wishes to vote has done so. If no one still needs to vote, the chair announces the polls closed, and the tellers proceed to count the ballots.

- *Digital Balloting.* Each participant downloads an app to their mobile device or computer to digitally transmit their ballot to the teller. The vote is private and tallied immediately, making it an efficient voting process.

Prepping Quickly: Impromptu Meetings

Spur-of-the-moment meetings can — and do — occur regularly in today's fast-paced corporate environment. Co-workers bump into each other in the hallway or cafeteria and start a conversation, and the next thing you know one of them says, "We should discuss this in more detail. Meet me in the boardroom (or on a video call) in 20 minutes."

When this situation occurs, you can do three main things to improve your chances of having a successful impromptu meeting:

>> Develop a quick list of topics to be addressed at the impromptu meeting. This step ensures that all topics are covered and begins to give form to what could otherwise be a disorganized exchange of ideas and information. It will also speed the meeting along.

>> Whenever possible, keep impromptu meetings short, sweet, and most of all, focused. By their very spontaneous nature, they are likely an interruption of the participants' previously planned day, so do your best to minimize the inconvenience.

>> If the meeting begins to become overly complicated or too long, consider ending it and rescheduling a formal meeting as soon as possible. You will allow participants to gather their thoughts and prepare any information or material that wasn't available when the impromptu meeting popped up.

Chapter **3**

The ABCs of Meeting Preparation

Mention the word "meeting," and chances are you receive an onslaught of negatives, many of which I wouldn't dream of putting into print. Suffice it to say that meetings aren't on the top of everyone's hit parade. Why? Because historically, meetings have been plagued with sloppy planning, weak agendas, and nebulous expectations. But there are many practical and beneficial reasons to hold meetings, such as when you need a group consensus on a project, or when you need to brainstorm ideas.

This chapter focuses on the necessary components for preparing a small business meeting that can be held in-person, virtually, or as a hybrid of the two, so that it accomplishes the planned objectives. For that to happen, every detail of your meeting needs consideration. Everything you do helps lay the groundwork and sets the scene. Even though, as the planner, you may not actually participate in the meeting, what you do behind the scenes is critical to the meeting's success. And the smoother things run, the more credit you can take for your meticulous planning.

You may be asked to organize small meetings with very little notice. (Sales managers are notorious for calling last-minute get-togethers and expecting you to pull miracles out of a hat.) You'll be the hero if you adopt a be-prepared attitude.

TIP

As soon as you can, start to build a comprehensive resource file identifying all the various components you need to pull a small meeting together (such as site checklists, suppliers and services, food and beverage checklists, and technical needs).

The sections that follow focus on what actually goes into your planning.

Identifying the Purpose

Knowing the purpose of your meeting equips you with a blueprint — a detailed plan of action — that you can operate from. By knowing the meeting's purpose, you eliminate the guesswork and make your life much easier.

REMEMBER

The primary purpose of any meeting is to exchange information — for example, to brainstorm ideas, communicate vital information, plan a strategy, make decisions, provide training, or solve a problem. Be careful not to confuse the purpose with the subject of the meeting, which might be launching a new product, going over the annual sales review, or creating better customer relationships. The purpose is the vehicle that drives everything about the meeting, including who should attend, what the agenda items should be, what materials and equipment are necessary, and the direction of a subsequent meeting. Get together with the person(s) requesting the meeting and obtain detailed answers to the following questions:

>> What is the purpose of the meeting?

>> What exactly do you wish to accomplish?

>> What messages do you want to communicate?

>> How do you want people to feel when they leave?

>> When will the meeting take place?

>> How long will it last?

>> Who will be involved?

>> What preferences do you have for the meeting location?

>> Do you want a virtual meeting, an in-person, or a hybrid of the two?

>> What specific materials and equipment will you need?

>> What refreshments and snacks are necessary?

Armed with this information, you can set about planning your strategy. But first ask yourself whether what you're being asked to do is realistic in the given time frame and whether you have the necessary resources available. If not, find out what you need to do to make the meeting happen.

TIP

If the requester's expectations are unrealistic, break down your project into its different components and decide what *you* can do and what you need to outsource — either to someone in your company or to an outside supplier.

One of your tasks may be to help assess whether a meeting is really necessary. Often people call meetings out of habit without considering that the information can be communicated in another way, such as an e-mail or a brief one-on-one discussion. Suggest that people ask themselves, "What would happen if we didn't hold this meeting?" This simple yet potent question identifies the true purpose of a meeting.

Planning the Agenda

Be aware of the direct correlation between preparation time and meeting productivity, specifically when it comes to preparing materials and the agenda items.

Identifying the purpose of a meeting is the first step in putting together an agenda. Knowing the result (or results) you want to achieve by the end of the meeting determines what agenda items the meeting must cover.

REMEMBER

An *agenda* is simply the list of topics that need to be discussed. Keep it short, sweet, and to the point. The average agenda usually fills one page. If an agenda has many subtopics and presentations, you may need to run to two pages. Your goal is to make it compact and easy to follow so that people can see, at a glance, exactly what they need to know.

Every agenda should include the following items:

>> **The meeting objective:** State right up front what the meeting is about. Write the objective in such a way that everyone knows exactly what needs to be accomplished. Be specific in how you word it, and use action verbs such as *decide, improve, create, develop, complete,* and *determine.*

Here's an example of a meeting objective: "To develop a plan to improve our after-sales follow-up."

>> **Logistical information:** Be clear about the exact date, time, length, and location of the meeting. Consider calling the meeting at an odd time, such as 8:57 a.m.

People take more notice and are less likely to be late that way. If people are unfamiliar with the location, attach a map or specific written directions.

>> **List expected attendees and their roles during the meeting:** Inviting the right mix of participants is crucial to the success of a meeting. (The section "Inviting Attendees," presented later in this chapter, gives you some essentials for choosing the best-suited group to help achieve your objectives.) Assign roles to each participant, such as facilitator, timer, recorder, and presenter. As a rule, the meeting leader should not be the facilitator or timer because they could be too emotionally involved in the outcome.

>> **What you expect participants to bring with them:** Remind attendees of what they need to bring to the meeting, such as reports or monthly sales figures. Never assume that people know what you want or expect them to bring to the meeting; the last thing you want is for them to arrive unprepared.

>> **The agenda items:** The meeting leader and participants help put together the agenda items. These should appear in a logical and sequential order and obviously help to achieve the objective. Next to each item, list the participant(s) who will present the topic and the time allotted for that agenda item.

If you want people to read or review some background material on any given agenda item before the meeting, let them know and include it when you send out the agenda prior to the meeting. Be realistic about the amount you can expect them to do. Most people tend to leave any preparation until the last minute.

A well-prepared written agenda circulated in advance helps participants understand the objective of the meeting, gives them a better idea of what will be discussed, lets them form questions about it beforehand, and allows them an opportunity to do any necessary preparation. This makes them more invested in the meeting and the outcome. An agenda acts as an official invitation, and participants are more likely to consider the meeting more seriously because of its businesslike tone.

TIP

Consider getting a few people's comments and suggestions for your agenda based on the meeting objective. When you involve people in the planning process and they have a specific role to play in the meeting, they're less likely to brush it off as unnecessary.

WARNING

Don't try to do too much at your meeting. Otherwise, you're likely to dilute its effectiveness. In addition, you increase the odds that you'll run past the allotted time, frustrating and upsetting attendees. Nobody minds ending early, but ending late is usually unacceptable and is likely to give you and the meeting a bad rap. Stay on topic and out of the weeds. Because meetings already suffer from low popularity, running late just adds fuel to fire.

SAMPLE AGENDA

The following is a sample agenda that gives you all the necessary components in an orderly manner. An agenda does not normally run longer than one page.

THE DINKY DOO COMPANY
Customer Service Department Meeting

Date: Monday, June 4, 20XX

Time: 8:57 a.m.

Location: Conference Room 2 (2nd floor)

Meeting Length: 1 hour

Meeting Objective: To develop a plan to improve our after-sales service

Participants:

Annie May (Facilitator)	Peter Piper (Timer)
Joe Blow (Recorder)	Suzie Cue
Spring Water	Tom Boy

What to bring:

April and May sales reports

Examples of good after-sales follow-up ideas

Your thinking cap!

Agenda items:

1. (8:57 a.m.) Welcome and good news overview — led by Joe Blow (5 minutes)

2. (9:02 a.m.) Review present after-sales service — led by Suzie Cue (15 minutes)

3. (9:17 a.m.) Review April and May sales — led by Spring Water (10 minutes)

4. (9:27 a.m.) Brainstorm new and improved after-sales service ideas — facilitated by Annie May (15 minutes)

5. (9:42 a.m.) Review ideas generated and plan implementation — led by Tom Boy (15 minutes)

6. (9:57 a.m.) Meeting over. A light continental breakfast will be served.

Inviting Attendees

When you start thinking about the right mix of attendees, review your meeting objective and select only people who can help achieve the results you're looking for. For total effectiveness and efficiency, each person selected needs to make a specific contribution.

When evaluating your prospect list, ask yourself the following:

>> Who do you need to provide specific information?

>> Who do you need to offer specific advice?

>> Who do you need with specialized expertise?

>> Who do you need that has authority to make decisions?

>> Who do you need that can see the big picture?

>> Who do you need as a practical nuts-and-bolts person?

>> Who do you need as an innovative and creative person?

Based on your needs, find a diverse mix to fit the roles. Include as many points of view as possible in your decision making or problem solving. When it comes to planning sessions, your team should include a variety of thinking styles, primarily big-picture and futuristic thinkers combined with practical nuts-and-bolt people. These two types complement each other well: One envisions the big picture, and the other sets out the step-by-step guidelines to achieve the plan.

Each person at the meeting should have a specific purpose for attending. The fewer people involved, the more successful you'll be in achieving your objectives.

TIP

For meetings that normally include the same people time and time again, consider inviting someone different once in a while to add new life and a new perspective to the discussions.

Discovering the right number

Figuring out how many people to invite to the meeting is part of your role. Unlike events, which can be successful no matter how large the guest list, business meetings are most effective when the number of participants is kept to a minimum.

REMEMBER

The larger the group, the more complicated the meeting. Many meetings are just too big, mainly because the leader does not want to leave anyone out or hurt anyone's feelings. However, the most effective size for most meetings is under ten participants, usually around seven or eight. This number of attendees allows for ample flexibility and is an optimum size for problem solving.

Business meetings that approach 20 participants start becoming somewhat complex and need careful management and facilitation to accomplish objectives. For meetings involving close to 30 people, consider breaking them up into subgroups, especially if you're looking for idea generation for planning or problem solving. You may also want to hire a professional facilitator to help maximize the meeting efficiency; as an outsider, a professional facilitator is not involved in any office politics that may sidetrack the meeting agenda. Meetings of more than 30 people should be used only for presentations, panel discussions, training seminars, and voting sessions.

Fitting into busy schedules

Finding a meeting time that suits everyone can prove challenging. Because meetings are often a low priority, many employees find something more important to do when given a choice. (But, of course, with your planning savvy, you'll soon convince them to think otherwise!)

Make sure that the key players can attend the meeting. If they have other commitments or are out of town or on vacation, schedule the meeting to a more convenient time or offer a virtual option to connect them to the in-person meeting.

The best time to meet is early in the morning, before the craziness of the workday begins. Another good time is toward the end of the day, around 3 p.m., when the crises have often been taken care of and the phones and e-mail inboxes start quieting down. If you do decide to meet at a later time, make sure that you're not infringing on people's need to get home by a specific time, to pick up the kids from the sitter, or avoid major rush-hour traffic.

Many companies arrange lunchtime meetings, which can work well, especially when you provide food or people brown-bag it. Be sure to communicate the eating arrangements when you send out the meeting agenda.

WARNING

The period immediately after lunch is the worst time to meet because people often suffer from food fatigue, and their brain cells function less effectively.

Assessing Your Needs

Based on the answers to the questions in the "Identifying the Purpose" section, earlier in this chapter, you should have a pretty thorough idea of what your needs are for the meeting. Now your job is to meet those needs, specifically with regard to meeting location, materials and equipment, and refreshments.

Meeting location

No matter how large or small the meeting, location is key. The meeting environment, whether formal or informal, helps set the appropriate mood and ambiance. Think about choosing a comfortable yet stimulating environment that encourages attendees to concentrate, but beware of making it so cozy and relaxing that they're likely to fall asleep.

When thinking about the right location, consider the meeting objectives, the length of the meeting, and, of course, your budget. Decide whether it might be appropriate or necessary to hold the meeting off-site. For example, sometimes a neutral, off-site location is necessary for confidential, top-secret discussions.

The following sections present the four primary location options for small meetings.

On-site meeting space

This is often the best of all four options. Most small meetings (ten or fewer participants) are usually conducted in the company office environment. On-site meetings can be quickly and easily arranged and, above all, are cost-effective. In addition, you also have most reference material readily available. And, unless employees from other office locations are expected to attend, you don't have to worry about travel time and expenses. An office, boardroom, or small conference room often works well. Whichever you pick, take steps to prevent distractions like ringing telephones or employee interruptions. A "Meeting in Progress" sign on the door works wonders to keep the distractions to a minimum.

Local off-site meeting space

Getting away from the office environment can stimulate creativity and generally makes a nice change from the often-mundane day-to-day office surroundings. This is a good option when you want some privacy to discuss sensitive or secretive issues, away from possible prying eyes and ears. Also, be aware that in some environments employees must deal with territorial issues. If this is a concern in your organization, a neutral off-site meeting location may solve the problem.

When selecting an off-site location, whether you're looking for a local hotel conference room, a restaurant, or another meeting space, your budget dictates your options. Will it be a two- or a five-star facility? To play it safe, always inspect the space first-hand before finalizing any decisions. In Chapter 5, I cover site inspections in greater detail.

Make sure that the space is the right size for the meeting. Avoid the tendency to *up-size* — selecting a space big enough to seat 200 for a 20-person meeting. (For more on this topic, see the section "Setting the Scene," later in this chapter.)

Out-of-town on-site meeting space

This option applies only if your company has offices in other locations around the country or world. These kinds of meetings often take place when another company location has something, such as new equipment, that employees at your facility need to see.

If possible, visit the site beforehand to set up the necessary details. Alternatively, if you have a counterpart at the facility, coordinate with that person to make all the arrangements. A thorough checklist to help ensure that you don't forget anything is especially vital in this situation. (For checklist suggestions, see the Appendix.) Stay on top of all the arrangements, and double- and triple-check with your liaison that everything is going according to plan. You may be the one held accountable if plans go awry.

Travel and accommodations, if necessary, will naturally increase your meeting expenses.

Out-of-town off-site meeting space

This option is usually reserved for extra-special meetings, such as sales meetings, because costs will inevitably be much higher. These kinds of meetings may last for several days, so you'll have more details to take care of. If you want to make this type of meeting rate high on the popularity poll, consider using a resort facility that offers enjoyable relaxation options such as golfing, swimming, or a fitness center. A site visit is essential so that you don't encounter any surprises.

Organizing this type of meeting takes a good deal of time, energy, and attention to detail. See the Appendix for examples of various checklists to use so that you don't have to reinvent the wheel.

Transportation

I cover this subject in more depth in Chapter 6, but right now, remember that if your meeting is held away from your business premises, transportation must be addressed.

Consider various options, including letting participants use their own vehicles, relying on local transit, and hiring a shuttle bus. Whichever option you choose, let the participants know the exact details. Send them a map or GPS location with precise directions and information about parking availability and costs. You might even arrange to have parking fees waived, especially if the parking garage is attached to a hotel facility and the hotel has the clout to do so.

If you plan to meet at a downtown location, notify the participants about any potential traffic difficulties, such as construction works or rush-hour bottleneck areas. If they need to use local buses or trains, give them the exact information, especially where to get off and how to find the meeting location from the bus stop or train station. Hiring a shuttle bus overcomes all these inconveniences, but, of course, it's your most expensive option.

REMEMBER

Your main objective is to have people arrive in the right frame of mind. If they run into surprises along the way because of poor planning, they may not arrive with their business brain turned on and ready for action.

Specific material and equipment needs

Your primary role regarding audiovisual equipment is to ask meeting presenters what they plan to use and, if they don't know, to find out what they want to achieve in their presentations so you can help them decide what equipment they need.

If the meeting is on-site and the company doesn't have the necessary equipment, find a trusty local supplier that offers rentals. Send e-mails to the rental companies stating your needs and checking their pricing and availability. Be sure to ask about the age of the equipment they rent. You don't want old beat-up stuff that's going to break down during your boss's keynote presentation.

If your meeting is held at an outside facility, check the facility's ability to provide the equipment you need. Most hotels used for meetings have equipment available for rental. If not, they usually have an arrangement with a local rental company.

Here's a list of the pieces of audiovisual equipment most commonly used at meetings:

>> **LCD (liquid crystal display) projector:** The most common piece of equipment these days is a laptop computer that uses an LCD projector to project images onto a screen. Programs that come with ready-made templates, such as Microsoft's PowerPoint, make it easy to look highly professional.

Compact LCD projectors are relatively inexpensive and can be used in daylight settings. If you use the projector frequently, it may be better to invest rather than rent. It will pay for itself very quickly.

>> **Flip chart:** Flip charts are particularly good for capturing ideas in brainstorming sessions, and they're easy to stick on the walls for reference. Make sure that plenty of extra paper and markers are available. Again, black and blue are the best colors to use because they're easy to read from a distance. Test the markers beforehand to make sure they're not dried up.

>> **Microphone:** If the meeting room is larger than a classroom, you should have a microphone. Also, even if the room is smaller, for longer meetings it will save the speaker's voice and make it easier for everyone to hear. You can choose one of the following options, and whichever one you choose, make sure you test it out beforehand.

- **A stationary podium/lectern microphone:** This is a good option for someone who is going to read notes, is nervous about giving presentations, and needs to stand behind, grab, or hold onto a podium. It's particularly good for the sweaty-palm types of people who don't know what to do with their hands while they're talking. Plus, the microphone is easily transferred between speakers.

- **A handheld microphone:** Only people who are confident speakers or aspiring comics or singers should use this equipment. The speaker really needs to know how to work with this type of microphone. You have to hold it vertically against the chin with the top of the microphone level with the bottom of the lower lip. Many people unfamiliar with its use tend to hold it away from their mouths, diminishing the sound and defeating the purpose. Remember to school your speakers in the proper technique if they have never used a handheld mic.

- **A corded or wireless lavaliere/lapel microphone:** This option is most suited for presenters who walk around and talk with their hands as they speak. It's a small microphone that's clipped to clothing, usually high up on the collar of a jacket, as close to the mouth as possible. Keep in mind that anything that brushes against this type of microphone — such as a scarf, tie, or piece of jewelry — creates an irritating noise for the audience.

TIP

From personal experience, I recommend placing a strip of tape over the handheld mic's on/off switch so that the speaker cannot accidentally turn it off mid-flow! And remember to turn off your mic when you head to the restroom!

>> **Laptop computer:** Ensure that your computer is compatible with the presenter's visual (and audio) format: MPEG-4 (or mp4), Windows Media Video (.wmv), PowerPoint (.pptx), MOV (PowerPoint on a Mac), Canva, Prezi, and YouTube are commonly used. Do a test run of the presentation to confirm your internet, audio, and video connections.

In Part 4 of this book, I discuss all your technology options: conference calling, videoconferencing, webcasting, and other cool stuff.

Refreshments

Most people enjoy being fed, so include food whenever possible at your meetings. Food gives the meeting a warm and fuzzy feeling.

Unless you have an on-site caterer, you have to bring in food from a local bakery, deli, restaurant, or catering service. Based on the length of the meeting and the time of day, you may need doughnuts, muffins, Danish, sandwiches, a buffet, boxed lunches, fruit and cheese, or just munchies. At a minimum, you'll need coffee, tea, soft drinks, and plenty of water. If you need to serve luncheon foods, ask attendees about their dietary restrictions and food allergies.

In Chapter 7 I go into great detail about food and beverage planning and management, particularly concerning the use of outside facilities. In a nutshell, discuss your requirements with the venue's catering manager. Find out what you need to purchase through the meeting facility and what you may be able to bring in yourself. Venues occasionally allow you to bring food or beverages in from the outside. It never hurts to ask (one of my favorite mottos). If you do get the green light to provide your own refreshments, you'll greatly reduce your costs because you always pay a significant surcharge when facilities supply what's needed. This fact shouldn't come as a shock to you — they're in business to make money just like everyone else!

Assisting Guests with Special Needs

When making arrangements for a guest with a disability, go the extra mile to make sure that their experience at your meeting is productive and enjoyable. In this section, I address the special needs of guests who are deaf or hard-of-hearing, visually impaired, or mobility impaired.

Be sure to read up on the Americans with Disabilities Act (ADA). This is one of America's most comprehensive pieces of civil rights legislation that prohibits discrimination and guarantees that people with disabilities have the same opportunities as everyone else to participate in the mainstream of American life — to enjoy employment opportunities, to purchase goods and services, and to participate in State and local government programs and services. For information on the ADA, visit the ADA website (https://www.ada.gov/ada_intro.htm).

Accommodating deaf & hard-of-hearing participants

If a guest attending your meeting is hearing impaired or deaf, you have to make a few special arrangements. For your deaf participants, you need to provide a sign language interpreter. Visit the websites for The Registry of Interpreters for the Deaf (www.rid.org) and for the National Association of the Deaf (www.nad.org) for information on sign language interpreting and a searchable database of nationally certified freelance interpreters. You can also check your phone book and online for companies such as Sign Language Associates, Inc. (www.signlanguage.com) that provide interpreters for meetings around the world.

Be certain that the interpreters you hire understand that they should:

>> Keep all information that they translate *completely confidential*. This is especially important in business meetings where sensitive issues and information are being discussed.

>> Translate without interjecting personal opinions into the translation. This is a rule that should be adhered to by all interpreters, sign language or otherwise.

Hard of hearing guests may have assistive devices to compensate for their hearing loss, but they still may prefer to be seated near the speaker for better reception and less room-noise distraction.

If you're arranging lodging for a hearing-impaired meeting participant, you can make a few preparations to ensure that their stay is enjoyable. Choose a hotel that is ADA compliant.

Guests who are deaf or hard of hearing won't be able to hear fire alarms or other emergency alert sounds. You should make arrangements so that your team will personally alert them in the event of an emergency.

Accommodating visually-impaired participants

If a guest attending your meeting is blind or visually impaired, you'll likely want to translate all written meeting material into Braille. The National Federation for the Blind offers a list of companies that translate written material into Braille (check their website at `https://nfb.org/resources/braille-resources/braille-transcription-resources`.

When choosing a venue for your event or making hotel reservations for a guest with a visual impairment, inquire about the following:

>> Does the venue or hotel have an audio tour of its facilities that can be sent to your guest?

>> Will a hotel employee be able to give your blind guests a tour of the hotel when they arrive?

>> Is the hotel and its website ADA compliant?

If a guide dog will accompany your guest, let the hotel know ahead of time. Service animals, such as guide dogs, are allowed in hotels, motels, and resorts, as well as on buses, trains, and airplanes.

Accommodating mobility-impaired participants

If a guest attending your meeting is mobility impaired, you need to address the following questions:

>> Is the main entrance of the meeting venue wheelchair-accessible? The main entrances of some hotels and conference centers are not wheelchair-accessible, but they likely have an alternate entrance for mobility-impaired guests. Find out in advance.

>> How deep is the carpeting in the meeting room and throughout the venue? Deep carpeting is very difficult for wheelchair users to push through.

>> Are meeting room doors staffed or are automatically accessible?

>> Will stairs or narrow doorways affect access inside the venue?

>> Are the hotel's restaurant and other on-site facilities ADA compliant?

In addition, think about the following considerations when setting up the meeting room:

>> Make sure that aisles are wide enough to allow for easy mobility of your guests.

>> If seating is pre-designated, consider removing the chairs in front of the seats of mobility-impaired attendees prior to the event, for ease of access. If seating is not pre-designated, make sure that someone is available to remove chairs to accommodate this.

>> If the guest speaker or presenter is mobility-impaired, ensure the stage is accessible.

Setting the Scene

Setting the scene means creating the right ambiance for your meeting. This involves taking care of everything in the room, from the seating to the heating. Most items that I discuss in this section are ones that attendees don't usually notice unless something goes wrong. You know you've done your job well if you hear no mention of any of them.

Seating

Most of us are creatures of habit and, given the choice, generally like to sit in the same place at every meeting. Consequently, people get very irritated if someone decides to sit in *their* seat. They also find that sitting next to a friend, friendly colleague, or someone of influence is comforting, whereas they often sit as far away as possible from someone they consider unpleasant.

For problem solving, you want to encourage a high level of interaction and participation, so a round-table setup works best. In this arrangement, all seats are considered neutral, thus avoiding any head of the table. This setup promotes a participatory, open-discussion environment.

A U-shaped table arrangement works best for training. It allows presenters to see everyone clearly and have participants easily accessible. Presenters can choose to stay in or out of the U, depending on how comfortable and close they want to be with the participants.

For decision making, select a rectangular table arrangement with the leader at the head of the table. Definitely seat participants strategically and avoid seating conflicting personalities next to or even across from one another. Sprinkle them throughout the group. For the best discussions, seat people with opposing viewpoints opposite each other. Also consider a hierarchical seating arrangement, which positions attendees in order of descending authority, starting with the meeting chairperson who's seated at the head of the table.

TECHNICAL STUFF

Seating arrangements can psychologically influence your overall meeting effectiveness. Someone who wants to exert influence needs direct eye contact with the person they want to influence, so sitting opposite that person is considered the most strategically powerful position. People who want someone to take notice of them sit to the right of or opposite that person. Another power position for achieving notice is the seat to the right of the leader; as people look at this person, they also look at you, thus creating a subliminal link between the two of you.

Heating and cooling

Trying to control the HVAC (heating, ventilating, and air conditioning) system is one of every meeting and event planner's biggest nightmares. In many modern facilities, the heating and air conditioning system is centrally operated or adjusted on a thermostat and often difficult to regulate on a room-by-room basis. So finding a temperature that everyone likes is almost impossible. The result is that you end up with either Saharan or Arctic conditions.

TIP

If the room temperature is warm when no one is in it, then it's only going to get warmer with extra bodies. It's best to opt for a cooler environment at the beginning of the meeting. In addition, people are less likely to fall asleep when they're feeling slightly cool. Have plenty of warm drinks available to increase the comfort level.

Room noise and other distractions

Eliminating all room noises and distractions is probably impossible. Still, by getting rid of as many as possible, you can help create the best meeting environment.

Check your meeting room for outside traffic noises, extraneous ventilation sounds, or distractions from the audiovisual equipment or sound system. Doing so is particularly important at an off-site facility that's a new venue for you. Also make sure that the room is away from kitchen noise or other presentations that are being conducted at the same time as your meeting.

TIP

A common distraction comes from ringing, dinging, singing mobile phones. Advise participants to turn them off during the meeting, or at least put them on vibrate mode. There is always one who is likely to forget! One way to encourage compliance is to announce a monetary fine that goes to a local charity for anyone who disrupts the meeting when their phone rings.

REMEMBER

Fire alarms don't usually give you the honor of a dress rehearsal. Whether or not the alarm is for real, you have to take it seriously. Before your meeting, make everyone aware of the available exits in case of an emergency.

When choosing your venue, be cognizant of the room décor. Hotel meeting rooms often have themes and are decorated accordingly. Mirrors and large murals or pictures create a distraction not only for presenters but also for the participants. Wherever possible, face chairs away from the diversion.

TIP

Want to prevent the sound of those slamming doors every time someone goes to the restroom during a meeting? Apply duct-tape over the catch to deaden the sound.

Many other distractions can disrupt a meeting. For example, consider how irritating it is when someone crinkles wrappers from candy or other snacks during a movie, show, or concert. This noise is just as annoying during a meeting, so don't hand out wrapped candies, at least until the meeting is over. The same applies to noisy snacks such as potato or corn chips, pretzels, or apples. See Chapter 7 where I discuss food and beverage options in detail.

BEWARE OF UNINVITED GUESTS

A friend of mine once took his children with him when he was conducting a sales meeting at an off-site location. The meeting room overlooked the swimming pool where the kids were playing during his presentation. During the session, they thought it was fun to peer through the window and make funny faces at their dad, hoping to make him laugh. The consummate professional that he was, this behavior didn't faze him in the least.

The moral of this story is to make sure that all outside distractions are eliminated. Most meeting rooms with windows either have curtains, blinds, or shades. Use them!

Remember to draw your virtual blinds, too! When holding an open virtual meeting another friend had an uninvited guest show up. Before the meeting started, she politely explained to the interloper that since they had no connection or direct interest in the group that they would be muted and not able to participate in the meeting. With that, the gatecrasher opted to drop out of the meeting. Most online-conferencing platforms allow password protection or let the host determine who may enter the virtual room to prevent stalkers and uninvited guests.

Lighting

If the light is too bright, it strains and possibly irritates people's eyes. If the room is too dark, the participants' eyes slowly shut. Whenever possible, use natural light. However, be on the lookout for outside distractions, and face chairs with their backs to the windows.

You still need artificial lighting when using audiovisual equipment so that participants can take notes and remain engaged. Make sure that the light doesn't wash out the screen. If you can, either position the screen away from direct lighting or eliminate lights that are directly above the screen. When meeting off-site, ask the meeting facility to remove or unscrew troublesome bulbs.

PERFECTING YOUR PERFORMANCE

Want to make sure that you perform well at your meetings? Here are 12 tips:

- Listen actively and give direct answers to keep the meeting on target and avoid wasting time.
- Clarify issues and ensure that all participants share and understand all relevant information.
- Be prepared to change strategy whenever necessary. Watch and listen for reactions.
- Be supportive of your colleagues, allowing them to make their points first.
- Critically question exactly what people are saying.
- Supply accurate supporting data whenever you want to make a point.
- Avoid any unnecessary interruptions and take control of outside disturbances.
- Make your feelings known, whenever necessary.
- Be aware of distracting behavior, such as finger tapping or side talk while others are speaking.
- Keep your temper under control at all times, unless you deliberately want to lose it!
- Answer questions truthfully. If you don't know the answer, say so. Bluffing gets you into trouble every time.
- Make sure that the meeting accomplishes its purpose in the stated time frame.

Essential details

The small stuff often can have the most impact on a meeting. Here are a few things that may give your in-person meeting that little something special:

>> **Providing name cards:** For meetings where participants don't all know each other, provide name cards. Have people use adjectives to describe themselves as a way for others to remember their names — for example, "Savvy Susan" or "Comical Colin."

>> **Taking minutes:** Find out whether someone is responsible for taking minutes or, in fact, whether this may be something you can do. Use a digital recorder to help ensure that the minutes are accurate (and notify all participants that the meeting is being recorded!).

>> **Adding spice:** Suggest ways to liven up a potentially dull meeting. Games, brainstorming exercises, and activities that foster interactive participation help make things more exciting. You can find ice-breakers for all sorts of meetings by searching for them online.

>> **Uncluttering the space:** Working meetings can easily become cluttered with leftover food or soft drink cans. Periodically arrange a cleanup session. Removing the clutter often helps to calm people's minds and stimulate extra creativity.

>> **Evaluating the success:** As part of your preparation, compile a short meeting evaluation form or online survey so that you avoid making the same mistakes over and over again. Try to improve each subsequent meeting based on participants' feedback. Suggested questions to ask include the following:

- How did the meeting go in relation to our goals?
- How well did we follow the agenda?
- How well did we stay on schedule?
- What should be done differently the next time to ensure a quality meeting?
- What were some of the challenges we faced?
- What conflicts or disagreements were or weren't resolved?
- What was the quality of decisions made?
- How well did we utilize participants' expertise?
- What happened that was unexpected?
- What areas need more preparation?

Also consider critiquing the meeting from your standpoint. Examine what you would do differently the next time around. Now that you know what you know, what mistakes would you avoid making?

Chapter **4**

Mixing Business with Pleasure: Events

The dictionary definition of an event is "a significant occurrence or happening; a social gathering or activity." In fact, an event is like a stage production. It has a cast of characters; often delivers messages and scripts in an entertaining medium; requires sets, scenery, lighting, and sound; and has a director, a producer, an audience, and critics.

There are two important components to running a successful event. First and foremost is the creative side, which includes themes, décor, food, and so on. Then there's the planning and organization that includes budgets, programming, and logistics. Subsequent chapters, starting with Chapter 5, walk you through the fundamentals of creating a successful event.

In this chapter, I explore some of the special events you might find yourself organizing. I address the "need to knows" about planning a destination event, hosting a media visit, arranging an awards dinner, organizing a product launch, and other showy events.

Heading to a Destination Event

Destination events require a considerable amount of planning. Guests are flown or driven to an out-of-town location and provided with lodging and entertainment for several days. Destination events are especially appropriate to show appreciation for employees, customers, or suppliers and also serve as excellent incentive events. Guests relish the idea of a weekend at a spa and golf course or an amusement park with their families. You can be as extravagant as you want with these events, depending mostly upon your budget. Some large companies provide their guests with full-service pampering at the costliest of resorts, and others fly them halfway around the world. You can also do a destination event with a smaller budget, but it takes more careful planning and forethought.

When planning a destination event, arranging activities for everyone to enjoy is an important part of your job. For example, if you're arranging a destination event at a golf course and resort, keep in mind that not all participants will be avid golfers. To plan an enjoyable experience for those who aren't, schedule alternate activities such as sightseeing tours of the surrounding area, massages and facials in the resort's spa, or golf lessons for guests who want to learn the game.

Alternate activities are especially important when inviting the family members of guests. If kids are involved, be sure that they have plenty to do. Luckily, entertaining children is relatively easy and inexpensive (see the nearby sidebar "Including children in a special event").

Destination events can incorporate work. You can take a business meeting out of the boardroom and turn it into a weekend that participants will enjoy and appreciate. If you choose to do this, schedule your meetings in the mornings and leave the afternoons and evenings free so that participants can enjoy their surroundings and the activities you provide for them. If participants' families have been invited to accompany them, provide activities to occupy them during the meetings, and then arrange for everyone to regroup in the afternoon and spend the rest of the day together. Spouses, partners, and children will appreciate your thoughtfulness so they don't have to wait in a hotel room or fend for themselves while their spouses, partners, or parents are working.

If you do opt for a destination event with a stay at a hotel, you can arrange certain amenities and special touches to make your guests' stay extra- special. Ask your hotel representative or the event sponsor about a complimentary welcome reception, complimentary gifts or welcome baskets in the guests' rooms, complimentary admission to the hotel's spa or health club facilities, and early and late check-in and check-out times.

INCLUDING CHILDREN IN A SPECIAL EVENT

Including guests' spouses, partners, and children in your event may make invited guests more likely to come. If you decide to invite children to your event, you have a few extra things to think about.

You need to decide whether the children will remain with their parents the whole time or whether they will be entertained separately while the adults do their thing. If you opt to entertain the children separately, consider the extreme importance of safety and security. Hire licensed and screened childcare professionals to watch the children. Develop a system to effectively match parents to their children (identification bracelets work well), and collect cellphone numbers and daily agendas to reach parents quickly in case of an emergency. Ask the parents to fill out a permission and information form when they leave their child. Make sure that the form asks for information about food allergies, medical conditions, and any other pertinent information.

Children are relatively easy to entertain. Popular diversions include sports instruction, video games, clowns, face painters, storytellers, photo booths, arts and crafts activities, popcorn and cotton candy machines, ice cream stands, and other sillyness. Think about creating a special menu just for the kids, such as hot dogs, nachos, and pizza. Use your imagination to make your event fun for guests of all ages!

Finally, if alcohol is served at an event that children and teenagers attend, work with your bartending staff to develop a reliable system of identifying which guests are old enough to be served and get unattended drinks removed immediately!

Connecting with the Media

Another very different type of event involves inviting the media to visit your facility. Media representatives, just like everyone else, enjoy being entertained. However, they need to know that the event will be worthwhile, especially if they give up time during their normal working hours.

The media has the power to influence your company's business efforts, be it on online, in print, or through broadcast and cable radio and television. When hosting a media visit, your job is to target your endeavors to create a positive company image and brand awareness of your products and services.

How do you do that? The following sections outline some ways to help maximize your media event.

Before the event

There's plenty to do before your event begins. You want to generate excitement, and educate and engage your team. Check out this handy list of actions:

>> Defining the reason for this event and what you hope to achieve. What information do you want the media to have? What ratio of business and pleasure do you want?

>> Deciding whether you have some major announcements or new product introductions that you want the media to know about.

>> Realizing that editors are interested in timely, newsworthy information, including industry trends, statistics, and new technology or product information; interesting material such as do-it-yourself tips, techniques, or strategies; useful advice; and human interest stories.

>> Compiling a comprehensive media list complete with contact names, phone numbers, and e-mail addresses of all trade, business, and local print outlets, key online connections, and broadcast media.

>> Investigating other media connections that may be interested in your company, products, or services. For example, consider chamber of commerce magazines and newsletters, local and regional business magazines, industry-specific newsletters, and cable television and local talk-radio programs.

>> Putting together a press kit to e-mail out prior to the event. A press kit should include interesting and timely information, including the following material:

- A press release that they can use in case they cannot attend your event they will still be able to get the content they need

- A one-page company bio sheet that includes the corporate structure, executive staff chart, and sales figures

- Complete product information, such as specs, distribution methods, and pricing

- Good-quality product photos and company logo in jpg and png formats

- Case studies

>> Including contact information so that the media can follow up after the event.

>> Briefing your upper management on how to respond to the media, especially if reporters ask awkward questions. Having a plan in case a crisis, such as the resignation of your CEO or a takeover bid, occurs immediately before your event.

>> Briefing employees about the media visit and explaining what you expect from them.

>> Preparing a handout of the presentation that includes frequently asked questions (FAQs) and their answers.

During the event

The excitement continues as the event progresses! Be prepared to wow the media with information and to woo them with food and beverages:

>> Having a media spokesperson — hopefully your CEO — and top management readily available at all times. They should be prepared to explain your products and their importance in easy-to-understand, nontechnical terms.

>> Involving the management in a brief presentation that highlights the company, its products and services, and any local community involvement, sponsorship, and so on.

>> Making sure that your speaker, ideally your CEO, is prepared to give an interesting and informative presentation.

>> Serving simple and tasteful food and drinks. But don't be too lavish — you want the media to focus on the factual information you're providing, not on fancy, expensive refreshments.

>> Planning tours of your facility and having designated employees available to speak to the media.

After the event

No event is complete until the paperwork is done, so consider the following actions:

>> Sending hand-written notes thanking people for attending, and including a contact name and number in case they need further information.

>> Creating a special company newsletter to inform employees of the media's response to the event.

>> Thanking employees for their participation in this important public relations exercise.

Honoring Employees

At some point, you may be asked to plan a dinner event to honor a respected employee who is retiring from the company, celebrating an important employment anniversary, or getting a significant promotion.

Consider planning an audiovisual retrospective of the honoree's life, framed by commentary from a live narrator. You might also recruit friends and family of the guest of honor to say a few words.

So where do you go to find information about the honoree to include in your presentation? Here are a few suggestions:

» Interview people who have been a part of the honoree's life, now and in the past. Talk to their family, friends, co-workers, assistants, current and past bosses, former teachers, and classmates. Maybe you'll surprise them with an unexpected speech by their high-school teacher!

» Ask for access to the honoree's keepsakes, such as photo albums, yearbooks, trophies, other awards, and so on. Ask the honoree directly, or check with a spouse, partner, or another family member, to gain access if you want to keep the tribute a surprise.

» Go through company records, such as newsletters and photos taken at company functions. Although individual employee records are usually kept confidential, through the proper procedure you may be able to get some additional useful information.

While you're digging for information, keep in mind that you want to highlight the following key areas in the honoree's life:

» Career history, including early jobs and important promotions

» Noteworthy career achievements

» The honoree's life outside the office, including volunteer interests, hobbies, and activities with family and friends

As an added touch, you can compile the information you gather during your research into a high-quality keepsake book to present to the honoree at the end of the evening.

HAVE FUN AND DO GOOD

With a little extra planning, you can add a charitable twist to just about any event. Arrange to donate leftover centerpieces and other flowers to your local hospital or convalescent home. Leftover food can go to a nearby homeless shelter.

You can involve guests at your event in charitable activities. For example, you can ask guests at your employee appreciation event to bring something such as clothing, school supplies, or toys to donate to a local children's charity. You could even break the guests into teams and create a competition to see who brings the most donations.

Launching a Product

Launching a new product is a significant milestone for any company. It might take months or even years to bring this baby into the world. How your boss and the sales department choose to celebrate this momentous occasion could take many different forms, from a huge hoopla for everyone and their uncle and aunt, to a small intimate gathering for the company's nearest and dearest. The following 12-step process will guide you through the critical components you need to consider:

>> **Step 1:** Define your launch strategy and objectives.

>> **Step 2:** Decide on a date and location.

>> **Step 3:** Develop a budget.

>> **Step 4:** Put together your "dream team."

>> **Step 5:** Verify the guest list.

>> **Step 6:** Formulate the creative ideas.

>> **Step 7:** Make decisions about outside vendors/suppliers.

>> **Step 8:** Plan the program.

>> **Step 9:** Go over program details with participants.

>> **Step 10:** Double-check the details.

>> **Step 11:** Direct the event.

>> **Step 12:** Critique the results.

The sections that follow walk you through each of these steps.

Define your launch strategy and objectives

The objectives for the product launch help determine whether this is going to be an "all frills" or "no frills" event. Communication with your boss and the sales and marketing departments will help define the importance in the marketplace for this new product. A new and improved version of an existing product is probably going to demand less hype than a revolutionary new invention.

Decide on a date and location

Before finalizing any date, make absolutely sure that the product is truly ready for its debut. The last thing you want is to organize the festivities only to find that the product hasn't passed all the necessary tests or is plagued with some other glitch. Also, decide where this launch will take place — in your facility or at an outside venue. If an outside venue is needed, then finding the right one that fits your criteria will be crucial.

Develop a budget

If your budget is contingent on the launch strategy program, the bigger the product announcement, the more money you'll need. On the other hand, you may have a set budget that dictates the size of the shindig, in which case you need an added dose of creativity to stretch those precious dollars.

Put together your "dream team"

The bigger the celebration, the more you need a band of reliable, compatible, and creative team players. A mixture of co-workers and outside vendors often makes a good combination for your "dream team." Hand-pick people who offer the skills and talents you need and with whom you know you can work well.

Verify the guest list

One of the biggest questions for any event is "Who needs to attend?" Your program objectives determine your guest list. You need to find out whether the event is intended only for company employees or whether your audience will include other people as well. If the intent is the latter, consider inviting groups with a vested interest in the company and the product, such as stockholders, local dignitaries, community leaders, customers, and vendors. Then work on groups within the company who need to attend, such as upper management, key employees, the production team, sales, and marketing. Whenever possible, include the media. (See the section "Connecting with the Media" earlier in this chapter.)

Formulate the creative ideas

Now's the time to let those creative juices run wild so that you can turn your event into something truly special and meaningful. This is particularly important when you're looking to impress outside guests. The media, on the other hand, might criticize you if they think your spending is too lavish and unnecessary. Do some creative brainstorming with your "dream team" to pull together ideas that will give this product the right send-off.

Make decisions about outside vendors/suppliers

An event the size of a product launch will almost certainly require the assistance of some outside vendors. Your first step is to determine what services you need. Next, look for the most reputable, reliable, and service-oriented suppliers within your price range. Obviously, reliability is key. But even if you find a vendor whose track record is impeccable, I strongly recommend that you have a backup plan just in case of the unforeseen. The last thing you want is to be left stranded without an essential piece of equipment on the day of the launch. In Chapter 12, I discuss how to most effectively work with outside vendors.

Plan the program

Meticulous planning is crucial to the smooth flow of your event. Discuss details with management and make sure that you fully understand who needs to do what, and when. Following are a few questions to ponder:

>> Who should be invited to make speeches?

>> How long should each speech last?

>> Who is responsible for the actual launch or unveiling of the product?

>> How will this take place?

>> What food and beverages should be served?

>> Should the food be served before or after the official program?

>> What other activities need to take place?

>> What promotional materials are needed on the day of the launch?

>> What else do you want guests to leave with?

>> Do you want to include any entertainment, such as a harpist playing background music while guests socialize?

> » Do guests need badges?

> » Do you want to include a facility visit with the launch?

Go over program details with participants

After the event plan is in place, contact all the program participants and go through what's expected of them. Stress the importance of adhering to a strict time schedule, which means that a ten-minute speech must take ten minutes or less. Send participants a written copy of the program including a breakdown of the timings, and highlight where each participant appears. For outside dignitaries, consider sending another reminder a few days before the event. Make sure participants have all the information they need before attending, such as details about the product to be launched. Have backup copies of all the speeches and presentations, just in case.

Double-check the details

Double-checking details should be an integral part of all your event planning. Consider doing this about two weeks prior to the event. This should give you enough time in case you need to put some aspect of Plan B into action. Contact your outsider service providers to make sure they have everything they need. Remind them of the program schedule and, if you haven't done so already, send it to them so they can easily access it on their devices (or print if necessary). Also, communicate with upper management and go over essentials. Remind them of the precise timing for their particular speeches and stress the importance of sticking to the schedule. Finally, scrutinize your plan to make sure you've covered all the bases.

Direct the event

By the day of the event, you've done just about all that you can do, but this doesn't mean you can sit back on your laurels. On the contrary, you need to be bright-eyed and bushy-tailed with a big smile on your face throughout the event. You've now donned the director and stage manager hat to make sure the program runs smoothly and according to plan. Ensure that your technical team is ready to support any of your audio/visual needs. Take care of your outside guests and make them feel welcome. Connect them with upper management or key employees, and make introductions whenever necessary. No one should be left alone at the event.

TIP

Stylish yet comfortable shoes are an event planner's best friend! You'll be covering a lot of miles on the day of your event, so wear shoes that will help you keep going all day.

Critique the results

Even when the event is complete, you still can't completely relax. After the event comes the critique and evaluation. Here are three key questions to ask:

>> Overall, how did the event go?

>> Did it accomplish the set objectives?

>> If you were to do the event over, what would you do differently?

Get feedback on these questions from company employees who attended the event. Then pull all the answers together, remembering to add your two cents, and compile a short report for upper management.

Now, at long last, it's time to relax and to treat yourself to a massage and some pampering. Perhaps your boss might even consider picking up the tab — you deserve it!

IN THIS CHAPTER

» Selecting the best time and place

» Creating the right atmosphere

» Understanding audience needs, wants, and interests

» Zeroing in on themes

» Deciding on entertainment

Chapter 5

Bringing an Event to Life

Your job as an event planner doesn't stop with the meeting in the company boardroom. You may be called upon to organize an employee appreciation event, an awards dinner, a product launch, the celebration of a company milestone, a gala recognizing a longtime employee's retirement, an incentive event for the company's sales force, a fundraising event, a holiday celebration . . . the list goes on and on.

These types of affairs differ from your typical corporate business meeting, and you face unique issues and pitfalls when planning them. Rave program reviews are generally the result of the blood, sweat, and tears you devote to the project. A well-designed and well-orchestrated program is analogous to a good stage production. It's all about getting your act together and performing the right show for the right audience.

This chapter zeros in on the nitty gritty elements that can help earn your efforts glowing reviews (and make your mom really proud of you). It covers bigger events that involve entertainment, themes, and venues that can accommodate large groups of people. From choosing a date for your event to selecting a theme that will make it memorable, this chapter gives you the tools to set your event planning in motion.

Larger events require multifaceted programs — which means planning a variety of activities such as keynote speakers, educational sessions, receptions, gala events, and tours. (Chapter 8 has helpful suggestions for hiring the best speakers.)

You want to constantly ask yourself how each activity you plan can engage the participants' interest.

REMEMBER

As you plan, keep in mind that people yearn for both passive and active participation. *Passive participation* is an activity such as listening to a motivating speaker. An example of active participation is a hands-on workshop, which requires participants to use skills such as interacting with fellow participants, brainstorming, and writing. When participants use as many of their skills as possible, they're more likely to have a memorable experience. And that, ultimately, is the goal of your planning efforts.

Deciding When to Stage Your Event

Perhaps you've been asked to organize an employee appreciation event or a dinner party celebrating your company's twentieth anniversary in business. Once you know what type of affair you're planning, your first task is to decide when and where to hold it. These two factors require careful consideration because of the impact they'll have on the success of your event.

The decision about when to hold your event is determined in large part by what type of event it is. For example, an outdoor carnival to show employee appreciation works best on a day or evening during a time of year when the weather is expected to be nice. A formal dinner honoring a respected vice president's retirement is best held on a Friday or Saturday evening to reduce the number of people who call in sick the next day after a late night of schmoozing and partying.

Here are some basic questions to ask while deciding when to hold your event:

>> **Is the event better suited for the day or evening?** When the sun is out, it's a great time to throw picnics, brunches, and other informal events. Begin formal dinners and cocktail parties as the sun is setting.

Although these are good general rules, you can also throw a great informal event in the evening. For example, rent out a local theater for a casual movie night. Depending on your budget, you could even create your own trailer to play before the film. This is a great time to show a recorded message from the CEO to the audience or to present a "commercial" for a new product you're releasing.

>> **Do you want to hold your event during the week, or on a weekend?** Because many people have plans on the weekends or like to spend that time with their families, an event during the week may mean greater attendance. On the other hand, guests who attend an event that runs late on a weeknight

might arrive at work late and tired the next day. If your event includes guests who work for companies other than your own, you need to hold it in the evening or on a weekend to accommodate their schedules. The same applies to any event you'll be inviting spouses, partners, and children to attend. Take into account that they have their own jobs or school on weekdays.

>> **If your event doesn't have a deadline, would it be best to hold it during a specific season or time of year?** People are particularly generous during the holidays, so that may be a good time to throw a fundraising auction. Obviously, an employee picnic is best held in the spring or summer.

Take into account what other annual events or holidays are on the calendar around the time you're considering throwing your event. For example, I generally don't advise planning your event adjacent to major holidays, long weekends, or school breaks, because many people leave town and your attendance will suffer.

In addition, check that your event doesn't overlap with any religious holidays. Think about all major religions — Buddhist, Christian, Hindu, Jewish, Muslim, and so on — not just your own.

TECHNICAL
STUFF

On a lighter note, try to avoid scheduling your event during major sporting events. You don't want your guests sneaking off to the bar to watch game seven of the World Series or to check the standings in the basketball playoffs! However, you can throw an event during a major sporting event by making the game the theme of your party — rent big-screen televisions, decorate in the spirit of the sport, and serve food typically associated with that athletic event.

Choosing Your Venue

After you've chosen *when* to throw your event, you can turn your attention to *where* to hold it. You have plenty of options and are limited only by your own imagination! When you begin considering your venue options, it's essential that your main consideration is to match the venue to the type of event you're planning. The following sections help you do exactly that.

Mapping out a location

The first order of business is to decide whether to hold your event indoors or outdoors. Formal events are best held indoors where the elements can't damage expensive clothing and muss styled hair, and uneven ground can't trip guests wearing heeled shoes. Although you can take steps to make the great outdoors more hospitable for your guests (think tents, portable flooring, electric generators, and space heaters), you're probably better off having your formal event on the patio of a restaurant or hotel where guests can enjoy being outside but are significantly more protected from the elements. If you do choose to hold your event on the patio of such an establishment, you can also provide guests access to an indoor room in case it becomes too cold, hot, wet, or windy outside.

Speeches and audiovisual presentations are notoriously difficult to stage outdoors. In an enclosed environment, you can control the level and angle of lighting and its effect on your speaker or projection screen. At an outdoor event, the sun can wreak havoc on your guests' ability to see the presentation. It's also challenging for the audience to hear speakers outdoors, because their voices aren't contained by walls and a ceiling and can easily be carried away by the wind.

But despite the potential pitfalls of outdoor events, they're both appropriate and great fun on many occasions. For your next informal event, you might try planning a picnic, barbecue, or carnival. These are especially fitting for an employee or customer appreciation event.

Outdoor events

A park, the beach . . . Mother Nature has provided you with some of the most beautiful settings for your outdoor event. If you don't live near or have access to such a spot, however, you still have options. You can turn your company's parking lot into a carnival or, as some businesses have done, into a carwash where top executives wash employees' cars to show appreciation for their work. Barbecues and picnics are other popular outdoor events.

REMEMBER

As you're planning your outdoor affair, keep in mind that into everybody's life a little rain must fall — and it just may fall on the day of your event! Have a contingency plan in case the weather turns bad. Consider renting large tents to shield guests from both the sun and downpours. Also decide on the need for portable flooring to even out rough ground to accommodate women in heels and the disabled. You also must determine whether you need special lighting, electric generators, sound systems, running water, and space heaters, especially for those warm days that turn chilly at night.

Using disposable plates, cups, and utensils is often appropriate at an informal outdoor event and helps make cleanup easier. Consider using eco-friendly plates, cutlery, and glassware and set up recycling bins and separate trash and food waste containers. And while we're on the subject of cleanup, figure out in advance who'll take on that responsibility. You'll be expected to leave the venue in the condition you found it, or better!

You'll also need signage to direct guests to an outdoor location. Use waterproof paint such as enamel or acrylic in case of damp weather, and use fluorescent lettering for after-dark events. If you're making multiple directional signs, paint them all the same color so they're easy to spot.

Post location maps with prominently marked "YOU ARE HERE" indicators for outdoor events that spread over a large area. Have arrows pointing to the parking areas and (if necessary) the shuttle bus stops.

You can also use apps such as What3Words (https://what3words.com) and Google Maps (https://www.google.com/maps) to create a customized map or grid reference for your event that is easily accessed on a mobile phone, tablet, or vehicle navigation system.

Be sure to check on the laws in your state for serving alcoholic beverages outdoors, and look into any extra insurance coverage that you may need. All in all, you have a bit of homework to do before taking on outdoor terrain.

Indoor events

If you decide to hold your event indoors, you can choose from an almost unlimited number of different types of venues. Stretch your imagination! You can hold it in a convention center, hotel, restaurant, skating rink, movie theater, museum, art gallery, racetrack, aquarium, nightclub, or even on a boat. The possibilities are practically endless.

If you're considering a location that holds multiple events at once, such as a convention center or hotel, find out what other events will be going on in the building at the same time as yours. You don't want your guests' dinner conversation to be drowned out by music from the high school prom next door.

After you've decided on a venue, do a quick inventory of what the facility provides and what you'll have to bring in. Does it have adequate chairs, tables, tablecloths, and silverware? Check the quality of the event supplies, and if you aren't satisfied that they're up to your standards, consider renting and bringing in your own.

Ask the venue about its insurance policy. For example, find out who is responsible if a guest slips and is injured. In some cases, purchasing extra insurance to cover any accidents may be a wise move.

Will you want to stick with the venue's decor or add your own personal touch? Ask the venue about any restrictions it may have on decorations you provide. For example, many facilities won't let you hang anything on their walls or bring in helium balloons because of fire safety regulations.

Also be certain to research noise, maximum capacity, and other zoning regulations at the venue you've chosen. If you plan to serve alcohol at a location that doesn't normally do so, you will likely need to procure a special liquor license. See Chapter 7 for information on serving liquor and handling liability issues.

If you choose a venue that doesn't specifically cater to the type of event you're holding, make a detailed list of *everything* you need. Perhaps you've chosen a restaurant for an event that will include a guest speaker or video presentation. Because the restaurant's day-to-day focus is on serving meals and not putting on productions, it may not have all the equipment you need, resulting in a little extra planning on your part. Will you need extra lighting to illuminate the speaker? Audiovisual equipment? Extension cords? Determine whether the venue has the ancillary equipment necessary for your event or whether you need to bring it in. Some places may not allow the equipment you want to use, so ask in advance.

TIP

You want the wait staff at your event to look uniform and professional, so decide what you want them to wear. For example, you might request that the waiters and waitresses dress in black pants and white shirts. After you've made your decision, communicate your wishes to the venue *in writing*. If you want the staff to wear costumes or tuxedos that are not a part of their normal wardrobe, you'll likely have to pay for the rental of these items. You can always try to negotiate with the venue, however. For an outdoor event, get matching shirts for the event team emblazoned on the back with "I CAN HELP!".

When procuring a venue for your event, keep in mind the extra space you may need. For example, if you're going to have a band or other entertainers, they probably need an extra room to get ready and store their equipment.

Finally, arrange to have access to the venue several hours before your event starts so you have enough time to set up. Don't run around putting up last-minute decorations and dealing with crises when your guests are arriving because you didn't know that another party was held in that same space up until an hour before your event!

TIP

Be very clear about what is and isn't included in the cost of the venue before signing any contracts. Find out whether the fee includes the following or whether you must pay extra for them:

>> Wait staff

>> Bar tender(s)

>> Tips

>> Cleanup

>> Audiovisual equipment

A NOTE ON, UM, BATHROOMS

Nothing can ruin an event faster than a lack of adequate bathroom facilities. As a rule, provide at least one bathroom for every 50 persons. Any fewer, and you'll quickly end up with long lines and unhappy guests. Too many people using one bathroom can also cause trouble.

When renting a venue, ask to see the bathrooms. No matter how great an atmosphere you create in the room you arrange, guests will forget it the moment they're forced to use a dingy restroom, especially if they have to wait in line to do so.

Also, many outdoor venues such as parks and beaches may not have adequate facilities. Scope out the lavatory situation before the event and consider bringing in portable toilets if necessary. You can even rent high-end portable bathrooms that look like mobile homes and have lights, flushable toilets, and running water. Check the toilet paper, soap, and running water before your event starts so that it has a happy ending.

See Chapter 11 for more detailed information about negotiating and signing contracts.

PARK YOUR CAR HERE

Convenient parking at your event, particularly at a night-time formal gathering, is key to starting the event on the right foot. Guests appreciate being able to simply step out of their cars and into the facility. Consider providing valet parking as an extra guest benefit, or arrange for door staff with umbrellas during those unexpected rain or snow showers. Your guests will feel pampered and appreciated.

No matter what time of day or year you hold your event, find out whether the venue offers adequate parking and whether it will waive parking fees for your guests. Negotiate a discounted or flat fee in advance to save guests the hassle.

Beware of independently owned and run parking garages. Check to ensure that they won't close before your event ends, trapping attendees' cars inside. Also find out whether the independent lot that serves your venue actually serves multiple venues, and what the chances are it will fill up before your guests arrive.

Looking at some venue options

Consider only venues that are large enough to handle the event you're planning. Determine up front whether you're looking for a local meeting space, an out-of-town meeting space, or either one. The sections that follow present some of your options. Keep in mind that much of your choice will depend on the purpose of your event, the number of participants, and the complexity of the program.

TIP

A good resource for U.S. hotels, conference centers, resorts, convention centers, and retreat centers is Cvent (www.cvent.com/venues). If you are looking for something a little quirky, consider Giggster (https://giggster.com) where you can track down a techy conference room or a spacious mansion. And, of course, always check with the Destination Management Company or visitor and conventions bureau in the location of your choice.

Hotels

With more than 91,000 hotels in the U.S. and over 290,000 hotels and resorts worldwide, you shouldn't have a problem finding the right venue for your event.

Hotels fall into three main categories:

>> **Well-known and established chains:** Hotels such as Marriott, Hilton, Hyatt, and IHG Hotels & Resorts offer a certain level of service that you can expect worldwide. They also offer a wide range of amenities, especially if you need room for large banquets, trade shows, or exhibit areas.

>> **Independently owned properties:** These hotels include those belonging to the Preferred Group (www.preferredhotels.com), whose luxury hotels and resorts offer a unique character, one-of-a-kind ambiance, and the highest standards of quality and extraordinary service. Along with this type of service comes a price tag, so be prepared for some fancy figures.

>> **Boutique lodgings:** These hotels provide service to business travelers in search of a home away from home. They are small luxury hotels and resorts with individual personalities — eclectic, quaint hotels housed in historic urban buildings or romantic resorts with flowering gardens and beachside villas. (I'm ready to book a room right now!) Find out more at myboutiquehotel.com and similar websites. Although these lodgings sound nice, you definitely need to check what meeting facilities, if any, they offer.

TIP

Some hotels are so impressive that you want to tell the world about them; others make you want to *warn* the world. Find out some behind-the-scenes truth about those glossy pictures and tantalizing promotional copy from Tripadvisor (www.tripadvisor.com) and similar online review sites. I've found some great recommendations this way!

Conference centers

Conference centers encompass a gamut of venues that are often built specifically for meetings and events and offer state-of-the-art facilities, many including videoconferencing. (For more on this technology tool, see Chapter 14.) Corporate training centers fall into this category, as do some facilities at universities, resorts, and airports. Many urban and downtown areas also have conference centers.

As opposed to convention centers (see the next section), conference centers offer accommodation facilities. To find a suitable facility, your best bet is to start your research with the International Association of Conference Centers (www.iacconline.com). You can do a worldwide search based on your specific meeting criteria.

Convention centers

When you're looking for a combination of an urban location, plenty of meeting space, and substantial exhibition space, a convention center is a practical solution. They're geared up for large numbers and generally situated close to airports or in a convenient downtown location. The one drawback is that you need to use a nearby hotel for accommodations.

TIP

I'll let you in on a little secret: It's a jungle out there! One of the best ways to clear a path for an easier passage is to make contact with the local Convention and Visitors Bureau (CVB) or Destination Marketing Organization (DMO) in your destination city. No one knows the city and its attractions better than these organizations do. The CVB or DMO can help you handle all the lions and tigers and take the guesswork out of your decision making. They can also assist you with your site selection and supplier contacts. I highly recommend that you take full advantage of all the services they offer.

SECOND-TIER, NOT SECOND-RATE

When trying to arrange cost-effective meetings, nothing beats smaller destinations, both urban and rural. Many medium-sized cities, often known as second-tier cities, are fast becoming serious competitors to first-tier cities. They may not have the same allure as Las Vegas or San Diego, but they're certainly working harder to attract the lucrative meetings industry. Many of them, such as Columbus, Salt Lake City, Pittsburgh, Indianapolis, and Tampa, have comparable meeting facilities to some of the first-tier cities, but the prices are lower.

They may not offer quite the same variety in terms of dining, entertainment, and sightseeing, but depending on your participants' needs, these issues may not be important. Second-tier cities are definitely worth checking out.

Resorts

You'll probably consider a resort property only if relaxation and leisure activities rank high on your priority list. This environment works well for both formal and informal meetings. Resorts Online (www.resortsonline.com) allows you to choose the activity you're most interested in to find an appropriate selection of sites.

Retreat centers

These facilities generally work best for smaller, more focused groups who are looking for a quiet, serene meeting environment. They foster a get-away-from-it-all mentality that encourages people to engage in personal exploration, strategic decision making, communication, and self-improvement.

Cruise ships

Ships are an interesting and unusual venue option. A few companies specialize in cruise meetings and offer facilities worldwide for a wide variety of groups. Check out www.cruisemeetings.com. Some of these companies will work within your budget constraints to offer complete packages that include airfare, transfers, meals, and entertainment. What a deal! Just make sure that your attendees bring their Sea-Band® (small bands, available at most pharmacies, that you wear around your wrists to prevent travel sickness).

Unique environments

This section covers everything that really doesn't fit into the other categories. Unique environments make memorable meeting spaces, so it's worth doing your homework to find out about them. Some options to consider include museums, stately homes, sporting venues, and theaters.

WARNING

Although many of these venues work well for special functions, they may not have the technology you need for a full business meeting.

Visiting venue possibilities

The golden rule of meeting planners is to never select a venue without having seen it in person. But, as with all rules, people break them, and many who do suffer the consequences.

REMEMBER

After you make a short list of your venue choices, set up site visits. Don't rush in just yet, though, as you have one more important task to complete — putting together your list of all your venue requirements. It's like putting together a shopping list. Doing a major shop is a whole lot easier, quicker, and more efficient with a list than without one. Knowing exactly what you want and need is crucial.

One person who I have trusted for event planning insights is Diane T. Silberstein, CMP. Here's some of her expertise that I've gleaned into a highly effective site selection checklist:

>> **Planning:** Make sure that your meeting objectives (educational, social, or business) are clear and concise, and know your meeting format (flow of events). List preferred dates and times and have a few alternatives just in case your first choice isn't available. Have a realistic figure of the number of guests you're expecting, and know your guests' expectations.

>> **Function space:** Identify the number, size, and shape of the meeting rooms you need, and ask about storage area location and access. Locate and inspect the condition of restrooms. Be familiar with the kitchen location and access, and check the location of freight/passenger elevators (particularly important in exhibition halls). Question in detail all venue costs (rental, utilities, elevator, insurance, and so on), and ask about other overlapping functions. Finally, know the rules, regulations, and policies for installation and dismantle.

>> **Transportation:** Familiarize yourself with directions from major roads. Know distance/drive time for guests. Find out the approximate taxi fare for guests, and check on taxi availability after hours. Ask about parking facilities/costs for cars and buses.

>> **Policies:** Understand completely the booking and cancellation policy, as well as the deposit and payment policy. Ask whether gratuities are mandatory or optional. Discuss insurance requirements. And, finally, find out about any restrictions on time, décor, entertainment, and so on.

>> **Services:** Make sure that you know and understand all the services provided by the facility. Find out how many employees will be available during each of your various functions. Get a list of preferred suppliers the facility uses.

>> **Miscellaneous:** Get exact contact information for everyone involved during the event development stage, as well as those involved during the event. Find out if the facility is ADA (Americans with Disabilities Act) compliant. Discuss any renovation plans, completion dates, and what happens if renovation is going on during your event. Get references for three groups similar to yours that have recently held events at the venue.

TIP

Instead of taking copious notes and committing your venue visits to memory, use your phone's camera to visually record your visits. Those photos or videos come in handy when you try to recall what each site looks like after you get back to your office.

Scripting the Event

Your program planning is at the core of your event — especially if it's a large one. But before you can begin to plan your program, you need to consider your meeting objectives — the purpose of the event. The purpose dictates who the participants need to be and what kind of program plan you need to design. It all stems from the reason for having the meeting in the first place.

With your purpose in place, you can focus your attention on the people you want to attract, whether they're employees, members, shareholders, customers, or others. Do you want to encourage them to come with their partners or family members? This decision depends entirely on the business/educational/social split of your program. Refer to Chapter 1 for information on identifying meeting purposes and for tips on figuring out whom to invite.

The program plan you choose stems from the purpose and participants. The following questions can help determine your four main considerations before formulating an actual program:

» What is the main emphasis of the program? Is it educational, business, or social?

» What are the program's financial criteria? Should it generate revenue, break even, or be a company expense?

» What are the participants' expectations? (See the section "Analyzing Your Audience," later in this chapter, to gather information to address this question.)

» What is the optimum ratio of educational, business, and social programming?

Based on the answers to these four questions, you can set about designing the program and developing the topic areas that best fit the event's objectives and criteria. Your goal is to create an exciting and creative program that will persuade participants that this is a not-to-be-missed event.

Programming format options include the following:

» **General session speakers:** Sessions that all participants attend.

» **Concurrent sessions:** Sessions occurring at the same time.

» **Small group breakout sessions:** Small group sessions within a meeting, organized to discuss specific topics.

- **Panel discussions:** A group of two or more speakers, often with a moderator, having a purposeful conversation on an assigned topic in the presence of participants.

- **Labs, clinics, or master classes:** Workshop-type educational experiences where participants learn by doing.

- **Case studies:** Oral or written accounts of an event, incident, or situation used to develop critical thinking skills and to attain new perceptions of concepts and issues.

- **Roundtable discussions:** A group of experts meeting to review and discuss specialized, professional matters, either in a closed session or, more frequently, before an audience.

- **Demonstrations:** Presentations that show how to perform a task or procedure. These are often found in an exhibit area.

- **Poster sessions:** An opportunity to meet with authors, researchers, or key speakers to view their background information as displayed in an exhibit hall or designated area.

- **Formal or informal networking sessions:** Exchanges of information or services among individuals, groups, or institutions.

- **Receptions:** Social functions with beverages, usually with food displayed on tables for self-service or offered around the room on trays.

- **Award recognition functions:** Functions organized to reward individuals or organizations for their contribution to or sponsorship of something such as an event, a community, or an association. Examples include retirements, exceptional employees, or significant sponsorships.

- **Banquets:** Formal, often ceremonial, dinners for a select group of people.

A WORD ABOUT VIRTUAL TOURS

Many meeting venues offer the opportunity to see their properties on their websites. Some sites are incredibly sophisticated and enable you to "tour" the venue from many different angles. Although touring a site online is a convenient feature, it's never a substitute for seeing the property firsthand. Website tours are better than photos alone, but there are many aspects of a meeting location that you can observe only in person. If you have no choice and for budgetary reasons can't see the venue in person, at least have some extensive phone conversations with your key contacts. Use the checklist in the section "Visiting venue possibilities," earlier in this chapter, as you would in a face-to-face situation.

TIP

Consider putting a team of planning advisors together so that you can take full advantage of various people's experiences, both good and bad. Include other event planners, local meeting planning vendors, and internal company colleagues who have organized events. Instead of making the same mistake someone else did, profit from their blunders and expertise.

Analyzing Your Audience

Before you can think about putting a programming plan together, you need a good understanding of the demographics, characteristics, and interest levels of the people who'll be attending the event. By doing a relatively simple audience analysis, you can determine specifics that will help you plan your event more effectively. Analyze your audience by seeking answers to as many of the following questions as possible:

>> Who is the target audience, and how many people will attend?

>> What is the age, socioeconomic status, gender, and educational background of most audience members?

>> What ethnicities, races, and cultures do audience members represent? (What political and religious affiliations do they have?)

>> What occupations do the audience members hold? What is their level of seniority within their respective organizations? Are they support staff or top executives?

>> What are their interests, needs, and goals? What is their motivation for attending the event? What do they expect to learn?

>> How much does the audience already know about the major focus topic for the event? What useful new information should be included? (For example, consider including new industry trends.)

>> Does the audience need general or specific in-depth information? How will the audience use the new information?

TIP

To get the best responses to these questions, e-mail them to the invitees or post the questions on your website. Do so well ahead of the event; for some events you can get goodies in a matter of days or weeks, but for other items (and higher quantities) you may need to plan well in advance. Give people an incentive (such as an online gift certificate or a premium giveaway item like a T-shirt or pen) for completing the questionnaire because it's going to take them a little time. The result is some phenomenal information on which to build a substantive program just to their liking.

Creating the Atmosphere

One key to a successful special event is to seek out entertainment or decorations that are unique and fun to spark conversation among guests. As you begin envisioning your event, picture the mood you want the environment to create. For example, determine whether you want to create a jubilant, celebratory atmosphere or one that is more serious.

The ambiance you aim for depends a great deal upon the type of event you're having. If it's a product launch at which you hope to create an aura of enthusiasm and excitement, you'll likely lean toward a jubilant atmosphere. If you're organizing an event for your employees and their spouses, perhaps you want the mood to be somewhat romantic.

Whatever you decide, shape and enhance the atmosphere with the entertainment, decorations, and food you choose.

Planning the entertainment and decorations

Think outside the box when planning the atmosphere at your event. Consider all sorts of amusements — strolling musicians, magicians, chefs' demonstrations, palm readers . . . anything out of the ordinary. Novelty is the key to your success. Give your guests something to tell their friends about!

Keep in mind that your entertainment doesn't have to come in the form of people. An elaborate coffee bar or startlingly beautiful champagne fountain will have your guests raving.

TIP

Providing your entertainers and team with meals and beverages during the event is a nice gesture.

Your decorations will vary depending on the type of event you're throwing and the venue you choose. Remember to check all decorating plans with the venue in advance because many have restrictions on what they allow you to do in their establishment.

If you're planning to create a theme for your event, you can cut down on decorating costs by choosing a themed venue and then building your event around the décor rather than molding a venue to the theme you've chosen. For example, you may want to hold your event in an elaborately decorated world-food restaurant. That way, all you have to do is provide the musicians and entertainers from the appropriate area of the world. For more on this topic, see the section "Creating a Memorable Theme," later in this chapter.

WARNING

The only appropriate time to have dancing at a special business event is when spouses or partners have been invited. Otherwise, you may be creating an awkward situation for co-workers.

Choosing foods and beverages

Before making any decisions about your menu, please read Chapter 7, where I discuss this subject in depth. But I have one tip in particular that I like to emphasize for event planners: If you're throwing a cocktail party or any event where food is served while guests are standing and mingling, limit your cuisine to bite-size morsels that guests can easily eat with their fingers or a fork. Keep it neat!

TIP

Remember to include some interesting vegetarian or vegan selections in your menu for guests who don't eat meat.

If you're serving alcohol at your event, make sure that you have enough bartenders and liquor. You don't want to run out of beverages in the middle of the party or have long lines of grumbling, thirsty guests. If the venue you've selected is providing the liquor and bartending staff, and the business hosting the event — not your guests — is going to pick up the tab, discuss with the venue how the business will be charged. Will you be charged per drink or a flat rate? Consider whether you want to limit your guests to certain selections, eliminating expensive liquors and specialty drinks.

Creating a Memorable Theme

Another challenge for planners is developing a theme for an event. Creating a theme for a large event helps to make it more memorable, in addition to making it easier to organize programming, food, décor, and other accessories, such as giveaway items. For themes centered on a specific region of the world, seek out cuisine and entertainment native to that area. For example, if you choose a Mexican theme, consider hiring a mariachi band or arranging for a chef to cook and serve sizzling fajitas before your guests' eyes (and watering mouths).

Selecting a theme that fits

Plenty of themes are just waiting to materialize. Perhaps a Hawaiian theme would work for your event (think leis, ukuleles, and tropical drinks), or maybe a party reminiscent of the 1950s (*Rock 'n' Roll Revival* or *The Fabulous Fifties*).

Consider choosing a theme from the following categories:

>> **Fashion:** *The Roaring Twenties* or *An Evening at Ascot*

>> **History:** *The Garden of Eden* or *A Renaissance Fair*

>> **Politics:** *Fourth of July Celebrations* or *Women's Sufferage* (political *and* historical)

>> **Popular culture:** *Star Wars* or *An Evening with Dr. Who*

>> **The arts:** *An Italian Affair* or *A Night at the Opera*

TIP

If you're still at a loss, consider having a competition soliciting ideas from your target audience. Offer the winner a free trip to the meeting. Your best ideas often come from others. All you need to do is ask.

If you do decide to have a themed event, keep the following in mind:

>> Carry out your theme before, during, and after the event. Reflect your theme in the invitations and in any party favors that guests take home.

>> Be prepared to follow through with it. If you've chosen to have a theme, be thorough and go all in. From the minute your attendees arrive they should feel they have been transported to another time and place. Have fun with it!

>> Your theme should complement the tone and content of your event. Be sure to let speakers know about the theme and how they can incorporate it into their remarks. The theme should work with any speeches and presentations that are given. On the flip side, speakers shouldn't overuse the theme in their presentations and still expect to be taken seriously.

TIP

For those of you who want to avoid the brainwork of choosing a theme and are looking for the easy way out, check out Giggster's party theme ideas (https://giggster.com/blog/the-greatest-list-of-party-theme-ideas-ever) or SocialTables (https://www.socialtables.com/blog/event-planning/corporate-event-themes) for more specific ideas and the guidelines to make them work.

Integrating a theme into your event

When integrating your theme into the event, here are a few basic guidelines to consider:

>> Is the theme general enough that it is unlikely to offend anyone? Is it meaningful to your group? How will participants interpret it?

>> Will the theme motivate participants to action? For example, will it prompt them to register to attend the event?

>> Can you integrate your theme into all aspects of your marketing and promotional materials — before, during, and after the event?

>> Can you develop a meaningful message or slogan through the theme? (For example, one year the National Speakers Association had the theme "The Privilege of the Platform." This theme was used in all workshops and the annual convention, and it also became a poignant message to the members that being asked to speak to a group is truly a privilege.)

>> Can you have a logo designed to enhance the theme and its possible message?

>> How can you maximize the theme? For example, is it appropriate to produce and sell theme-logo merchandise?

TECHNICAL STUFF

SAY CHEESE!

A photographer is a great addition to almost any event. Guests appreciate a visual reminder of the fun time they had at your affair. Arranging to have family portraits taken at an employee appreciation event shows your employees that you care about them as individuals — and about their families and lives outside the workplace. Guests at more formal affairs enjoy having their pictures taken while they're dressed up for a night out.

Decide whether you want a photographer to roam among your guests taking candid shots, to set up in a central location to take posed shots, or both.

If you don't want to hire a professional photographer, you can always designate staff members to walk around the event to snap pictures with the guests' phones or their own. Provide a hashtag for the event so the photos can be shared and posted online through social media.

On a technical note, be specific when asking your photographer what their fee includes. Does it include their time, editing, prints, and digital files? It's also a good idea to have the photographer inspect the venue in advance to determine whether the lighting and background are acceptable, and if they will need to bring additional equipment.

Entertaining the Groups

Participants look forward to the entertainment segment of a program. They want to have fun, enjoy themselves, and let their hair down, particularly after stressful and demanding sessions. So guess what? Your participants' stress reliever now becomes your stress maker. You have a true responsibility to choose the right entertainment for your group.

Choosing appropriate entertainment

Keeping your budget in mind, use the information you gathered from your audience questionnaire (see the "Analyzing Your Audience" section, earlier in this chapter) to help define what best fits the bill.

Some options include the following:

>> **Music:** Your choices include a band with or without singers, a soloist (instrumental or vocal), a DJ, or even karaoke.

>> **Spectacle:** Consider hiring a magician, juggler, comedian, or mime.

>> **Theater:** Arrange a dinner theater performance, a one-person act, a murder-mystery experience, or corporate theater (which involves using professional or amateur actors to dramatize a company's image, a new product, or the history of an organization).

>> **Games:** Involve your participants by planning individual games, such as a treasure hunt, or an event with a game show format, such as "Jeopardy" or "Hollywood Squares."

>> **Video or slide show:** A picture *is* worth a thousand words. For a retirement dinner, consider creating a slide show featuring the guest of honor's accomplishments. For a sales meeting, you may want to provide a video demonstration of a new product.

Hiring the talent

As you think about hiring your entertainment talent, find out where and for whom they've previously performed. Make certain that you view a demo video. Watch for the quality of the entertainers' performance and the audience reaction. Check out their references and ask some pertinent questions.

Here are a few questions to get you started:

>> Would you hire them again?

>> How flexible, reliable, and easy to work with were they?

>> How would you rate their act on a scale of 1 to 5, with 5 being the highest?

>> What do they do well?

>> What part of their act could use improvement?

>> What were the demographics of your audience? (You want to make sure that this act would be a good fit for your participants.)

Find out whether the entertainers need extra staging, lighting, or décor to create the right ambiance. Special requirements add to your bottom line — watch out, this could get expensive. Be sure that the venue you'll be using approves any special requests. For musical entertainment, discuss various options, such as low-volume background music, light entertainment during the meal, and lively dance music.

Discuss how the entertainers involve the audience in their act. People enjoy both passive and active involvement. And the more they're involved with the entertainment, the more likely your participants will remember your event favorably. Check your entertainers' willingness to accommodate special on-the-spot audience requests.

REMEMBER

Double-check that the person you interview is the same person who will actually entertain on the day of your event.

If you don't have the budget for a DJ at your event, your venue may have piped-in background music or allow you to provide your own playlist of licensed music. Discuss fees and any extra charges, such as accommodations, travel, and food. Also check on the payment and deposit policy. Find out whether the entertainers are union members and what this means in terms of your working agreement with them. This may mean that you cannot record their performance, or you may be charged an extra fee if permission to record *is* granted. It may also mean that an entertainer cannot deviate from the original arrangement; you cannot expect entertainers to do more than they were contracted to do.

Make certain that you communicate your event objectives and any theme or message developed for the occasion. The better your entertainers understand your needs, the better the chances for a great performance.

JOCKEYING FOR POSITION

Many DJs will vie for your business. What do you need to know about them to find the one who will play your tunes in the best possible way? When interviewing a DJ, ask the following questions to help you make a final decision:

- What equipment do you use and what are your backup options in case of an emergency?
- How do you plan to dress for the occasion?
- Where is an upcoming performance I can see?
- How do I select the music for the event?
- What is your over-time policy if the event runs long?
- Do you plan to use strobe lighting? (This special effect is particularly dangerous for people who suffer from epilepsy.)
- Do you plan to use pyrotechnics? (You need to consider safety issues here.)

No matter what type of entertainment you choose, make certain that you have a written contract.

2

It's All Show Business

The fun really begins here because this part covers the concrete steps to making your meetings and events sizzle. From planning the program to ensuring high-impact presentations, you examine the myriad components that require your attention.

Knowing the best and most hassle-free way to get to the meeting or event site is a crucial first step, so I begin with a chapter on travel arrangements. After people arrive, you naturally want to make them feel good, and what better way than with some top-quality nourishment? Hence I offer a wealth of information on food that will help add some real zing to your events.

Creating a memorable and effective program is at the heart of your task, and the process begins with knowing what your target audience wants, picking the right location, and looking at the extras that will help you put together an appealing lineup and irresistible program package. The cornerstone of your program hinges on selecting the right speakers and arranging the appropriate environment. I guide you through some of the tricks of the trade and share important insider secrets so that you get the rave reviews you deserve.

Chapter **6**

Get Me to the Meeting on Time

They come by land and by air, travelers fighting their way through crowded airports and unfamiliar cities, making their way to your event. A smooth trip means they arrive relaxed, refreshed, and ready to focus; give them a poorly planned trip, and they walk in the door fatigued and frustrated.

When you make travel arrangements for people attending your meeting or conference, you have a certain level of control over their mental state when they arrive. If you follow a few simple tips and pay attention to detail as you set up their travel plans, you can help your travelers get to the meeting on time and ready to work!

This chapter tells you what you need to know about arranging air travel and ground transportation, and it helps you choose a reputable travel agent. The skills you learn here can also help you when you plan your own travel —perhaps a well-deserved vacation after the meeting is over?

Up, Up, and Away: Air Travel Made Easy

At any given time, the sky is full of commercial airplanes shuttling business travelers to and from meetings and events. For some passengers, the trip is easy and enjoyable. For others, the trip is an exhausting and frustrating experience. You can make sure your traveler is among the former group of passengers by knowing a bit about the airline industry, and by following a few guidelines when making air travel arrangements.

Understanding ticket classes

The first thing you need to know is the difference between the classes of tickets you can purchase. Most airlines offer four classes to choose from — economy, coach, business class, and first class.

TIP

Be aware that each airline has their own lingo for their ticket classes and they also have different seating plans. On Southwest Airlines for instance, everyone gets the same seat, but they may allow you to upgrade for earlier boarding, additional baggage, or a more fluid change and cancellation policy.

Here are their basic descriptions, but be sure to ask your airline representative or travel agent about the specifics of any ticket you are considering:

>> **Economy.** Although an economy fare is your least expensive option, the requirements and restrictions placed on this class of tickets make it difficult for business travelers to use. These tickets must be purchased two to three weeks in advance, require a Saturday night stay, are difficult and costly to change, and are nonrefundable.

>> **Coach.** A much better option for business travelers, coach tickets do not require as much advance purchase, and they do not require a Saturday night stay. Airlines do not apply a charge for changing these tickets, and refunds are possible.

>> **Business class.** Situated somewhere between coach and first class, business class tickets usually provide the passenger with bigger seats and more amenities than coach tickets. You're also more likely to be bumped up to first class when flying business class.

>> **First class.** You can't do any better than first class. As its name implies, first class is the best and, naturally, the most costly! First-class passengers have the luxury of more room, better meals, special amenities, and the best service.

Booking airline tickets

First determine when you want your travelers to arrive in town. Always allow enough time to get from the airport to your event, to avoid your travelers arriving winded and flustered just as the meeting begins. If attendees fly into town on the same day as the event, book the flight early enough to allow for possible delays and enough time to catch a cab or meet other transportation you arrange, check into the hotel (if applicable), park any luggage, and get to the meeting punctually. The best option, if possible, is arriving the night before the event starts, so they can turn up at the start rested and focused.

Before booking airline tickets, get to know your travelers by asking a few simple questions. Do they favor a window or an aisle seat? What's their meal preference? Airlines that provide meals will have options for special dietary needs such as diabetic, vegetarian, kosher, low-calorie, low-sodium, and low-fat meals. Check with the airline to see what it offers.

TIP

When you do make or change airline reservations, always write down the name of the person who helps you, the time of the call, and the outcome of your conversation. (Also make a point of doing this when you deal with ground transportation providers and make hotel reservations.) Be certain to record your confirmation number and keep it handy for easy reference. (In the travel world, your confirmation number is also known as your *recordlocator*.)

When booking a flight, ask your airline representative or travel agent the following questions:

>> What restrictions apply to this particular fare?

>> What is the refund penalty?

>> What do I need to do to change flights?

>> Is there a charge for changing flights?

>> Is this the lowest fare/rate available?

>> What special promotional fares are you presently running?

>> What does the travel agent charge for their services? (Back in the day, travel agents received a commission from the airlines and hotels for bookings. Now, due to travelers booking directly online, some travel agents charge a fee for services.)

You can reduce the risk that your traveler's flight will be cancelled by not booking them onto the last flight of the day.

If you have trouble finding a flight into a major airport, take a look at smaller nearby airports. They may have a cheaper flight or one that better fits your plans. For example, the Long Beach, Orange County, Ontario, and Burbank airports surround Los Angeles International. The Oakland, Sacramento, and San Jose airports are alternatives to San Francisco International.

Whenever possible, avoid booking flights that have connections in cities with chronic weather conditions that cause flight delays. For example, the fog in San Francisco is notorious for fouling up flight schedules there, and Boston is not much better.

Buying tickets online

Perhaps the biggest advantage to shopping for flights online is the immediacy of the information you get — enter a few particulars about the trip, press a button, and up pops a list of flights matching your needs.

Be aware, however, that the internet may not be the answer to all your air travel needs. Many things you just can't do online. If you're booking a complicated multi-leg or international flight, or if your traveler has special needs or preferences for his meals or seating, you're better off working directly with the airline or a travel agent.

Despite these areas for caution, the internet often is still a good place to shop for airline tickets. You can visit the websites of individual airlines, as well as travel sites that almost instantly give you flight options on numerous airlines.

Popular internet travel sites include:

» CheapTickets.com

» Expedia.com

» Hotwire.com

» Kayak.com

» Priceline.com

» Travelocity.com

TECHNICAL STUFF

NONSTOP VERSUS DIRECT FLIGHTS

While they sound deceptively similar, *nonstop* flights and *direct* flights are actually quite different. As its name implies, a nonstop flight does not make any stops en route to its final destination. A direct flight does stop. The term *direct* simply indicates that you will not have to switch planes when it does. (Sometimes, you end up changing planes anyway because of the infamous "equipment" changes airlines make when they get to a hub.)

You can ask your airline representative for the on-time performance of any flights you're considering. The one-digit code they give you will indicate how often a flight arrived on time during the most recent reported month. The codes range from 0 to 9, with 9 being the best. For example, an on-time performance rating of 7 means that a flight arrived within 15 minutes of its scheduled arrival time between 70 and 79.9 percent of the time.

You can find the performance data on flight tracking websites such as Flitestats.com. These stats can be especially helpful when you're choosing between flights with similar times and fares.

Using a travel agent

Travel agents can take care of any changes or problems that arise. If you book your ticket online and then need to change your traveler's flight (as often happens in business travel), or if you encounter a problem with the ticket you purchased, you're stuck handling it yourself. If you go through an agent, you can call them for help making the changes or resolving the problem with minimal inconvenience to you or your traveler. For information on selecting a reputable travel agent, see the "Working with a Travel Agent" section, later in this chapter.

Organizing Ground Transportation

Now, turn your attention from the friendly skies to *terra firma*, better known as solid ground. Whether you're arranging a ride from the airport or renting a car to be placed at your traveler's disposal, the following sections offer key information on your ground transportation options.

Airport shuttles

Hiring an airport shuttle from the airport to the hotel is a convenient way to move solitary travelers or groups of people.

Super Shuttle Express (www.supershuttle.com) is a popular national chain that offers its services 24 hours a day, 7 days a week. You can also find local shuttle services on the internet with a quick search for "airport shuttle" and the name of the city.

Before you pay for any shuttle service, check to see if your hotel offers a courtesy bus service to and from the airport. If the hotel charges, it's usually worth the $5 or $10 extra.

TIP

Save on your group's ground transportation costs by arranging a central meeting point at an airport hotel. Provide a small reception while people wait for others to arrive, and then transport everyone in a hired bus. This tactic can potentially save you hundreds of dollars on individual transportation fares, especially if your destination is 10 miles or more from the airport.

Chauffeured vehicles

When you want to provide your guests with ground transportation that's a step above shuttle service, consider arranging a chauffeured vehicle to transport them from airport to hotel to event. If you don't want to rent a limo, you can also choose from sedans and town cars that are every bit as luxurious, but draw less attention. These cars come with professional drivers and allow your guests to sit back and enjoy their ride in the comfort of a luxury vehicle without the stress of driving in an unfamiliar city. The privacy and elevated service of chauffeured vehicles make them an excellent option for transporting VIPs and guests you want to impress, but they're also a great way to spoil your regular guests if you have the budget!

Super Shuttle Express offers ExecuCar (www.execucar.com), a business-class sedan service, in select cities. It advertises "courteous, professional drivers" and "consistent and reliable service" — things to look for in any chauffeured car company.

A number of other companies offer comparable services. When choosing a transportation service, make sure it has three key things:

>> A good safety record

>> Experienced, professional drivers who dress appropriately

>> Clean, well-maintained vehicles

Check with the local Convention and Visitors Bureau at your event site for reputable companies. You'll find the bureau by entering "convention and visitors bureau + location" into your favorite internet search engine.

ARRANGING TRAVEL FOR ATTENDEES WITH SPECIAL NEEDS

Traveling is difficult for anyone, but especially for people who are mobility challenged, visually impaired, or hearing impaired.

Whenever possible, try to get your special needs traveler on a nonstop or direct flight. When you must book them on connecting flights, schedule the arrival time of the first flight and the departure time of the second flight at least an hour apart, allowing plenty of time to make the connection. You can also arrange to have an airline or airport employee meet your traveler and assist them from one gate to the next — an employee can provide a ride on a motorized vehicle, push your traveler in a wheelchair, or simply offer assistance with carry-on luggage. Ask your traveler for their preferences.

When choosing a seat on the plane for a traveler with a disability, try to get one at the front of the aircraft so they won't have to maneuver down the long, narrow aisle. For travelers in wheelchairs, ask the airline or your travel agent for an aisle seat with movable or removable arm rests. This will enable your traveler to move from wheelchair to seat with greater ease.

Look for shuttle services that offer accessible vans. You also can opt for a private limousine company that has a track record of providing exemplary service to customers with mobility issues.

Finally, when booking a rental car for a traveler with a disability, it's often best to opt for one with four doors. The larger doors make it easier to maneuver and to get a wheelchair in and out. Ask your traveler whether they have any special needs when it comes to a car (such as hand controls).

Rental cars

In most cities, you can transport your travelers with the help of shuttle services, taxis, ride shares, and chauffeured vehicles. Occasionally, however, people may need or want the independence of having their own vehicles. That's when you turn to a car rental company for help. A few things to keep in mind when renting a car:

>> Reserve rental cars far in advance.

>> Get the class of rental car and the guaranteed rate in writing.

>> Verify the reservation the day before your traveler needs the car.

>> Arrange for the car to be picked up early in the day, so your traveler doesn't get stuck with an inferior vehicle — or no vehicle at all!

Car rental agencies that are located away from the airport terminal are generally cheaper but also less convenient. You can decide which is more important, cost savings or convenience.

TIP

You can help guarantee your traveler a newer, cleaner car by asking for a car with low mileage while making your reservations. Also, check if your traveler needs a smoking or nonsmoking car.

WARNING

Although a rental car provides your traveler a significant degree of independence, it may not be the best option. Keep in mind that taxi fares or ride-share services may be less than the cost of parking a rental car, and your travelers wouldn't have to worry about finding their way around an unfamiliar city. Many hotels also offer transportation services that can get your travelers to and from your meeting or conference at minimal cost.

Working with a Travel Agent

Sometimes the bother of travel planning can get to be too much, and you need to call in the ground troops. Here are some advantages to hiring a reputable travel agent:

>> Travel agents do all of the tough and tedious work associated with your travel planning. They also handle any problems that arise with minimal inconvenience to you and your traveler.

>> These people are experts, and they know the ins and outs of arranging successful air and ground travel at the best possible price.

>> Travel agents often have access to package deals, wholesalers, and specials not available to the general public. Also, because they bring airlines and hotels repeat business, their clients are often given the best accommodations.

>> Years of experience in the business result in travel agents having a pool of knowledge that they often share with you, from recommendations for the best restaurants and local attractions in your destination city to suggestions about what to pack.

>> Agents are adept at understanding and explaining the fine print on your travel tickets. They can alert you to restrictions, extra fees, and other potential pitfalls you should be aware of.

>> Some travel agents wield a lot of power and are surprisingly successful at getting you what you want — whether you need a hotel room with a view or a specific airline seat.

Hiring a travel agent takes most of the responsibility off of your shoulders, but how do you go about finding a good one? The best way to find a travel agent is to solicit recommendations from friends and colleagues. From there, your job is to do your homework and select the best of the bunch. Note that I mean the best travel agent for *you* — the travel agent that best matches your needs and personality. While your friends and colleagues will give their recommendations in good faith, you may have very different service needs and preferences.

Here are four key steps to finding the best travel agent fit:

1. **Make a list of your travel planning needs.**

   Begin by writing down what you need and expect from a travel agent. Determine what services you need: Are you looking for package deals that include air and ground travel, plus hotel accommodations and special perks for your travelers? Next, decide if you'll be using the agent primarily to make airline reservations, or if they'll be arranging a lot of ground transportation as well. Be aware that some agencies offer different services and specializations. Find the one that best fits your needs.

2. **Interview prospects.**

   Take the time to interview the travel agent you're considering. See if your personalities and tastes are in harmony. This step is important because the agent becomes an extension of you, and the arrangements they make for you and your travelers will reflect upon you and your company. To see if your tastes are similar, you might ask potential agents for comments on a hotel or city that you're familiar with. You can then compare their opinions to your own.

3. **Check affiliations.**

   Find out if the agent you're considering is a member of the American Society of Travel Agents (ASTA) or the Association of Retail Travel Agents (ARTA). While you don't need to base your final hiring decision on membership in one of these groups, this step is an added safety precaution for you. These organizations insist that their members follow certain professional guidelines and provide mediation in the event that you and the agent experience problems.

4. **Test their capabilities.**

   One final step you can take when shopping for a travel agent is to ask each candidate to price a specific trip for you. You can then compare the deals they offer you, the quality of their work, and their level of service.

TECHNICAL STUFF

MAYBE YOU *CAN* TAKE IT WITH YOU: PACKING TIPS

You try desperately to cram it all in — your clothes, toiletries, a picture of your kids. It's useless; you don't have enough room in your suitcase. You take everything out, look at it disgustedly, discard a few items, and try again.

Packing can be quite a chore, but turn to the experts for advice. Santa knows how, so follow his example. Below are a few tips on successful packing that you can use and pass along to travelers at your next event:

- Pack clothes that you can mix and match into several outfits. Black, beige, and other neutral colors are the most versatile and can be dressed up or down.

- Packing toiletry bottles and shoes in plastic bags can protect your clothes from leaks and smudges. Throw an extra bag into your suitcase to hold dirty clothes.

- Check the current TSA rules for the items you can pack in your carry-on and checked luggage (www.tsa.gov/travel/security-screening/whatcanibring/all).

- Try rolling your clothes carefully in plastic bags from the dry cleaner rather than folding them. Fans of this method of packing say it minimizes wrinkles and creases and is very space-efficient.

- Each airline has maximum baggage weight and dimensions. Smart frequent flyers always check the airline's website for their current allowable limits for carry-on and checked baggage.

After you pack your bags, be sure to tie a brightly colored piece of fabric to the handles of any suitcases you plan to check; you can spot them easily as they whiz by on the luggage carousel.

TIP

Check if your travel agent has a 24-hour, toll-free emergency number. This sounds like a perk, but it's actually essential in the event that problems arise or last-minute changes to your traveler's itinerary become necessary.

Timing It Right

When orchestrating travel plans, timing is everything. To secure a bargain rate with an industry supplier and to avoid as many travel frustrations as possible, planners need to consider the time of week and the time of year of their event.

Considering the time-of-week demand

As you're trying to figure out when to schedule your event, keep the following in mind:

» Hotel demand in urban centers typically tails off on Thursday and plummets on Friday and Saturday. In cities such as New York and San Francisco, where tourism is a major component of hotel demand, weekends may be heavily booked at certain times of the year.

» Hotel demand in entertainment and recreational areas such as Atlantic City, Reno, and Las Vegas tends to peak on weekends for much of the year, particularly where a large population is within driving distance.

» Airline demand patterns do not, unfortunately, coincide with those of lodging suppliers. Peak times for airlines are Friday and Sunday afternoons because of a convergence of VFR (visiting friends and relatives) and leisure travelers trying to get home to return to work and business travelers coming home Friday and leaving again on Sunday. The best time to schedule uncrowded airline travel is Saturday afternoons, except in ski resorts where packages typically run from Saturday noon to Saturday noon.

» Car rental demand peaks sharply between 11 a.m. and 2 p.m. on Wednesdays, reflecting the rental companies' dependence on business travelers. Significant discounts are offered on rentals beginning after noon on Thursdays and ending as late as 6 p.m. on Mondays.

» Ancillary services, such as destination management companies and audiovisual specialists, pretty much mirror lodging patterns because their demand is often derived from hotel activity. However, weddings often tie up limousine availability and hotel banquet facilities on weekends. Restaurants are also heavily booked for Saturday nights.

Reviewing the time-of-year demand

Nearly all services related to travel have peak seasons. If your meeting plans are flexible, try to schedule when demand is moderate or low to get the cheapest rates and to provide the calmest possible experience for your travelers.

Table 6-1 presents an overview of seasonal activity for the major travel-related services.

WARNING

In some cases, service employees take vacations during low-demand periods; this may reduce the dependability of on-site services. In these cases, try to negotiate service standards into your contract.

TABLE 6-1   A Month-by-Month Look at Service Demand

Month	Hotels	Airlines	Car Rental Agencies	Ancillary Services
January	Generally light	Heavy first week; light thereafter	Generally light	Generally light
February	Heavy for resorts only	Heavy to ski and warm weather destinations	Moderate generally, heavy in resorts	Light, except in resorts
March	Heavy in resorts, moderate in cities	Heavy on most routes	Moderately heavy in resorts	Moderate
April	Lighter than March	Lighter than March	Moderate	Moderate
May	Variably light to moderate	Variably light to moderate	Variably light to moderate	Variably light to moderate
June	Moderate	Heavy but not packed	Moderate	Heavy (weddings and graduations)
July	Light in cities; moderate for resorts	Heavy with VFR and resort traffic	Heavy	Light
August	Light, except in summer resorts	Heavy with VFR and resort traffic	Heavy	Light
September	Moderate	Moderate	Moderate	Moderate
October	Heavy in cities, light in resorts	Heavy Monday to Friday	Heavy Monday to Friday	Heavy in cities
November	Heavy until Thanksgiving in cities	Moderate	Moderate	Moderate
December	Very light until mid-month	Very light	Very light	Very light

When negotiating with all suppliers, ask what may happen to prices if alternative dates are possibilities. Make sure meeting sponsors are aware of both supplier and destination seasonality. If you schedule a winter resort meeting, for example, avoid setting it up during ski season.

IN THIS CHAPTER

» **Figuring out how food fits into your function**

» **Delving into different types of dining**

» **Deciding whether to serve alcohol**

» **Getting what you want from the catering manager**

» **Nailing down every last detail**

Chapter 7

Food for Thought

A meeting without food is like a car without wheels.

In other words, meetings work much better with food than without!

Food and drink provide an opportunity to relax and encourage networking. People's meeting memories, both good and bad, often stem from their food experiences. However simple it may sound to organize food and beverage functions, tripping into some major pitfalls is easy if you don't know what you're doing. This chapter focuses on the basics of food and beverage management so that you can spice up your events with flair, creativity, and imagination.

Considering Food and Beverage Concerns

As you start thinking about your food and beverage requirements, consider these five major areas:

» The role of food in your meeting goals and objectives

» Your budget for the event

>> The meeting venue you've selected

>> Your audience

>> Timing

I give you more information on each of these factors in the sections that follow.

Fitting food into your meeting purpose

For starters, your food and beverage concerns depend on your meeting goals and objectives and what role you want these concerns to play. Do you need light refreshments to break up the day, or does your boss want to wine and dine the group sparing no expense? Or perhaps your needs fall somewhere in between these two extremes? Each approach requires a totally different mind-set and plan of action based on whether food plays a major or minor role at your event.

Keeping your budget in mind

Everything regarding food and beverage planning hinges on how much you have to spend. Recognizing that you can't serve caviar on a hamburger budget is possibly your number one guideline for realistic budgeting. If you don't know that now, you'll certainly find it out after you start discussions with the catering manager. The reality of costs can quickly knock the wind out of you. Providing sustenance for the masses doesn't come cheap, and the quicker your boss and management realize this, the better. If you educate them early in the process, you can nip some complaints in the bud.

Looking over your venue

You can serve food just about anywhere. Your major venue consideration is whether catering is available in-house or whether you need to find an outside resource. Hotels, restaurants, private clubs, and conference and convention centers typically have on-site catering facilities. However, alternative venues, such as art galleries, museums, theaters, yachts, nightclubs, historic buildings, stately or celebrity homes, sporting stadiums, or clubs, probably require an outside caterer. If you want to take on the challenge of using an alternative-type venue, then definitely consider the feasibility of serving food before you decide on the site.

Understanding your audience

When it comes to feeding people, keep in mind that not everyone likes the same type of food. Not only is variety key, but so is having a profile of your attendees.

Knowing the likes, dislikes, allergies, and dietary restrictions of your audience helps avoid embarrassing and stressful situations. Serving quiche to a hearty meat-eating crowd or meat to vegetarians or shrimp to someone who keeps kosher will not make you popular. So knowing your group's dining particulars can help you make menu choices.

It would be to an event planner's credit to accommodate individuals as well as the majority trend. If the caterer knows in advance (when the order is placed) that the wait staff is serving 91 chicken cordon bleu dinners, 3 vegetarian pasta dishes, 2 diabetic dinners, 2 lactose intolerant meals, and 2 kosher dinners, for a total party of 100, then everybody is happy.

An easy way to get this information is to have your participants fill out a special dietary needs form prior to attending the meeting. The easiest way would be to list the various preferences available, just like the airlines do. Some possibilities include:

» Strict Vegetarian

» Lacto Ovo Vegetarian

» Diabetic

» Gluten Free

» Low Calorie

» Low Fat/Low Cholesterol

» Low Sodium

» Non-Lactose

» Vegan

It is important to include a section on your form for information on any food allergies. Also, you may want to add a disclaimer that you'll try to meet their preferences but cannot guarantee it.

You may or may not want to get this involved. If you're coordinating meetings for the same group of people on a regular basis, consider starting an individual profile sheet on each person.

Timing it right

To get the right timing when serving food, consider where and when it will be served, as well as what types of food you'll be providing. Where your food is served dictates how much time you need to allow for the various breaks. For example, if a mid-morning refreshment break is located at the other side of a facility from where participants are meeting, you need to make some allowances. People need enough time to get there and back, make a restroom stop, check their phones, and, of course, eat and network without experiencing stress and indigestion. Fifteen minutes to a half-hour is the norm. Any longer may disrupt the flow of the meeting.

If you schedule an evening gala event after a day of meetings, allow ample time for your participants to rest up and get dressed up. Functions held at alternative venues require that you allow people additional travel time.

Exploring Eating Options

You can include anything from a light breakfast to a full-blown banquet in your meeting or event plan — depending on your budget, of course. In the following sections, I give you what you need to know about each of the most common food functions.

REMEMBER

When the food function is over, be sure to sign off on your food and beverage bills and take a copy with you. Make a note of any special items you ordered while they're fresh in your mind, such as a bottle of champagne to celebrate the boss's wedding anniversary.

Breakfast

Breakfast helps fuel meeting participants' energy. It can range from a full sit-down event, including fruit, eggs, bacon, sausage, muffins, and so on, to a simple continental breakfast that includes coffee, juice, and Danish. Knowing your audience profile can help in your decision making. For example, health-conscious dieters may want only fruit and yogurt, whereas lumberjacks may prefer a buffet table that's loaded with more substantial fare.

In addition to being a great networking opportunity, a full breakfast buffet is often a wise choice as it gives everyone the opportunity to pick and choose their favorites in varying degrees of quantity. You'll probably find that most hotels offer a wide range of buffet options at different price levels. Buffets tend to be a little more expensive as the hotel must build in surplus food because there's no portion control. Remember to read the fine print to find out what surcharges apply depending on your numbers and what additional services you may add, such as an on-site chef to prepare individual omelets, pancakes, and/or waffles. Personally, I thoroughly enjoy having breakfast as part of a meeting or event because it's a nice way to start the day with people you'll be spending time with.

When it comes to food, people hate surprises. Have the catering manager label the various dishes on the buffet table so that your guests know what they're putting in their mouths. (Also bear in mind the people who suffer from food allergies.)

If you opt to go with a buffet for breakfast, be sure to offer various types of cereals, especially those high in fiber as they help to keep blood sugar levels stabilized longer.

Another breakfast option that works well for smaller numbers of event participants is to have them eat in the hotel restaurant. Then you just pay for whatever they order off of the regular menu. This way you don't have to shell out for any special arrangements or worry about guaranteeing certain numbers of people. You can also arrange with the restaurant to provide block seating so that your group can enjoy the added opportunity to interact with their colleagues.

Brunch

If you host brunch, make sure that an equal proportion of proteins (meat, eggs, cheese, fish, and tofu, for example) and carbohydrates (such as breads, grains, potatoes, and corn) are served to your guests to sustain participants' appetites through the major part of the day. Again, buffet-style allows for more variety. Brunch is usually a good choice if you start your meeting late in the morning and don't want to stop again for lunch.

Refreshment breaks

Refreshment breaks are meant to refresh participants between sessions and meals. Most adults need a break every 90 minutes. Often coffee, tea, soft drinks, and bottled water are all that's necessary. A light snack, however, such as fruit or cookies, helps give participants' blood sugar a lift during an afternoon break. Always offer a healthy alternative such as whole fruit, granola bars, or popcorn.

Do remember to check when other groups at the venue are breaking so that you schedule around them to avoid any conflict. Otherwise, you may find that if you offer nicer break food than another group, some unexpected visitors may pilfer the goodies, leaving your group short. To stop this from happening, have the hotel put up a sign on the table indicating that this refreshment table is reserved for your particular group.

For a break with a difference, consider some different location options within the facility. For example, a meeting planner took a group of air conditioning engineers to a plant room on the roof of the hotel for a break and served them coffee and tea in tin cups. Creative food choices can also add some fun to your event. For example, consider an ice-cream sundae bar during an afternoon break.

As a rule, order coffee by the gallon as opposed to by the cup because the price differential can be significant. Figure on getting 20 cups (not mugs) per gallon.

Lunch

Your lunch options could include a sit-down meal, a buffet, a barbecue, a boxed lunch, or just a plate of sandwiches and fruit. Much depends on how important the lunch is in relation to your meeting. For example, if you have some type of entertainment and/or a speaker scheduled, a sit-down meal is the easiest and most appropriate. If lunch is just a scheduled break time, a buffet or barbecue makes a good opportunity for your group to network and exchange ideas. If, on the other hand, the troops plan on working through lunch, a boxed meal or a plate of sandwiches may suffice.

Keep your lunch foods on the lighter side so that they energize rather than put people to sleep. For example, fish, chicken, or turkey with a salad make better choices than steak and potatoes. Pasta is a cheap filler-food, but don't overdo it, especially if you're meeting for several days. Think variety!

REMEMBER

When you're discussing menus with the catering manager, make sure that the vegetarian alternative is more than just steamed vegetables or pasta. As a vegetarian, this is an area near and dear to my heart. I've suffered through more plates of steamed vegetables than I care to remember. They definitely get old quickly!

Again, for a smaller group, you can arrange to have a block of seats in the hotel restaurant and have everyone order from the regular menu. Another alternative is to have your group do their own thing and go off to local restaurants. Unless you want some astronomical receipts, give them a budgeted amount for this. This is only practical if the group has a leisurely afternoon to themselves. If you offer this option, make sure the participants have a means of transportation and that you give them a list of local restaurants.

Dinner

Because dinner usually brings closure to the day's activities, you don't have to worry quite so much about low-calorie and high-energy foods. You can make the meal as extravagant or as simple as you want. Again, budget rules supreme.

If you include some form of entertainment, then a sit-down affair works best. However, if you want something a bit different, look at alternative areas in the hotel, such as an indoor patio or pool area. Naturally, a plan revolving around an outdoor pool is contingent on the weather. It's best to have a back-up plan just in case the heavens decide to open.

Buffets and barbecues also work well, but watch the price tag. These kinds of food functions often require extra labor, which automatically means additional dollars.

REMEMBER

Always offer butter/margarine, sugar/sugar substitutes, and cream/nonfat milk at all functions. Guests who have dietary restrictions will appreciate that you are looking out for their welfare by these small kindnesses.

Receptions

If you include a reception in your meeting schedule, decide what specific role it plays. For example, do you want it to be the beginning of the evening's activities, or do you want it to be a meal substitute? Knowing your reasoning for this event dictates the types of foods you order. The food fare can range from snacks (such as nuts and pretzels) to cold and hot finger foods (such as cheese and fruit, fresh vegetable platters, shrimp, fancy hors d'oeuvres, pasta bars, and more).

When ordering your hors d'oeuvres, allow seven to eight pieces per person. People who don't often attend receptions tend to eat more food than professionals who attend them frequently. Hot hors d'oeuvres are far more popular than cold ones!

WARNING

People inhale shrimp, so there's never enough. Plus, it's one of the more costly items to include.

Parties

Everyone loves a party, and including one in your meeting agenda can add an extra sense of fun and excitement, especially when you include a theme (see the nearby sidebar, "Party themes"). Depending on how much detail you want, your costs can range from minimal to excessive. Find out whether the facility has house decorations that it's willing to provide at no additional charge. If you're holding your event at a resort facility, check out what themed parties they're offering their guests. As a savvy planner, think of tying into an existing theme as this could offer you a significant savings. Naturally, you want to tie your food into the theme; for example, if you go Mexican, serve tacos and provide a chili bar.

Banquets

A banquet or gala event can be your most expensive food function, unless an angel steps in and sponsors it for you. A gala is often a formal affair that encourages guests to dress up, and it should act as a culmination to your event. You may include awards, speeches, and entertainment (such as singers, a comedian, and/or a live band or disc jockey for dancing). If this is a celebratory event, make sure that you create a special ambiance with fine food, décor, and entertainment.

PARTY THEMES

Think through what you can do to create a fun, interesting, and exciting ambiance for your event. Items for consideration include stage settings, lighting, special scenery, music, ice carvings, flowers, centerpieces, candles, balloons, colored linens, printed menus, a photographer, and gift items. Budget determines how much of your wish list turns into reality. The following list is just a sampling of some of the themes you could execute:

- Caribbean Carnival
- An Evening at the Moulin Rouge
- A Ghostly Evening
- Downton Abbey Era
- Murder Mystery Mayhem
- A Night at Alcatraz
- Rockin' Beach Party
- Viva Las Vegas
- Wild West Saloon

For more theme-related ideas, turn to Chapter 5.

For an awards banquet, timing is critical, because you never want people to suffer through a program of never-ending speeches. Make sure that you rehearse beforehand to iron out any kinks so that everything runs as smoothly as possible.

TIP

Sponsorship can be a great way to extend your budget. Try to find a department, corporation, or individual sponsor for any portion of the food and beverages for the event, or for the entertainment. Just be sure to acknowledge their contribution in the program, at the podium, and with signage if possible.

Serving Drinks at Your Event

Serving drinks at pre-dinner functions such as receptions or cocktail parties provides a good opportunity for people to socialize and is often a welcome break from the meeting's formalities. However, from the event planner's standpoint, cost and liability are two issues that need serious consideration.

Whether you're hosting a formal gala or a simple buffet table loaded with light, bite-size finger foods, you need to decide on drinks. When it comes to purchasing liquor, here are your options:

» **By the bottle:** This applies to hard liquor, wine, and beer and makes the most economic sense when you cater to large groups. For wine, decide whether you want to serve the house wines, usually unknown and less expensive brands, or better-known brands, which are more costly. Make sure that all the mixers and garnishes, such as orange juice, olives, cherries, and so on, are included in your price.

» **By the drink:** As the term implies, you literally pay for each drink guzzled. This can quickly become very expensive if you don't set any limits, so you may want to consider keeping tabs on your guests' consumption by distributing tickets they can use to "buy" drinks. This provides far better control and avoids any real surprises on the final bill. After a guest has exhausted their tickets, they then pay for their own drinks.

» **By the person:** When you opt for this alternative, you pay a set price per person for a specific time period, during which there are no limits to the number of drinks consumed. Be sure you have a way to control turnout for the event, so you aren't surprised by how many people take advantage of the open bar.

» **Cash bar:** This is by far your cheapest option because your only costs include the bartender and possibly someone to handle the cash. (Hiring a second person to handle money is preferable, because you probably don't want the bartender handling money and then pouring drinks.) As a rule, allow 1 bartender for every 75 people. If you have over 100 people, then arrange for a second bar.

TIP

Here's a tip about tips! If the bartender is a venue employee ask for their fee to be waived with a minimum amount of beverages sold, usually $350 to $500 per bar. And have a tip jar available to reward the bartender for making your event positively memorable.

» **Open bar or hosted bar:** This is your most expensive option because you're responsible for the entire liquor bill. Open bars (sometimes referred to as hosted bars) attract excessive, expensive drinking. Limiting your hosted bar to beer, wine, and some nonalcoholic beverages can keep your costs down. Instruct the banquet captain to uncork wine bottles only as needed. If you serve hard liquor, insist on the bartenders using jiggers instead of free pouring, specifying one-ounce instead of one-and-one-half-ounce drinks. This soon adds up to a significant savings.

Don't announce a last call for drinks before the bar closes; otherwise, you're encouraging overindulgence. You may consider instructing the bartenders to inform you of any excessive drinking, which may turn hazardous. Allow for two drinks per hour for an average person.

>> **Waiter-served drinks:** This is a nice option if you want to offer champagne or wine as guests enter a reception. It's most cost-effective if the reception lasts around 30 to 45 minutes. However, serving drinks to guests as they enter is the most expensive option if you combine it with an open bar.

No matter what drinking option you decide on, keep the following tips in mind:

>> Plan for transportation or a sleeping room as a contingency plan for those guests who may become inebriated.

>> To keep tabs on the amount of wine served, consider counting the empty bottles after the event.

>> Check the rules at the facility to find out if you can provide your own wine for the event. The facility may charge a *corkage fee* — a cost for its staff to serve each bottle — if you go this route.

Check out the liability laws and the legal drinking age in the state/country you're in. Do you need additional insurance coverage in case of any accidents on the premises or during the drive home? Remember that some states prohibit serving liquor at certain times or on Sundays.

Working with the Catering Manager

Before you can start organizing any food functions, you need to meet with the facility's catering manager (CM) or your outside caterer or party planner if you hold your event at a unique venue without in-house facilities. Be prepared to build a good working relationship with this person. Share as many of your event details as appropriate — goals and objectives, programming, timing, number of guests (approximate if you're not sure of exact numbers — see the section on "Guaranteeing guests" later in this chapter), alternative venue arrangements, any specific menu requests, your participants' likes and dislikes, and so on.

If you don't already have historical information from past events, definitely start compiling a dossier for future reference. This document should include information on previous dealings with your food function catering; use it as a reference guide for all future communications. Why re-invent the wheel?

Set an appointment with the CM, letting them know beforehand what you wish to discuss so they, too, are prepared. If you want to see a meeting room or refreshment area or discuss sample menu ideas, let them know. Inform them if you're interested in meeting with the chef, head waiter/captain, or any other staff members. You maximize time when everyone's prepared. Site visits are covered in more detail in Chapter 5.

Make sure that you come to your first meeting prepared and knowing your budget and limitations. Like any good salesperson, a skillful CM wants to sell you as much as possible. Don't waste their time exploring wonderfully creative ideas when your purse strings don't stretch that far.

Avoid disclosing your budget too early in the discussions. Give the CM ballpark figures to work with rather than specific amounts. If you reveal a specific amount, then that's what the CM will quote you. If you just give a budgetary range, then you could get a quote for less. Be professional, understand your budget, and respect the CM's knowledge and guidance.

Use your first meeting to constructively discuss any prior food function problems or concerns, especially if you've used the facility for previous events. In addition:

» Discuss options for participants with special dietary needs, such as low-fat, low-salt, vegan, vegetarian, kosher, and halal. Request that no peanuts or peanut oil be used, as peanuts are the cause of many allergic reactions.

» Inform the CM of other specifics, such as what meals are needed on which days, whether your various meals necessitate separate rooms, whether you want plated or buffet-style food service, where you want to have the refreshment breaks (in or out of the meeting room), and what extras you may need for a mealtime speaker/entertainer (a raised platform and/or lectern).

The more the CM understands the essence of your event, the more they can help you plan. Remember, it's in their best interest to help you achieve a successful event. They want repeat business, and they want you to give great word-of-mouth recommendations to your meeting and event planner colleagues.

» Discuss complete meeting package (CMP) prices. Many facilities offer an all-inclusive package to help the meeting planner save money and budget for the event. A typical package may include the room rental, basic refreshment breaks, and minimally priced meals. Know exactly what is and isn't included in the CMP price.

You want to avoid any hidden surprises. For example, are soft drinks included in your refreshment breaks or is that an extra? What audiovisual equipment is provided? A great question to ask is, "What *specifically* is included in that price?" Verify if tax and gratuity are included.

>> Establish the extras that you'll be paying, such as tax and service charge/gratuity. Also find out if the service charge/gratuity is taxed.

>> Ask about any conflicting events being held at the same time as your event, and find out if the hotel will be renovating at the same time as your event.

REMEMBER

Don't underestimate the value of your business. Push, shove, and cajole the CM until you get what you want — within reason, of course! However, know your limits. You may win the battle, but doing so in an overly thoughtless or aggressive manner could jeopardize a relationship, which is definitely not recommended because you do need the CM's support and cooperation for your event.

In addition, you'll want to put on your food critic hat and get into the nitty-gritty of the menu and presentation. Realize the significant role the food and beverage arrangement can make to the success of your event. You want everyone to have a memorable experience. Together with the CM, plan well-balanced, nutritional menus that offer variety and are visually appealing. Remember that people eat with their eyes, and cover the following points:

>> Consider doing a food tasting beforehand, and, if you serve wine, definitely sample the CM's recommendations for both red and white wines. Always remember for whom you are catering — it's not yourself!

Match the wine to the menu. If you're not a connoisseur and feel intimidated at the prospect of choosing a wine, ask for help. The CM, the food and beverage manager, or the chef will gladly come to your aid.

>> Avoid choosing a standard set menu and then asking for it at a lower price. This won't make you popular. Instead, ask the CM to develop a similar menu at a reduced cost. It's best to give the chef an inclusive, per person budget and ask them to create a menu, as you're more likely to get better food and more creative options.

>> Ask to see a sample refreshment break station setup. Look for creativity and design. Do they use disposable or real crockery? Is there a selection of herbal as well as regular teas? Is soy milk available as a dairy alternative?

>> Find out if the chef has any specialties and look into local/regional/ national dishes that would be appropriate for your group. Using seasonal, locally-produced foods can often equal a cost savings. Ask that the chef be involved in your discussions regarding any unusual dishes you'd like created specifically for your event.

>> Find out if the foods served are purchased fresh, or whether they are canned or frozen. Also inquire if they have an in-house bakery.

>> When doing a taste test, remember that what you're sampling now may not be in season at the time of your event. Review this with the chef.

>> Ask about the portion sizes of each meal, particularly for luncheon and dinner entrées.

>> Discuss whether the luncheon dessert could be served at the afternoon refreshment break or whether the dinner dessert could be served in another location on the premises.

Getting It All in Writing

The *banquet event order* (BEO) is your official written confirmation of every detail of the food and beverage function that you plan with the CM. Whatever is written on the BEO is what will actually happen on the day of the event.

REMEMBER

Your job is to always double- and triple-check this document for accuracy, especially where detailed instructions are specified. Any changes need to be made in plenty of time prior to the event. Check the timing, menus, guaranteed numbers (more about that in a moment), various setup arrangements for meals and receptions, audiovisual equipment, service charges, and all other agreed details. I cannot stress this enough. If any changes are made, recheck them for correctness.

TECHNICAL STUFF

AND HOW WOULD YOU LIKE YOUR FOOD SERVED?

You can serve food in four major ways. Familiarize yourself with the following, and you should be well versed in the art of dishing up those tasty morsels:

- **American:** Diners enjoy a sit-down meal where their food is already served up on a plate.

- **Buffet:** Diners go to a pre-set table to help themselves to a variety of different dishes.

- **Butler/Russian:** Wait staff brings platters of food to the table so that diners can help themselves.

- **French:** For each course, servers spoon each item of food individually and directly onto the diner's plate.

Find out who will be in charge on the day of your event. Will the CM with whom you've worked so hard and built up a relationship be there? The following two sections on better understanding guarantees and room setups make up an integral part of the BEO.

Guaranteeing guests

A *guarantee* is the number of people who are expected to attend a food function and who you're obligated to pay for, whether they actually arrive or not. The CM needs to know the guarantee at least three days in advance so that the chef and the banquet staff can accommodate your food function in the best possible manner. Each meal requires a guaranteed number. Based on your menu pricing and your discussions, the CM often requests minimum numbers that they want you to guarantee. You need your attendance figures to be as accurate as possible so that the chef can prepare the right number of meals. You also need to find out what percentage of meals the facility will overset. This is your lifeline if numbers exceed your estimates.

An alternative method is to guarantee a quantity of food consumed; however, you'd better know what you're doing if you choose this option. It's usually an option used for buffets.

TIP

When hosting a dining event, estimate in favor of an overabundance of food or drink, which is much better than running short of food before every guest has been served. Besides, if after your event is over you find that you have enough cuisine left over for another party, this may be your opportunity to give back. Find out if and how you can donate the leftover food to a local soup kitchen or other charity, so the not-so-fortunate can also enjoy some tasty morsels.

Setting up the room

Decide what the best table arrangement and room setup needs to be for your various food functions. Round tables that seat six, eight, or ten work best for socializing. You could also consider U-, E-, or T-shaped table/seating arrangements. Know whether you need a head table and who will sit there. If you schedule some entertainment or a speaker, you may need a stage, a raised platform, a lectern, and/or audiovisual equipment. Make sure that the room you choose can comfortably accommodate all your needs. Definitely discuss this with the CM.

Tables are typically sized at 60-, 66-, or 72-inch rounds. Ask which size the facility has, and seat accordingly:

>> 8 people can fit at a 60-inch table.

>> 8–10 people can be seated at a 66-inch table.

>> 10–12 people will be comfortable at a 72-inch table.

REMEMBER

Keep in mind all the table embellishments when determining how many to seat at each table. If you have a formal place setting with wine and water glasses, bread and salad plates, chargers and dinner plates, plus centerpieces, programs, or other décor you may want either a larger table or fewer people seated at it.

Finally, work with the CM to manage the temperature of the room — comfortably cool — and to have easy access for everyone to move about the room and exit as needed. See Chapter 10 for more details on managing your environment.

Chapter **8**

Selecting Great Speakers

The success of meetings and events today relies more heavily than ever on the strength of program content and presentation. Nothing can spoil a meeting more than hiring the wrong speaker. Speakers are the main vehicles for communicating the overall meeting message. You look to them to provide insights, awareness, or cutting-edge information in an energetic, motivational, entertaining, and professional manner. The right speaker can emphasize an important message, offer inspiration, help people cope with new assignments, and lead the way toward change.

REMEMBER

Selecting the right speaker is one of the most important, and daunting, elements for creating a successful meeting. Your speaker can often make or break the event. If they bomb, your reputation not only takes a severe nosedive, but you also have the pleasure of dealing with the barrage of complaints from a disappointed audience. Yet, if they do well, you can walk away with many of the accolades, compliments, and rave reviews. This massive responsibility is not to be taken lightly.

Selecting the right speaker is not as easy as it may appear — the skill is determining what combination of education, motivation, and entertainment best fits your function. To help you meet this challenge, I devote a whole chapter to some tried and tested ways for you to single out the best of the best for your event. In this chapter, I give you guidelines to help simplify this intricate task, as well as some reputable resources for finding your golden nuggets.

Understanding Types of Presentation

First things first. Presentations primarily fall into four main categories:

>> **Keynote speeches:** For the most part, keynotes are used as official opening sessions, because their purpose is to rev up the troops and set the tone for the entire event. However, they can also be used at a luncheon, dinner, or banquet or to wrap up an event. Running time is commonly 30 to 90 minutes. Because the keynote speech is an inspirational and motivational tool, you may choose a celebrity; a best-selling author; a noted business leader; an expert in a particular field; a popular sports personality; or a professional speaker whose work, achievements, status, or thorough knowledge of an appropriate topic best suits the theme of your event.

Three main types of keynotes are given:

- **Motivational** keynotes offer a thought-provoking and useful message to arouse excitement in the group about themselves or their company. A good motivational speaker delivers a message that has a long-lasting effect.

- **Inspirational** keynote speakers often base their poignant messages on overcoming their life obstacles or accomplishing mammoth feats against all odds. Their speeches frequently consist of their life stories, which incorporate moving messages to encourage people toward higher aspirations.

- **Educational** keynotes concentrate on high-content information. A skilled speaker in this area delivers the message in an exciting and, at times, entertaining way.

>> **Workshops:** These presentations provide intense hands-on learning experiences. Workshops often zero in on coaching or training participants in how to tackle an issue or apply a new skill. Running time is usually from 90 minutes to a full day. Presenters for these sessions typically possess expertise in the area. When choosing workshop topics, consider "hot" industry issues or trends, areas that truly interest participants, or skill sets that attendees most need.

>> **Seminars:** This type of presentation is usually given to a small group (normally 30 people or less) whose members are expected or required to have a certain level of expertise in an area. The presenter, a subject authority, may also act as a facilitator. Seminars are often highly interactive and feature intense discussion sessions that can last several hours or days.

>> **Entertainment sessions:** These presentations are intended for pleasure. Possible choices for these sessions include humorists, comedians, musicians, hypnotists, magicians, and mimes. Entertainment sessions generally work

TECHNICAL STUFF

best as after-lunch or dinner attractions or wherever you need to lift spirits or add a touch of levity. Running time is normally 30 to 60 minutes.

People often confuse humorists with comedians, and vice versa. Just for the record, a *humorist* is a performer who uses amusing and witty material, some of which can include a motivational or inspirational message.

Selecting Good Speakers

Because nothing can spoil a meeting faster than booking the wrong speaker, I've put together these basic guidelines to help keep you away from the duds.

Know the program objectives

Before you can start looking for the right speaker, you must know the program objectives. Begin with the end in mind. In other words, step one is identifying exactly what you want to pull off with your event. Is this an annual meeting, a training program, an incentive get-together, an awards celebration, or another type of event? What are you trying to achieve? This is probably a committee or management decision, rather than one you have to make. But you may have to make their intangible concept tangible.

After you have a clear objective, you have a foundation on which to build your program. You want to consider the best combination of education, motivation, and entertainment to reach your objective. A common mix is 40 percent education, 40 percent motivation, and 20 percent entertainment. Another winning formula is 80 percent motivation and 20 percent entertainment. After building your presentation equation, consider what types of presentations (keynotes, workshops, seminars, or pure entertainment) are appropriate for your audience and fit the program format. The more thorough your plan, the better you'll be able to select the right speakers.

In addition to your program objectives, you don't want to forget two other very important factors that help shape your entire program. I'm referring to time and budgetary constraints — the time allotted to the program and the amount of money you have to spend. Both issues seriously impact the end result; make sure you have all the answers you need. (I cover speaker fees briefly at the end of this chapter.)

Understand audience needs

Along with the program objectives, consider the needs of your audience. Does your group need industry-specific or technical information? Will a mix of motivation and entertainment serve your group's purpose?

Today's audiences want content. They are generally younger, more educated, more diverse, and more sophisticated than those of days gone by. They want to learn, but they also want it to be fun. In choosing the right speaker, consider the audience needs and exactly what they expect. If management hasn't identified specific topics to be covered, I definitely suggest that you survey your audience. Ask them what they want or what skills would most help them in their jobs. For example, salespeople may ask for advanced selling skills, but managers may request teambuilding programs.

In the situation where you or your management team has already settled on specific topics or topic areas, your job involves finding the right speaker to handle the subject matter. The more you can pinpoint your needs, the easier your job of finding the perfect match will be. Your main objective is to narrow the search; otherwise, the process is a lot like looking for a needle in a haystack. Alternatively, you can find a speaker who may suggest a subject that would interest the group and meet the program objectives and needs.

Check for reputation

With countless speakers vying for your business, how can you possibly determine which one best meets your needs? Many speakers produce highly professional or glitzy marketing materials to help sell their services. Simply scanning a few website videos isn't going to land you a good speaker, unless you're very lucky. Ask pointed questions to find the right person. Here are three important questions to get you started:

>> What experience does this speaker have?

>> How familiar are they with your industry?

>> Who else has used them?

Depending on the topic area, it isn't always necessary for speakers to have worked in or be familiar with your particular industry. Ask them if they have addressed groups similar to yours. Often, if they have a broad industry background, they can easily deal with the idiosyncrasies in your environment. In addition, you can supply them with relevant material to help customize or tailor their presentation.

REMEMBER

It probably goes without saying, but just for the record, I'm going to say it anyway — never hire a speaker that no one you know has heard speak. Make this your golden rule! Get suggestions from people you respect. Ask your colleagues and friends. Find out who speaks at industry events such as annual conferences, and ask for recommendations.

Make a point of checking references. Ask questions about the type of audience the speaker presented to and the appropriateness of their message and style. If a reference says that the speaker was difficult to work with, recognize that this usually means that the speaker was inflexible. You only want to deal with speakers who are flexible and easy to work with. You're looking to develop a symbiotic relationship, one of mutual benefit and respect where you help make this person a star, and they do their utmost to make your event a huge success.

TIP

Check which professional organizations a speaker belongs to and what awards or certifications they have earned or have been awarded. For example, the National Speakers Association has two prestigious designations, Certified Speaking Professional (CSP), an earned award for extended speaking experience and client satisfaction, and the Council of Peers Award for Excellence (CPAE) Speaker Hall of Fame, a special designation awarded for professional excellence in the speaking business.

See a demo

If you don't have the opportunity to preview a speaker in person, review their audio or video on their website of a previous presentation (or request a link if there's nothing on their website). A session that was recorded before a live audience gives you a better sense of the speaker's real ability.

WARNING

Some demo videos highlight only small segments of a presentation, so you get only snippets of the best material. There's great parallel here with previews for upcoming movies where you see only the funniest or most exciting scenes. You then make a decision to go to see the movie and are disappointed because all the best stuff was in the preview. Don't let this happen to you. Talk to people who have heard the speaker you're considering, and, if at all possible, go and see them live before another audience so that you can form your own opinions.

Watch or listen to how the speaker builds rapport and interacts with their audience. Ask yourself if this person would be right for your group. Is their combination of education, motivation, and entertainment appropriate for your needs? Do they have a message that is appropriate, timely, and relevant to the theme or purpose of your event? Does it conform to your company's philosophy and policy? Do you feel they are genuine and have the expertise to deliver a solid presentation?

Watch out for celebrity speakers

If you want to hire a celebrity speaker, make sure they can speak. A person may be a celebrity in their area of expertise (sports, for example) but lack speaking skills. TV personalities do a great job on the air but often have little public speaking expertise. Know that the skills needed for being on TV and for speaking live are very, very different. I've experienced several embarrassing situations when associations chose TV personalities as their opening keynote speakers and were dreadfully disappointed.

However, many well-known personalities make excellent speakers and can add enormous value and clout to your event. Political, sports, media, or entertainment celebrities often share life experiences, offer advice, or have an inspirational message to impart.

Be aware that some celebrities have inflated egos. This can make them difficult to work with. Also, you may have to deal with special security arrangements. Just be prepared!

REMEMBER

A star may be a big draw to attract an audience, but if they flop, heads will roll. Do your homework so that your own head remains on your shoulders.

Be wary of grandiose claims

WARNING

The speaker who claims to be all things to all people is probably desperate for work. This person would probably sell their soul for a price. My advice: Avoid those people like the plague.

High-quality, professional speakers, on the other hand, usually have certain areas or topics of expertise. They would much rather refer potential business to another expert, rather than jeopardize their reputation by trying to do a program outside of their comfort zone. Many speakers can recommend a reputable colleague.

Ask for a biography, testimonials, and references, and make sure you check them. If it's important to you, ask for verification of any doctorate degrees or other titles the speaker uses. Unfortunately, some people out there on the speaking circuit use titles they haven't earned.

Request information on any published articles and books, and have speakers send samples of their work so you can verify their credibility firsthand.

Also, beware of the charismatic and fluffy speaker. Your audience wants good, solid take-away value. A speaker presenting a program on success should share examples of true success. A speaker on leadership should have actual experience as a leader. Check these real-life experiences out beforehand.

Provide and ask for good information

A reputable speaker wants to find out as much as possible about the meeting objectives, the audience, industry challenges, and so on so that they can tailor their presentation to the group. Share information on your organization and audience to help the speaker design a program to fit your specific needs. Send them web links and hardcopies of newsletters, catalogs, or any other publications that highlight industry trends, key people, industry jargon or buzzwords, and insider news and views.

Provide the speaker with as much information as possible about the size and demographics of the audience (age, gender, and positions, for example). Also, tell them about any other speakers you've hired and their presentations. Whenever possible, speakers like to build on what another speaker presents, especially when the other speaker is someone from your own management team or an industry expert. The last thing they want to happen is to duplicate what's already been said — an instant death knell for their credibility.

Other important information to share with speakers includes:

>> The purpose of the meeting

>> The length of time allotted for the presentation

>> The time allotted to Q & A

>> Meeting attire (business, casual, formal)

>> Events preceding or following the presentation

>> Any good/bad news about the company that should/should not be included in the presentation

>> Subjects that are taboo

>> Names of VIPs attending the event

>> Any ancillary media events (pre/post-meeting interviews)

Make sure that you have each speaker's travel information so that you can make any necessary arrangements. And, of course, you need to request each speaker's presentation requirements.

In addition, get the following information from each speaker so that you can promote them adequately before and during the event:

>> Biographical data.

>> A digital headshot as a .png or .jpg file.

>> The correct spelling of the speaker's name (and a nickname, if applicable).

>> A written introduction. Keep it short, aiming for 30 to 60 seconds (that's 75 to 100 words maximum).

>> Written permission to record the presentation. Be prepared to pay an extra fee for this privilege, as it can infringe on the speaker's ability to sell their products.

>> Audiovisual requirements.

>> Any special room setup arrangements.

>> The speaker's travel itinerary (arrival and departure dates and times) or travel arrangements that you must schedule.

>> Any special meal or accessibility needs that you should be aware of.

REMEMBER

Never be frightened to ask for information. Don't leave anything to chance.

Ask for an outline, handouts, and promotional material

Ask a speaker for an outline of the presentation to make sure they will be covering the material as you discussed. Communication has a habit of being misunderstood or misinterpreted. Seeing exactly what speakers plan to cover in the sessions should help to ensure that the material is tailored to your specific needs.

Let speakers know about specific deadlines you have for duplicating their handout material. Many speakers provide their own copies of handouts, because they want to ensure a certain quality. If they use workbooks or learning guides, they may have a per-person fee for these materials.

If you need help writing promotional information for a session, ask the speaker for help. Many speakers have this type of information available. They know the right words to use to highlight the benefits of their presentations, the learning objectives, and the take-away information. Why re-invent the wheel? You're trying to develop a mutually beneficial working relationship with your speaker.

Maximize opportunities

Look for ways to maximize opportunities with your speakers. Discuss different ways they can add extra value and be a significant resource to help improve your meeting's success. Brainstorm ways that you feel they can assist you in planning, preparing, promoting, and presenting. Some suggestions include:

- » Serving as an emcee.

- » Conducting special sessions or round-table discussions about current issues for select groups (such as company executives or the board of directors).

- » Participating in a spouse program.

- » Coaching key in-house presenters.

- » Working with the program committee on content and scheduling.

- » Holding a press conference.

- » Sitting with a select group during lunch. If participants are paying to attend your event, you may charge an extra fee for this privilege.

- » Conducting a special clinic or general discussion following the session.

Trust your instincts

Through your communication with the speaker, you will quickly form an opinion or have a feeling about this person. Your reaction can be summed up simply: You either feel comfortable about working with them, or you don't. This response usually comes from your gut — a very trustworthy organ. Have confidence in your instincts, and trust that so-called sixth sense. It has a good track record for accuracy and truth. If you experience any kind of negative feeling, think about looking for someone else or get another opinion from a colleague. You want to make sure that you can work with this person and that both of you are on the same wavelength.

REMEMBER

The true objective of hiring a professional speaker hinges on establishing a partnership where a mutually beneficial relationship grows and flourishes. When this happens, you know you've chosen well.

Using Help to Find a Speaker

Are you overwhelmed with the plethora of speakers to choose from? You may want to turn to a speakers bureau for advice and guidance. A good bureau should act as a consultant and partner to help your event succeed. Even though many hundreds of bureaus are out there, the numbers pale in comparison to the thousands of speakers. A bureau's sole purpose is to make your job easier and provide you with solutions. They want to find the best possible match for your event within your price range.

So, where do you go looking for one of these angels? Here are a few places to start your search:

» Professional associations

» Convention and Visitor Bureaus

» Industry colleagues

» Chambers of Commerce

» Customers and clients

» Friends

» Internet search

As with the individual speakers, check the bureau's references. Talk to past clients and find out how easy to work with and accommodating the bureau is. Ask the clients about the speakers the bureau recommended and the results, opinions, and take-home value from the presentations. I feel you can never ask enough questions.

When you find a bureau you feel comfortable working with, share as much information as possible with them. They want to know about your organization, the event, the size and demographics of the group, the results you're looking for, and (of course) your available budget. They also need time to process your request. I definitely recommend that you contact them many months in advance, primarily because the better speakers usually get booked early.

After you give the bureau a profile of the type of speaker you're looking for, they should be able to provide links to demo videos. Pay attention to how the speaker builds rapport and interacts with their audience. Ask yourself if this person would be right for your group. (Check out the "See a demo" section, earlier in this chapter, for more information on demo videos.)

Some bureaus may charge you a finder's fee for their services, especially for lining up celebrities and authors; a fee of around 10 percent is normal. However, the standard in the industry is that the bureau quotes you the same fee that the speaker quotes. The speaker then pays the bureau a commission for helping with their marketing efforts. As always, make sure you know what you're getting for your money. As ever, don't be afraid to ask questions!

The following are a few of the many names and website addresses of associations and speakers bureaus that can help you in your search for the ultimate great speaker.

Selected speakers bureaus:

>> **American Speakers Bureau:** www.speakersbureau.com

>> **Eagles Talent Connection:** www.eaglestalent.com

>> **Gold Stars Speakers Bureau:** www.goldstars.com

>> **Harry Walker Agency:** www.harrywalker.com

(This bureau specializes in celebrity speakers.)

>> **Speakers Unlimited:** www.speakersunlimited.com

>> **Washington Speakers Bureau:** www.washingtonspeakers.com

(This bureau specializes in celebrity speakers.)

General resources:

>> **International Association of Speakers Bureaus:** www.iasbweb.org

>> **National Speakers Association:** www.nsaspeaker.org

(Find samples of a speaker engagement agreement and a speaker evaluation form on this site.)

>> **Toastmasters International:** www.toastmasters.org

Understanding Fees

Examples of typical speaker fees are impossible to give, as they can range from nothing to thousands of dollars. Speakers who speak for free usually do so because they want to donate their services to support the industry, or for charity, or because they value the exposure they can get from the engagement. But expect to pay expenses, which usually include travel, accommodations, ground transportation, and meals.

Celebrity speakers are definitely a horse of a different color and fall at the other end of the spectrum. Expect to pay big bucks for the privilege of having a celebrity present at your event. I mean really big bucks in many cases — $50,000 and upward for some of the more popular celebrities who frequent the speaking circuit.

Don't get discouraged though. Many really good speakers have fees that fall within the $3,000 to $6,000 range. Check what their fees include and exclude. Realize that you are not only paying for a speaker's time while presenting, but also for the hours devoted to research, preparation, and customization.

TIP

LURING YOUR FAVORITE SPEAKER

Is negotiating a speaker's fee an option? Offer a speaker a good deal, and chances are they'll be willing to listen. Here are some extras that may entice your favorite speaker to lower their fees:

- Provide opportunities for the speaker to sell products. (Limit the infomercial to one minute or less, or you'll get complaints from the audience.)

- Offer to send an e-mail on their behalf to the participants with a link to the speaker's website.

- Personally refer the speaker to colleagues in other companies/associations.

- Write a letter to association chapters around the country/world with a recommendation.

- Provide free advertising space in your newsletter or the event program.

- Link the speaker's website to yours through a banner ad.

- Place the speaker's articles in your newsletter or other publication or on your website.

- Pay for the speaker's spouse/significant other to attend the event.

- Offer one or more extra nights of accommodations at the meeting location (always nice if it's a resort area).

- Offer stock options in your company (if it's publicly held).

- Offer one of your products. (This only works if you sell something the speaker would use, such as a computer.)

- Give the speaker a digital recording of the event.

- Offer multiple engagements.

- Plead poverty as a nonprofit organization. (This is your absolute last resort!)

WARNING

You shouldn't go bargain hunting when it comes to selecting a speaker. If you do, you may pick a real dud and pay heavily as a consequence. Just think about all those unhappy, complaining people when you consider choosing a bargain-basement speaker — that should keep you levelheaded. Remember that experience, knowledge, and reputation should always come first.

TIP

If providing a thank-you gift to your speaker, be sure it is easy to transport — light, small, and packable. For a larger or heavier item, once it is publicly presented, privately offer to ship the gift to their home or office so that they can enjoy it. Word will get out that you are a wonderful and considerate host.

Confirming Arrangements in Writing

Make sure that all your arrangements are in writing and signed by both parties. (It wouldn't hurt to have a lawyer check them.) Your contract or letter of agreement should clearly outline all the agreed-upon arrangements and the expectations of both you and the speaker. Check that your written agreement includes arrangements for the following:

>> Travel and ground transportation

>> Accommodation and meals

>> Fees, payment terms, and your reimbursement policy

>> Cancellation policies

>> Audiovisual requirements and handout material deadlines

>> Expectations for the speaker to attend any social events

>> Arrangements for the speaker to sell products

>> Any legal implications included in your contract

Speakers usually have their own working agreements that confirm details of the engagement, the payment terms, and the cancellation policy. Expect to pay up to a 50 percent deposit as a confirmation for the speaking engagement and the balance of the fee on completion of the presentation.

Chapter **9**

It's the Extras That Count

Trekking to and from meetings and conferences can fast become tedious for frequent business travelers. Show them a good time while they're in town for your destination event to help them break free from their travel-induced weariness. The things that happen outside of the meetings make your event stand out!

This chapter touches on some of the things that you can do to make your next event memorable — from organized outings to recreational offerings to great meals and hotel service. Read on to find out how you can send your participants home raving about the great time they had at your event.

Helping Guests Get a Good Meal

They say the way to someone's heart is through their stomach, and the same may well be true of your meeting participants. Point them in the direction of a good meal, and they'll be awfully appreciative. Whether you arrange dinner out for a group of meeting participants or simply provide suggestions for individuals who want to dine on their own, several resources can help you choose a winning restaurant in almost any city:

» **Frommer's and Fodor's:** Frommer's guides and Fodor's guides don't stop with their reviews of select restaurants. They are comprehensive travel guides to specific destinations. While these sites can really help you plan, they also make wonderful resources for visiting meeting participants who have some extra time on their hands and may want to explore the local area. Their respective websites are www.frommers.com and www.fodors.com, and both offer a wealth of travel tips and useful information.

>> **Michelin:** Having started as a road-touring guide, the Michelin guide to restaurants is based on a three-star rating system. Restaurants that are worth a special trip are awarded the three-star rating; those worth a detour on your way to another destination have two stars; and those you should stop at only if they're on your path have one. Check out www.guide.michelin.com.

>> **Internet:** Ask Google for "restaurants near me" and see what pops up to your liking. Check in with TripAdvisor, Yelp, and look at local "foodie" accounts on Instagram. Then check the reviews, get directions, make reservations, or even order online for delivery to your room.

You can always ask the concierge or staff at your meeting venue for restaurant recommendations. However, make an effort to check out the recommended restaurant in person beforehand to make sure that your opinion of the establishment is on par with that of the person who suggested it. Everyone has different tastes, and perhaps you'd prefer something more upscale or a menu with more variety.

TECHNICAL STUFF

MIND YOUR MANNERS

Even though everybody eats several meals each day, some diners may not have the best table manners. Here are a few tips for you and your dinner companions to keep in mind:

- Courtesy dictates that you wait to begin eating until everyone at the table is served. However, if the person who hasn't been served insists that you eat, go ahead and do so.

- Keep your napkin in your lap when seated at the table, and place it on your chair if you must leave the table during the meal. When you're done with your meal, place your napkin to the side of your plate (never on top of the plate).

- When presented with numerous pieces of silverware lined up on the sides of your plate, your best bet is to start at the outside and work your way in.

- Pass items such as the breadbasket, salt and pepper, and salad dressing to your right. When passing liquid items, such as a creamer or gravy boat, be sure to pass it with the handle pointing toward the recipient.

- When you are finished with a course, do not push your plates away or stack them. Simply leave them in their original position until they are cleared.

TIP

For gourmet dining brought to you, you can hire Wolfgang Puck to cater your next meeting or business event. For an extra fee, Mr. Puck himself will come and prepare his delicious food for your guests. Talk about tasty! You can find more information on his website at www.wolfgangpuck.com.

Showing Off the Location to Your Guests

Participants who travel to a new city for your event may like to experience the area and get a taste of the local flavor. Doing some research and offering them information can enhance their experience. Checking out one of the travel guides that I mention in the previous section or visiting www.worldtravelguide.net can help you find information on numerous destinations. Or use your favorite web browser and drop your heart's desire followed by your event or meeting location.

Here are some areas that you may want to cover:

>> **Amusement parks:** These can make a real change of pace and add a get-away-from-it-all mentality for your meeting participants. The child in everyone loves to have fun, so give people the option. For something a little different, you may even consider holding an after-hours reception at a local amusement park.

>> **Art galleries:** Whether they're just looking or thinking of purchasing, art lovers enjoy glimpsing work by local artists. You may be amazed at the pockets of incredible artistic talent around the country. For example, the Adirondacks in Upstate New York, are a haven for talented artists.

>> **Eating:** Help your guests *literally* get a taste of local flavor by providing them with a list of restaurants serving food native to the region they're visiting. Include a range of prices and styles from small hole-in-the-wall establishments that serve startlingly good food to upscale restaurants that provide a lavish dining experience. Your guests will be grateful to experience the best Cajun food New Orleans has to offer, and they'll tell their friends about the great Chicago pizzeria they discovered!

>> **Historical landmarks:** Every city has historical landmarks — valuable historical locations preserved through time that offer visitors a glimpse of the past. The National Park Service has a searchable database of national historic landmarks on its website at https://www.nps.gov/subjects/nationalhistoriclandmarks/search.htm. States and communities also designate their own landmarks, so ask around! Remember that the local Convention and Visitors Bureau has a wealth of information.

- **Museums:** From museums with art exhibits to those specializing in natural history and everything in between, let your guests know what's available in the area.

- **Parks and nature preserves:** After sitting indoors at a meeting, your guests may relish the idea of getting back to nature.

- **Shopping:** Whether buying for themselves or someone at home, most travelers love to shop for gifts from the region they're visiting. Provide your meeting participants with information on local shopping opportunities. When doing so, include not only information on shopping malls and chain stores, but also information on swap meets, flea markets, local bazaars, auctions, shops, and shopping districts that specialize in unique items, such as antiques, handicrafts, and art by local artists.

- **Sightseeing tours:** Arrange for guests to tour the area around your meeting by bus or even helicopter. Contact local tour operators to find out what they offer. Some tours focus on themes, such as local history, native plants and animals, regional food and wine, and so on. Some tour operators specialize in tours for people with special needs — a great option if applicable to any of your meeting participants.

Never assume that your guests know what to bring with them when going on a sightseeing tour or other outing. Remind them to bring the following:

- Bottled water (As a nice extra touch, you can provide your guests with this amenity as they head out for the day.)

- PWK: Phone, wallet, keys!

- Hat

- Identification

- Sunglasses

- Sunscreen

Putting Sports and Exercise on the Menu

Many travelers will jump at the opportunity to stay in shape while at your event. After long flights and time spent sitting in meetings, they'll welcome the chance to stretch their legs and get the blood flowing.

Arrange for them to have access to their hotel's health club. If the hotel doesn't have an on-site health club, it may arrange for guests to use a local gym at discounted rates.

You can also arrange sports for your guests to participate in, including:

>> A round of golf at a local course

>> Tennis matches between meeting participants or time on the court with an instructor

>> One-on-one or three-on-three basketball games

>> Walks and hikes

Some guests may prefer to observe rather than participate in sports. For this type of sports enthusiast, you can arrange a broadcast of a sports game in a hotel lounge or hospitality suite. Offer food and beverages, turn on the game on a big screen television, and guests will feel right at home. The only thing missing will be their favorite recliners!

You may also consider arranging an outing to a local sporting event. Whether it's a major league, minor league, or college event, give your guests an opportunity to cheer for the local team. At least one sport is always in season, whether it's baseball, basketball, football, hockey, soccer, volleyball . . . you get the idea.

For guests who aren't very interested in sports or working out but still need a little pampering, set up time in the hotel's spa or at an off-site facility.

Welcoming Spouses and Partners

Many business travelers bring along their spouses or partners when they attend out-of-town meetings. What a nice, considerate touch to develop a spouse or companion program aimed at making your event enjoyable for them, too. While your meetings are in progress, you can provide activities for the partners. Providing a selection of things to do ensures that there's something for everyone! In addition to the other options mentioned in this chapter, you may want to consider:

>> **Arts and crafts:** You provide the room, refreshments, and craft-making materials, the spouses and companions provide the manual labor and take home a handmade bauble to remember the trip by.

>> **Classes and instruction:** Avid cooks would love a gourmet cooking class in the hotel's kitchen or at a nearby restaurant, and aspiring golfers might jump at the chance to spend some time with an instructor on a local course.

>> **Speakers:** Arrange a special speaker or entertainer to address the spouses and companions of your meeting participants.

In Chapter 12, I touch on the role a Destination Management Company (DMC) might have in helping you arrange your event. When it comes to spouse/companion programming, a DMC really could be of service to you, especially as you probably have more on your plate than you can cope with.

TECHNICAL
STUFF

DMCs frequently have an extensive list of full- or half-day tours that would be of interest to spouses/companions, youth, and other groups. A tour can usually be tailored to a group's specific interests, and professionally trained tour guides are often available to escort. Also, DMC tours often offer unique programs and topics that are educational and entertaining, such as self-help programs on personal safety, effective communication, and stress management.

TIP

If spouses or partners accompany your participants, it's a good idea to plan your meetings in the morning and leave them the afternoons and evenings free to enjoy their surroundings with their travel companions.

Chapter **10**

Lights, Camera, Action!

Your meeting success depends on many factors. The greatest presentation can be ruined by physical logistics, such as room setup, audiovisual equipment, and ambiance. Ignore these factors at your peril.

In this chapter, I show you how to select and arrange a room for your meeting or presentation, ensure appropriate lighting, determine what audiovisual equipment will do the best job for you, and figure out what to do in several special presentation situations. Quite a lot of stuff to grasp in one sitting!

Taking Control of Your Environment

If you've ever suffered through a meeting in a stuffy room, craning your neck to see the speaker and being startled every few minutes by loud voices in the hall outside, you know how miserable and unproductive a poorly planned meeting can be.

Creating an environment conducive to your meeting or event is fundamentally important to its success. The following sections contain some general guidelines on how to choose and arrange the room suitable for your event, a room that will accommodate participants in comfort and enable you to accomplish the established goals for your meeting.

Setting up the meeting room

When the time comes to pick a location for your meeting or presentation, whether in your own office environment or at an off–site location, pay attention to the following characteristics of the room or rooms you're considering:

>> **Space:** Will everyone be able to fit comfortably into the room after you set up chairs, tables, aisles, a stage or other presentation area, and any audiovisual equipment you need? If you're a novice in this area, definitely ask for advice from your venue contact.

>> **Temperature:** Does the room have air conditioning or heating? Can you control the temperature during the meeting in case body heat causes the temperature to rise uncomfortably?

Unfortunately, windows aren't a good substitute for air conditioning because they let in outside noises and distractions along with fresh air (which may not be so fresh). Many large facilities, especially convention centers, have temperature controls that are centrally located, and you may be hard-pressed to find a happy medium between the Arctic and the Sahara in the individual meeting rooms.

>> **Lighting:** How much control do you have over the room lighting? Can you make the room dark enough for the audience to see images projected on a screen? Can you make it light enough for participants to take notes?

>> **Sight lines:** Will you be unable to seat participants in any areas of the room because a column, low ceiling, or other impediment obstructs their view? You can best glean this type of information from a site inspection. You can't rely on room specifications to give you this data. However, if a site visit isn't possible, grill your contact with specific questions so as to avoid any on-site surprises.

>> **Potential distractions:** What potential distractions make the room a less-than-ideal setting for your meeting? Is the air conditioner too loud? Is the room situated on a busy street? Does noisy foot traffic intrude from the hallway outside? Is the room located adjacent to the kitchen or above a general session auditorium where dress rehearsals may be taking place? Are the walls thick enough to block out distracting noises? How about the sound system — can you hear feedback from one room to another?

The only way to know the answers to many of these questions is to test things out. Make sure that all windows have workable blinds to avoid distractions from outside activities, especially at resort facilities.

>> **Seating and tables:** Does your room have all the tables and chairs you need, or will you have to rent them? Are you required to rent them from the venue, or can you use an outside provider? If the room has any furniture that is inadequate or inappropriate for your meeting, will you have to move it out

and store it? Will the venue provide this service free of charge, or does it charge an additional fee?

>> **Rental time:** Be sure you have access to the room early enough to set up and troubleshoot any unanticipated problems before the meeting begins. Build in time for audiovisual technicians, lighting specialists, chair and table suppliers, caterers, and any other service providers to do their thing before attendees arrive. You may also want to give presenters rehearsal time in the room to become familiar and comfortable with their environment and to run through their presentations in search of potential problems. If your meeting covers multiple days, consider putting the meeting rooms on 24-hour hold to eliminate room equipment teardown and reset for each day.

WARNING

>> **Room capacity:** Room capacity charts provided by the event venue are often optimistic. Find out about the legal capacity of the room you are renting, and do not exceed it. Also check out all emergency exits, and work them into your planning, being careful not to obstruct them with a stage or seating. Make sure that all the exits are clearly marked and illuminated.

>> **Essential items:** Find out in advance whether your venue provides the following essential items either free of charge or for an additional fee. Any of the items not included, provided you need them, ought to become part of your contract negotiations:

- Coverings for any tables you're using, such as tablecloths and/or table skirts.

- Water and glasses for attendees.

- Notepads and pencils.

- Dishes of candy at each table.

- A stage and stage props, such as a lectern or podium, greenery, and an American flag if it's appropriate.

- Water, tissues, and mints at the lectern or podium for the speaker.

- Easels or sign holders and signage to direct attendees to the proper room.

- Flip charts or easel-sized sticky notes that can be placed on the walls, blue and black marker pens plus spares for the presenters.

- Blue and black marker pens for participants to take notes, complete worksheets, or use for team projects.

- Extension cords, power strips, and extra tables for projection equipment.

- Extra lighting, should it be necessary.

- Audiovisual equipment, such as a microphone, projector, screen, and so on. If the venue provides these, does it also provide technical staff to set up and handle any problems with the equipment?

- Laser pointer and remote control for the presentation, if necessary.

- Extra batteries for microphones and other equipment.

- Stanchions and ropes, for crowd control and managing movement.

Find out early which items you'll need to rent from an outside supplier to give yourself time to make arrangements.

Planning your seating arrangement

Different presentations and sizes of audience, together with the room dimensions, dictate the seating arrangements you need to consider. Following are the six most common forms of room setups:

» **Theater-style setup:** In this setup you simply seat participants in rows facing the speaker, as in an auditorium or theater. This arrangement is most common for large audiences and meetings that last less than half a day. It is an effective way to focus the viewer's attention on the presenter or screen. In this layout, you don't expect participants to write anything down because they have no writing surfaces other than their laps — not the most conducive for copious note-taking!

» **Curved-style setup:** This arrangement is a variation on the theater-style setup where instead of straight rows of chairs, the rows are curved in a hollow shape — slightly more informal because people can see each other.

» **Classroom-style setup:** In this setup, you seat participants in rows with a writing surface in front of them — either a table or desk. If you use individual desks, they can be rearranged for any breakout or brainstorming sessions you have planned.

This setup works best when the main portion of the conference is a lecture or speech, and the presenter wants participants to either take notes and/or refer to a manual. The most popular form of a classroom-style setup is to arrange the tables in an angled chevron design. This arrangement adds a friendlier ambiance that encourages networking and works well for small group interactions.

If possible, allow two people per 6-foot table or three people per 8-foot table for maximum comfort.

REMEMBER

>> **U- or V-shaped setup:** In this versatile room setup, you arrange the tables into a U or V shape and seat the participants all around the outside edge. A presenter then positions themself at the open end of the U or V. If you're using a television monitor or screen, place it at the opening.

This setup is an excellent arrangement, allowing the speaker to walk into the U and directly engage with individual participants. It is ideal for meetings arranged for a relatively small number of people, such as board meetings. I recommend no more than 30 people for this arrangement.

If you use this arrangement for a banquet, you can arrange seating on both sides of the table so people are on both the inside and outside of the U or V shape.

>> **Workshop-style setup:** In this setup, you seat participants in small groups around individual tables. This arrangement works best for meetings in which participants interact in small groups away from the main group (such as breakout or brainstorming sessions). It works for all sizes of meetings because the number of tables is limited only by the available space. Round tables seating six to eight per table are preferable. The ability to see one another encourages group interaction.

>> **Crescent setup:** This variation uses round tables where you seat participants using one half of the table. You may use this arrangement when a presentation is divided between lecture and small group interaction. Participants face the presenter for the speech and then easily team up for the group work.

>> **Hollow-square setup:** Similar to the U-shaped setup but with the open side closed with tables. This setting can handle from 30–60 people in a United Nations-style setting, where all participants are facing each other with equal rank and visibility.

>> **Conference-style setup:** This is similar to the hollow-square setup but with no space in the middle, instead using a large conference table or multiple portable tables grouped together. This is suitable for board-meeting style events with usually no more than 20 attendees. Observers can be seated around the periphery if needed.

Realize that if you're planning to use the same room for several presenters, you need to decide the best configuration for all the different presentations. If you're dealing with only one presenter, insist that they provide you with a preferred room layout. This step allows you to avoid having to reconfigure the seating when the presenter arrives because the layout isn't suitable for their presentation format.

TIP

To make your life a little easier, get a copy of the blueprints for the room you are using. The blueprints help immensely when you are trying to figure out how to arrange seating, the stage, and equipment. For a small investment, check out the viability of purchasing your own event management software. These programs give you the ability to design your own room setups, thus eliminating the guess-work. Check out www.dea.com/layout.asp for options.

Setting up a stage

For small, intimate meetings, you don't need to place your speaker on a raised stage to give their presentation. However, as the size of the room and audience grows, so does your need to elevate your presenter.

REMEMBER

In even a moderately-sized room, if your speaker is not raised, only the top quarter of their body is visible to attendees as close as three or four rows back from the front of the room. For those poor souls stuck at the back, forget it — the presenter is nearly (if not entirely) invisible. As a rule, use a riser when more than 100 people are in the audience.

If your situation requires a stage, consider the following key questions:

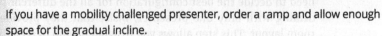

>> How big do you want the stage to be? Common sizes are 6 x 8 feet and 4 x 8 feet. How much space does your presenter need to work in? Are they going to be positioned behind a lectern or moving around the stage?

>> Will one stage be sufficient for multiple presentations?

>> If presentations using audiovisual equipment are back-to-back on different stages, do you need separate equipment for each stage? It can be problematic to move a projector and screen from one stage to another, and then set it up, while the audience is waiting.

>> Do you want the stage to be accessible from the front, side, or back? Where do you want the steps leading up to the stage? These questions may seem trivial, but they determine how your presenter makes an entrance. If the only steps are up the front of the stage, your speaker will have to enter from the audience, or walk around the stage from the side or back to ascend.

If you have a mobility challenged presenter, order a ramp and allow enough space for the gradual incline.

REMEMBER

>> What stage backdrop is appropriate? Will what's available be satisfactory, or do you want to invest in special drapes to add a certain ambiance to your meeting?

Let your presenters know about any color scheme, so their outfits don't clash with the stage backdrop — definitely an eyesore for your audience!

>> How appropriate or necessary is it to accessorize the stage with greenery, a lectern, an American flag, or other props? A lectern limits the movement of the presenter and hides most of their body from the audience, but many speakers like to hide behind them or use them to hold notes. You want to keep the accessories as simple as possible so as not to detract from the presentation.

TIP

If, despite your best planning, it will be impossible for everyone in the room to see a speaker, consider sharing the presentation live to screens placed strategically around the room.

Also, when you're conducting a hybrid meeting with attendees watching via their computer screen, be sure their feed clearly shows the presenter and the presentation. You can check the feed by logging into the hybrid meeting from another computer — providing you with the exact visual your online participants are viewing.

Handling Your Audiovisual Needs

Some facilities, such as conference centers, offer the luxury of built-in audiovisual (AV) capabilities that often contain highly sophisticated equipment. However, if you have to rent the necessary gear, it helps to have a little knowledge. You need to have a clear sense of how your AV equipment will enhance your event. Make sure that AV elements — and difficulties — don't overpower the message being conveyed.

In this section you discover some elementary points about AV equipment and a few tricks of the trade so that you feel more comfortable understanding what equipment to use, and when. The following sections concentrate on the fundamentals. For detailed information about more sophisticated technology, see the chapters in Part 4.

Microphones

Let your presenters know what room setup you've organized, and then ask whether they have any specific needs — speakers often prefer a certain type of microphone. (See the sidebar "Meeting your presenter's needs," later in this section, for a list of other equipment that a presenter may request.) Some common microphone setups include:

>> **Lectern/podium microphone:** This type of microphone is usually attached to the lectern with an adjustable arm. Speaker introductions are often conducted

from this location, and speakers who use notes often feel more comfortable positioned here.

>> **Table microphone:** As the name suggests, this type of microphone is used when the speaker is seated at a table. You often find these microphones used for panel discussions where the panelists are seated at a long table on the stage. You want to provide each participant with their own microphone, or at least one microphone between two people. It gets rather awkward and cumbersome when four people share one microphone and need to pass it to one another.

>> **Standing/aisle microphone:** Entertainers, especially singers and comedians, prefer this kind of microphone, which is positioned on a stand. These microphones are also commonly placed in the aisles so that during a question-and-answer session, participants can walk up and speak questions or comments directly into the microphone for all to hear.

>> **Hand-held microphone:** As the name says, this microphone is held in the hand. Corded and wireless versions are available. Entertainers and speakers who don't need to use their hands during their speeches often choose to use these. The hand-held mic is not the best choice for an inexperienced presenter or one who needs to write notes or perform a demonstration.

>> **Lavaliere/lapel microphones:** These microphones are small and easily clip onto clothing, preferably as close to the speaker's mouth as possible. They can be corded or wireless. Speakers who need to use their hands throughout their presentations often prefer this type of microphone. Remind your speaker not to turn their head away from this microphone when they speak — their audibility will fade.

TIP

Should you use a wireless or corded mic? There are advantages and disadvantages to both. The corded mic keeps the speaker on a short leash but offers the most reliable connection. The wireless mic enables the speaker to move even off the stage, but may encounter more feedback. Rely on an experienced audio tech to help you identify your best option.

Projection screens

Any time your presenter uses visuals during the presentation, you need a screen. The common projection screen format is letterbox (similar in shape to a modern television with a 16:9 ratio). The key here is to have one that is large enough, so everyone can see clearly.

MEETING YOUR PRESENTER'S NEEDS

The following is a typical list of audiovisual needs that speakers often request:

- LCD projector
- Screen
- Table microphone
- Hand-held corded microphone
- Wireless hand-held microphone
- Corded Lavaliere microphone (with 50-inch cord)
- Wireless Lavaliere microphone
- Flip chart or oversized sticky notes with markers

Remember to give presenters a deadline date for their requests because equipment ordered on-site is often more expensive, if it's even available.

Follow these helpful guidelines to get what's best:

» Decide whether you need a square or rectangular screen format. Choose a screen format that matches the projection equipment you're using. Ask your AV supplier for help with this.

» Order a nonglare screen that is video-format with a matte-white surface and is either a tripod or fastfold.

» Place the screen in the center of the audience's view, to the side, or in a corner. Much will depend on what's more important: the speaker or the projected visual information.

» Seats should be located a distance that is no less than double the width of the projected image, and the farthest seat from the screen is no more than five times the width of the image.

» Make sure that the bottom of the screen is at least 5 feet up from the floor to ensure that those backbenchers get a good view.

» Place the screen on the stage if the ceiling height permits, but make sure that it's dressed appropriately — side curtains, bottom skirt, and top valance. Naked screens are aesthetically uninteresting.

Projectors

You should anticipate that your presenter will have digitized visuals for their presentation. It is up to you to confirm that their format and your technology are compatible.

Select your projector first by their *lumens*. The minimum lumens for a small to medium-sized meeting room with a 100-inch screen is 2,500 lumens. The larger the room, the more lumens you need.

The latest digital video projectors offer wireless and Bluetooth connectivity while also featuring HDMI, USB, and micro-USB options. For the best connectivity, have a computer handy to support the apps being used (such as PowerPoint, Keynote, or Prezi).

TIP

Audio is available on some projectors and this may work well for a smaller setting, but using additional speakers and a mixing board to bring the sound clearly into a large conference room or auditorium is your best bet.

Here are some options for video projectors:

>> **DLP:** *Digital Light Processing* technology uses micro-mirrors to project images from a monitor onto a large screen. DLP is seen in stand-alone projection units, in rear projection TVs, and in most of the digital cinema projections. DLP provides excellent images, is compact and low maintenance, and works well in large rooms. Get one with LEDs for illumination.

>> **LCD:** *Liquid Crystal Display* projectors send light through a prism to display video, images, or computer data onto a screen or flat surface. These projectors tend to be bulky and pixilated. Be sure to have an extra lamp on hand as they are sensitive, hot, and can burn out during your presentation. Newer LCDs are available with an LED light source.

>> **LED:** *Light Emitting Diode* projectors are identified by their light source, the LEDs. They are compact — a little larger than your hand — very portable, and a great workhorse for meetings in close quarters.

The old-school overhead projector has been upgraded to make it compatible with digital technology (called a Digital Document Camera). These cameras (also known as visual presenters, visualizers, digital overheads, or docucams) are real-time image capture devices for displaying paper, transparencies, or an object to an audience. They come with a light to illuminate objects or surfaces below the camera so you can feed live content into your computer to share online. For live events, you can elect to send the images to a projector, delivering the picture to the screen.

The brighter the projector, the more versatile it will be under different lighting conditions. Projectors that provide brightness ratings of 1,000 lumens or more can produce excellent images in larger rooms, even without dimming the lights.

Lighting

Don't leave your meeting participants in the dark! Good lighting is essential to a good meeting, particularly when it includes a visual presentation or speech. Your goal is to light your meeting room unequally, following these basic guidelines:

>> For a keynote or general session, most of the light ought to be channeled onto the main presentation area enabling the audience to see as much of the presenter's facial features as possible. To avoid creating a spotlight effect and blinding your speaker, use cross lighting with two separate lights, one on either side of the presentation area. Less lighting is needed on the audience.

>> For a presentation where participants are expected to take notes, allow enough lighting to cover the audience so that they can do this without strain.

TUNING IN TO LICENSING

Before you crank up that oldies-but-goodies playlist to entertain your meeting audience or add a little life to a presentation, familiarize yourself with some of the legal know-how to save yourself from any problems that may occur down the road. Copyright law states that you must get permission from the copyright holder before you play a piece of music either live or from a recording. You don't have to track down the recording artists in an attempt to get their blessing before using the music — thankfully, the process is much simpler than that.

To get permission to play a piece of copyrighted music, all you need to do is pay a fee through one of two major performers' rights organizations: BMI (www.bmi.com) or ASCAP (www.ascap.com). Both of these nonprofit groups collect license fees on behalf of the composers and performers they represent. They then distribute the funds as royalties to the appropriate writers, composers, and copyright holders.

Note that the law does not apply to music over 75 years old that has not been revised and copyrighted. For music licensed after 1978 the copyright protection expires 50 years after the death of the last surviving author or composer.

For more detailed information about copyrights and trademarks check out: www.uspto.gov/trademarks/basics/trademark-patent-copyright.

>> You should have no light directly above or on any screens or monitors showing slides or other video or computer presentations. Definitely avoid fluorescent lighting near screens and monitors because this washes out any of the images you want to project.

Ideally, you should be able to control and dim individual lights in the meeting room. If you can't control the lighting, you can arrange to have venue management unscrew specific bulbs ahead of time to achieve the desired effect for your event.

REMEMBER

To avoid any washed-out images on a screen, arrange to have bulbs unscrewed that shine directly above or onto the screen. This task is particularly easy with recessed halogen spotlights.

Exploring Special Presentation Situations

As you organize various meetings and events, you're likely to come across many different presentation situations. Each requires a unique approach and attention to detail. This section prepares you for some of the most common scenarios.

Team presentations

Flip to almost any popular television morning show or sports coverage, and you likely find that it features an assemblage of co-hosts working as a team. Television networks and producers have caught on to the fact that different personalities and styles complement each other and provide the audience with more perspective, variety, and entertainment than a single host ever could. You can use this knowledge to *your* advantage by including a team presentation in your next event.

A team presentation is a highly coordinated effort given by two or more individuals trying to convey a common message. A team presentation is more complex than a solo presentation and requires extra planning to work successfully.

Knowing when to team up

Quite often, no one person has a complete understanding of all the details of a complex project or subject. Turning to a team presentation enables individual team members to speak about information they are familiar and comfortable with, rather than forcing one person to present information they have to struggle to learn and then speak about authoritatively.

Team presentations also give your audience a better overview of your organization by introducing them to more than just one presenter, and they make long presentations more interesting. For these reasons, team presentations are particularly appropriate for project proposals, progress reports, and training seminars.

TIP

Here are four tips for successful team presentations:

>> Select one team member to take charge and to coordinate all necessary details.

>> Plan the presentation carefully so that each team member fully understands what's expected of them.

>> Make sure that all team members direct their part of the presentation to the overall theme or message being conveyed.

>> Take time for a dry run through the material for timing and content.

Understanding the planner's role in team presentations

Your job is to find out what each presenter needs in the way of support material and audiovisual equipment, and to establish where each member wants to sit when they are not presenting. Make sure the speakers have plenty of water and their own glasses. It wouldn't be a bad idea to remind team members to pay attention to other presenters who are speaking and not be seen fidgeting, yawning, or playing with their notes. Most importantly, make sure the participants know the procedures and assignments and adhere to a tightly planned time schedule.

Presentations read from a script

Speeches read directly from a script can often seem unnatural and flat, usually because the speaker fails to listen to their own voice as they read, and they eliminate all natural pauses and inflection. Because their eyes are glued to the script, they often eliminate natural movement, gestures, and eye contact with the audience. As a result, audience members may wonder why they didn't just read a copy of the speech themselves.

Academics at professional meetings seem obliged to read their papers. However, many business presenters know just how to deliver a scripted speech and make it look as if they were speaking extemporaneously. A major technique is writing the manuscript the way you talk — informal and personal.

Encourage the presenter to practice reading the speech out loud before the actual presentation so that they can make any necessary adjustments to the tone, pitch, phrasing, and pauses. In addition, as they become more familiar with the speech, suggest that they work in a few physical gestures so that they're not seen as a statue behind the lectern. Convince them to *talk* to the audience rather than to *read* to the audience.

Scripted speeches often contain a high proportion of dense, substantive material. You may suggest that the presenter produce a summary of the speech or make a full copy of the actual wording available to participants.

Limit the speaker to 30 minutes maximum, or 20 if they are likely to lull the audience into a soporific state.

Q & A sessions

Most audiences like to be an active part of a presentation and contribute through their questions. Many speakers allow for Q & A sessions as part of their presentations, which can result in a mutually beneficial interchange of ideas, information, opinions, plans, and concerns. Alternatively, you could plan a stand-alone Q & A session as a separate element of your programming. The following rules help create an environment where participants can feel safe asking questions:

>> For large audiences, consider having standing microphones in the aisles for participants wanting to ask questions or make comments to the presenter(s).

>> Help presenters plan for anticipated questions, especially if they are addressing a controversial topic.

>> Pass out 3 x 5 cards for the Q & A session. Some people prefer writing a question rather than approaching the microphone. It also allows the question to be anonymous.

>> Arrange for questions to be submitted prior to the session to avoid the possibility of no one asking a question. This step is particularly important for stand-alone Q & A sessions.

>> Instruct presenters to listen to the entire question before responding. If they begin to formulate an answer while the question is still being asked, they may miss the point the questioner is trying to make, and their answer could appear inappropriate or incomplete.

>> Make sure that questions are repeated before they are responded to, especially for guests who use English as a second (or third) language.

» Encourage presenters to avoid arguable issues, especially as they relate to the organization or a political situation. They should agree to disagree rather than be sarcastic or belligerent with the questioner.

» Suggest that presenters keep their responses brief and relevant. Long-winded answers are boring! Have presenters defer questions that require lengthy answers. They may offer to talk to participants individually after the session.

» Tell presenters to treat each question seriously, however dumb it may sound. They should also deal with a convoluted question by asking the questioner to repeat it more succinctly.

» Avoid ending the session with someone's question. Have the presenter recap key points to wrap things up.

TIP

To keep the program moving along, establish a *10-second rule:* You have 10 seconds to ask your question. This prevents fans from raving about the presenter or explaining the impact their work has had on the questioner's life. Also, place mics and stands (with or without moderators) at the front and the middle of the audience for easy access.

No Guts,
No Story

If you really want to master being a highly effective meeting and event planner, I suggest that you memorize the first chapter in this part, which includes a discussion of negotiating a contract. My goal is to make you a negotiating maven so that you can strike the best deals around.

If you're feeling overwhelmed, check out the various vendors who can come to your aid. There are definitely enough of them out there vying for your meeting and event planning business.

The final chapter in this part focuses on putting together a realistic budget so that you know exactly what you can afford and what you can't. The best part, though, is all the wonderful cost-cutting tips that show you how to drink champagne on a beer budget. What are you waiting for? Start reading!

IN THIS CHAPTER

» **Getting the best deal with an RFP**

» **Conducting effective negotiations**

» **Recognizing the complexities of contracts**

» **Being aware of safety and security issues**

» **Covering yourself with insurance**

Chapter **11**

Nuts and Bolts: Negotiating, Contracting, and Ensuring Safety

Much of your meeting and event success hinges on the behind-the-scenes logistics. If you plan, position, and prepare your strategy, the results should speak for themselves.

This chapter addresses some of the most challenging aspects of your pre-meeting/event preparation — the terms and conditions that affect all of your arrangements. Clear these hurdles, and you can take home the award for meeting planner superstar.

In this chapter, I focus primarily on working with hotels because this is where most meetings and events are held. The information is applicable to other venues and suppliers as well.

WARNING

You need to perform extra research and study up on each of the topics in this chapter, as they are too involved and complex to cover fully in the space available here.

Finding the Best Supplier with RFPs

The first step to take when buying a big-ticket item — a bundle of hotel rooms, for example — is to send out a request for proposals (RFP). An RFP asks a supplier to provide its best possible price for your specific meeting/event needs. RFPs are most frequently used to assess hotel facilities. However, you can also use them for Convention and Visitors Bureaus, destination management companies, independent meeting planners, audiovisual companies, and any other company with whom you may spend a significant amount of money.

If you have a vendor that you've used in the past and are totally happy with, or you have one that comes highly recommended, you may want to skip the RFP stage. However, if you want to make comparisons among different vendors, then I suggest you go the RFP route. When you do look at the various proposals submitted, make sure that you compare like with like. For example, when comparing the cost of renting audiovisual equipment, make sure it's the exact same equipment.

In the sections that follow, I show you how to locate potential suppliers and create an effective RFP.

Determining who gets the RFP

When you start creating your list of possible suppliers, begin with recommendations from people you respect, such as industry colleagues, other meeting and event planners, or chambers of commerce. Research supplier listings in industry magazines or online, and ask your present suppliers if they offer services in other locations or can make a suitable recommendation.

With so many potential suppliers, it's easy to get overwhelmed with your choices. When you're interested in a supplier that no else you know has used, make sure that you check references.

Your best bet is to send an RFP to only a small, select group of suppliers that you are considering seriously for your meeting or event. Otherwise, much of the work that goes into your RFP can be wasted time. The exception is if you want to get extra figures for comparison — you may be able to use the information to negotiate a better price with the supplier you really want to do business with. Naturally, that's up to you!

Writing an RFP

Whether you design your own written RFP or use an online version, make sure that you keep it simple, concise, and to the point, including only your meeting/

event essentials and the services that you actually plan to use. Take a spin around the internet searching the term "RFP for events" to find a variety of resources for RFP solutions. Also see *Writing Business Bids and Proposals For Dummies* by Neil Cobb and Charlie Devine (John Wiley & Sons, Inc., 2016).

TIP

Check out www.cvent.com/venues for an online RFP solutions program. It's free and provides information from the initial search for the perfect meeting venue through the final budget reconciliation. This online application enables planners to do their jobs more efficiently and helps control costs.

Basically, four elements comprise an RFP, usually in this order: background information, a list of things that you need pricing information for, a list of perks you hope to receive for selecting a particular vendor, and a request for references.

Background information

The first part of your RFP includes all the necessary background information about your group, organization, or company:

>> Your group/organization/company name.

>> The meeting name (if you have one), such as Dinky Doo's 5th Annual Sales Meeting.

>> Your contact information — name, address, telephone and fax numbers, and e-mail address.

>> Meeting location.

>> Meeting budget (optional).

>> Meeting dates (offer alternative dates if possible).

>> Meeting goals and objectives.

>> Estimated number of participants.

>> Participant profile — particularly important if you want the prospective vendor to organize tours or any other type of entertainment.

>> Previous meeting locations (city and facility used) and previous meeting histories. This can give the potential supplier some useful information about any trends, such as always opting to use a major city location.

>> RFP deadline, a decision date, and your decision-making criteria. For the RFP deadline, allow a minimum of ten days from the time you send out the requests. This gives responders time to complete the information and return it to you.

Areas for which you want pricing

The second part of your RFP contains a list of all the areas for which you want pricing. The information included in this section must be very specific. I highly recommend that you make separate lists for each type of vendor. For example, develop a separate, detailed list of needs for hotels, audiovisual companies, transportation companies, and so on.

For a hotel, you may have needs in each of the following categories:

>> Meeting-room space needs — include information about the number of people scheduled to attend, preferred room setup styles, and start and stop times.

>> Audiovisual requirements — you may want to request pricing for internet access if you don't plan on using an independent vendor.

>> Internet and Wi-Fi bandwidth, coverage, and fees.

>> Sleeping room block — indicate approximately how many rooms/suites you need and your desired rate range.

>> Food and beverage necessities.

>> Any special dietary and accessibility needs.

In addition to these considerations, you may want to include some other specific questions for the facility to answer. Here are a handful of questions that may be important to you:

>> What airport transportation do you offer?

>> What parking facilities are available to guests?

>> What business center and/or health club amenities do you offer?

>> What is the breakdown of applicable taxes (sales, occupancy, and so on), service charges, and gratuities?

>> What's your policy on complimentary rooms? (It's fairly standard to ask for 1 comp room per 40 room nights you pay for.)

>> How are your reservations handled?

>> How do you handle pickup reports (a report prepared by the hotel that shows the number of rooms actually utilized out of the contracted room block)?

>> What, if any, additional charges apply for using outside contractors or suppliers?

>> Does your facility comply with ADA (Americans with Disabilities Act) requirements?

>> What's your cancellation policy?

Note that this is not a comprehensive list, but rather just a few basic questions for you to consider. Take your time and do your research so that you cover all the bases needed for your specific event. In addition, make sure you include any concessions you are requesting in your RFP instead of asking for them after proposals have been submitted.

Special perks to ask for

I think you'll like this part! The third step in the RFP process is making a list of all the possible extras you'd benefit from the supplier/contractor providing. Of course, you want these extras for free or, at least, at a discounted rate, in exchange for giving the supplier your business. But don't confuse this with blackmail! Naturally, you very easily can go overboard with some far-fetched requests, so please be reasonable. For example, can the facility offer complimentary rooms for your guest speakers? Can an audiovisual company provide complimentary portable two-way radios for you and your staff to use during your event?

Request for references

The last thing on your RFP is a request for references. It definitely pays to take the time to check out potential suppliers before making your final decision. Develop a list of pointed questions to ask the references so that you find out exactly how well your potential supplier has performed in the past. Some sample questions may include:

>> What are the supplier's greatest strengths?

>> What are the supplier's areas of weakness?

>> What criteria did you use to evaluate the supplier's performance?

>> If you were to use this supplier again, what would you ask them to do differently?

>> What advice would you give me if I decide to use this supplier?

Negotiating the Deal

After you receive the proposals, you need to come up with a short list of two or three suppliers with whom you want to negotiate the best deal. If you select at least two, you can often play one supplier against the other to get more bang for your buck. But remember to play fair.

This is a point in the process where you really have to show your smarts. You can't only compare prices — you need to carefully examine the various packages and equipment potential of each provider.

For example, are two comparable audiovisual companies offering you the exact same equipment? Are two comparable facilities offering you the exact same menu options? Never take the items on the proposal at face value. Talk to the service providers and ask in-depth questions to find the best price–value relationship. And don't forget the importance of the human element. It may be worth spending a few extra dollars to have a satisfying working relationship — one where the supplier provides everything you need for a successful, smooth-running event.

Narrowing the list

Before you start negotiating, you need to decide which suppliers to negotiate with. Money isn't everything, so never just compare prices. Examine every aspect of what you need and what the potential service provider offers.

The following is a list of questions to ask yourself to help make the right decision for hiring an outside contractor:

>> How professionally did this company handle my requests?

>> How well can they handle my event?

>> Do they have the resources to handle the project completely, or do they need to subcontract portions of it?

>> What similar events have they handled?

>> Who are some of their major clients?

>> Do they have satellite offices or affiliate companies they work with around the country?

>> What relationship do they have with the hotel/facility we're considering?

>> How long have they been operating this business?

>> What industry or trade associations do they belong to?

>> What additional services did they offer me, either complimentary or at a discounted rate?

>> What is their payment policy?

>> How do their prices compare to my budget?

>> How comfortable do I feel doing business with them?

Playing the negotiating game

Negotiating a deal is both a serious business and a game that you either love or hate. Negotiating has rules, just like any other game. To get what you want, I highly recommend that you practice and perfect the rules of negotiating.

The following are nine general negotiating rules to be familiar with:

>> **Start with a plan.** Know exactly what you want out of your discussions. Prepare a list of items you really, really want and a list of ones that you'd be willing to concede if necessary.

>> **Do your homework.** Understand the value your business brings to the supplier. Find out as much as you can about the company, especially how it makes its money. The more it wants you as a customer, the harder it'll work to give you what you want.

>> **Use bargaining power.** Have another supplier in the wings that you can use to help influence your negotiations.

>> **Be methodical and meticulous.** Make careful notes of everything discussed and agreed upon so that all aspects of the negotiation appear accurately in the final written contract.

>> **Avoid vague, confusing language.** Make sure that you agree on specific pricing or numbers. Steer clear of words such as "reasonable," "anticipated," or "projected," which reek of ambiguity.

>> **Question preprinted contracts.** Hotels often use preprinted contracts to save time. Stick to what you want, and challenge anything that's "standard" policy. Remember, your trump card is to use an alternate supplier.

>> **Read the fine print.** It's easy to skip over the small print, especially when you're told that it's standard operating procedure. The time to discuss and agree is prior to signing on the dotted line.

>> **Insist on shared responsibility.** Avoid any agreements that are one-sided and allow the facility to change arrangements without your consent. You always want a say in any variation to the original agreement.

>> **Assume nothing.** Remember that *ass-u-me* stands for "making an ass out of you and me." Make sure that you're never put into that situation. Ask questions, more questions, and still more questions to clarify points.

For more information on negotiating tactics, see Chapter 23.

Knowing which areas to negotiate

Every book you read on negotiating skills says that "everything's negotiable," which is a sound premise for you to work from. Realize, however, that making deals involves an element of give and take. If you want something really badly, you'd better be willing to give up something in its place.

Because you'll probably invest most of your negotiating efforts with venue facilities, following are the major areas to consider:

>> Meeting dates

>> Guest sleeping room/suite commitment

  - Room/suite configurations (such as king-size, queen-size, or double beds)
  - Room rates

>> Check-in/check-out times, luggage handling, and gratuities

>> Complimentary rooms

>> Reservation procedures

>> Pickup reports

>> Master accounts

  - Billing and credit arrangements
  - Deposit fees
  - Refunds

>> Meeting rooms

  - Audiovisual equipment
  - Labor for setup

>> Food and beverages

  - Prices
  - Taxes

- Gratuities/service charges

- Bartenders/wait staff

>> Staffing

>> Meeting stoppages

>> Renovations

- Current

- Future

>> Other groups with overlapping meetings

>> Exhibits (if necessary)

- Move-in/move-out costs

- Exhibit-hall rental — included and excluded services

- Insurance

- Licenses and permits

- Security

>> Miscellaneous services

TIP

You can increase your success with negotiating these perks into your contract by calling in a good travel agent. Even if you're booking a relatively large group of people into a hotel, you probably won't have as much bargaining power as a travel agency that deals with that hotel on a regular basis and books numerous groups there throughout the year. The International Association of Exhibitions and Events (iaee.com) has a tremendous resource library that can help you with RFPs and hotel contracting.

REMEMBER

Negotiate wait service ratios (how many people you want/need to have serve your food and beverages) before signing your contract. Good service won't necessarily happen automatically. Match the service you need to the type and quality of your function.

Requesting perks from hotels

When making hotel arrangements for your meeting participants, try to get the hotel to throw in a few of the following perks:

>> Reduced (or eliminated) fees for parking and valet services

>> Separate check-in with extra bell staff for your group

- A welcome reception with beverages and snacks for your meeting participants as they arrive

- Room upgrades for your special guests

- Special hospitality suites and receptions (a private cocktail and hors d'oeuvre party for your meeting participants, for example)

- Small gifts and special services for your special guests (like the daily newspaper delivered to their rooms)

- Special amenities in your guests' rooms (such as coffee makers, workspace, or a kitchenette.)

- Nightly turn-down service

- Discounts for on-site services, such as the spa or health club

- Use of the hotel limousine or van service to shuttle your participants to nearby attractions

- No charge for late checkout on the last day of the event

Signing on the Dotted Line

After you've negotiated your best deal and made your final supplier selection, your next step is to put all your discussions and agreements in writing. I highly recommend that you consult with a contractual lawyer if you are in any doubt about taking responsibility for signing a contract on behalf of your organization. Although I refer primarily to hotels in the following sections, the points are also relevant to any other facilities and vendors you use.

WARNING

Unless you have some kind of legal background and feel totally confident, you probably need plenty of help understanding the legal elements of your contract. This is not the time to have a proud, cavalier, "I can do it" attitude. You should definitely seek professional aid. We live in a litigious society, and you want to do everything possible to avoid any ramifications that may lead to litigation.

In addition to understanding the contract legalese, you need to know the correct way to amend and sign your contracts. You also want to ensure that all terms are clearly defined and you leave nothing open "to be negotiated" or "to be determined." With the constant change of company personnel, one individual may not honor the discussions you had with a predecessor, unless a firm contract is in place. And finally, watch out for merger and/or renovation clauses and their implications. Renovations in particular can disrupt your event, so remember to discuss any plans for construction or refurbishment — start and finish dates. If construction occurs during your meeting, discuss what actions the facility will take to ensure no disruption to your arrangements.

REMEMBER

Under no circumstances should you sign a contract that leaves key points, such as room rates or food prices, for negotiation in the future.

Your contract should also include what are known as "The Big Three" or "ACT" clauses — Attrition, Cancellation, and Termination.

>> **Attrition:** The attrition clause in the contract allows you to decrease the originally agreed-upon number of sleeping and/or meeting rooms and food and beverage functions. The size and timing of the reduction will determine the percentage change in fees. For example, if you reduce your numbers six months prior to your event, the hotel will probably be able to resell the space or services, which means a lower penalty, if any, to your organization. However, if you lower your numbers a month before your event, the hotel is less likely to be able to resell the space or services, and you'll pay for the originally agreed-upon terms to compensate their loss.

>> **Cancellation:** A cancellation clause in the contract is usually one-sided in your favor. It specifies dates by which you can cancel the meeting without penalty and after which the provider can charge a penalty for cancellation. If you have a signed contract, the hotel is usually unable to cancel your meeting without your consent.

>> **Termination:** The termination or *force majeure* clause allows for either party to terminate the contract without liability because of an unforeseen and uncontrollable occurrence such as strikes, fires, or severe weather conditions — tornadoes, hurricanes, earthquakes, blizzards, and so on, often called "Acts of God" — all of which make it impossible to conduct your meeting as planned.

For more information on contract matters, consult with your corporate legal advisor (if you have one), reach out to an attorney through your Chamber of Commerce, or contact LegalShield (www.legalshield.com) which provides an online connection to local attorneys who can assist with your concerns.

HOTEL BILLING ERRORS

TIP

After your meeting is over, you may see some unexpected charges on your invoice. A few areas to watch include:

- Items added to the master account
- Obscure charges
- Incorrect guaranteed numbers
- Additional taxes
- Unitemized billing

Make it a rule to sign off on each individual meal bill after each individual function so that you don't forget what was originally ordered. Furthermore, always remember to pick up and sign your final bill before leaving the hotel. Dealing with any disputes in person is easier than via the phone.

Put on your Sherlock Holmes hat and be on the lookout for hidden costs that may be included automatically on your bill — for example, garnishes used in preparing drinks, audiovisual setup, or meeting room cleanup. Be meticulous so as to avoid any surprises. Always remember to ask your service provider while negotiating, "What charges haven't we yet discussed?" Before the meeting begins (at preconference meetings you hold with the facility), inform the hotel of who has master account signing privileges and instruct them that you will not pay for any charges signed by unauthorized signers.

Creating a Safe and Secure Event

Savvy meeting planners know that risk management is an area that needs serious consideration. Your primary concern is keeping all participants as safe and secure as possible. Part of your location decision should incorporate assessment of weather conditions, the political environment, and any history of crime. What are the chances of serious weather disrupting your meeting? How stable is the political environment? (This is particularly important when meeting overseas.) How safe are the hotel and surrounding areas?

In addition to choosing a safe and stable location, make sure you do the following:

>> **Familiarize yourself with the hotel and surrounding area.** Take time to check guest rooms to find out what door locking system is used, if doors have

peepholes, and what security devices are on windows and sliding doors. Familiarize yourself and your staff with the locations of emergency exits, fire extinguishers, and first-aid stations. Make certain that you have a security contact and phone numbers in case of an emergency. Know how to get in touch with a doctor and the location of the nearest hospital. Also, have an evacuation plan in place and communicate it to all participants.

>> **Gather information on participants.** When participants register for your event, insist on getting an emergency contact and any allergies or accessibility issues that may need consideration. Of course you should also gather their basic contact information: phone(s), e-mail, mailing address, and company.

>> **Protect your VIPs.** If you have some very important people — company executives, speakers, or celebrities — as part of your event, assess your security needs and make sure that you have adequate precautions and appropriate protection in place. The level of risk will determine whether you need to hire bodyguards or simply have one of your own staff act as an escort. You may even consider consulting with a security professional for advice on dealing with possible demonstrations or confrontations, especially if your meeting is politically, scientifically, or environmentally sensitive.

>> **Have contingency plans.** What if there was a hurricane, a hotel fire, or an outbreak of food poisoning? What if a participant had a heart attack or was physically assaulted during your meeting? Would you or your staff know what to do? As part of your preparation, take time to develop contingency plans. Instruct your staff accordingly and rehearse emergency and evacuation drills. And it would certainly be a good idea if you or one of your staff were proficient in CPR and first aid. (For more information about emergency readiness and crisis planning, visit InEvent at `https://bit.ly/crisis-mgt-guide` for a comprehensive step-by-step guide.)

TIP

Always designate a team spokesperson to handle all the social and local media. You want to be in control of your messaging about your event and the people involved.

Liability and Insurance Issues

Another area of concern involves liability and insurance. Once again, consider consulting an expert to make certain that you cover all eventualities. The most common types of insurance coverage available to limit your liability and protect against losses are included in the following list.

Check what insurance your company policy includes, especially as it pertains to off-premise insurance. This will be a guideline to help you decide what additional coverage you need. For example:

>> General liability insurance

>> Fire

>> Medical

>> Independent contractor liability

>> Host and liquor liability (may differ from state to state)

>> On-site office

>> Exhibits

>> Worker's compensation

>> Employee's liability

>> Travel and accidents

>> Equipment (hired or borrowed)

>> Non-appearance of speakers or entertainers

>> Event cancellation

In addition to these areas, investigate any additional insurance for other items or instances that may not be covered, such as renting a charter bus for a special excursion. You always want to err on the side of safety. And finally, you want to ensure compliance with all regulations and bylaws, such as association, municipal, state, and federal statutes.

REMEMBER

Leave nothing to chance. Consider taking out weather insurance to protect against any losses due to unforeseen and uncontrollable weather conditions. The policies are a valuable investment for the success of your event.

Chapter **12**

Working with Vendors

O
utsourcing can be a lifesaver for the busy meeting planner. Caterers, florists, and many other vendors and service providers are just waiting to help with your next event.

Although turning over the responsibility for part of your event to outside contractors may be nerve-racking, what would you do without their help? Without a caterer, would you consider cooking lunch for meeting participants yourself? I know I wouldn't! With companies vying for your business, you have little reason to worry about finding vendors. By making some intelligent choices when you hire your contractors, you can rest easy knowing that you've placed some of the responsibility for your meeting's success in dependable hands.

Most meeting and event planners rely on a network of vendors and service providers that they develop relationships with over time. Whether you're just starting out or already have some event planning experience, this chapter gives you some helpful tips on choosing the best product and service suppliers. It also gives you an overview of the types of contractors available to assist you, some of whom you may not have known existed.

Teaming Up

If you choose the right team of vendors and suppliers, they can provide you with goods and services that make your event sparkle. The following tips and suggestions can help guide you through the hiring process and aid you in choosing your vendors and service providers wisely.

Searching for vendors

Here are several ways to begin your search for a vendor or supplier:

>> Keep an eye out when you attend parties and business events. When you see something you like, ask your host or the event planner for details.

>> Ask trusted friends and colleagues whether they've worked with a vendor they can recommend.

>> Ask people at the venue you're renting for the event to recommend a vendor. Note that some venues will let you use only their own preselected list of approved vendors.

>> Contact a professional association affiliated with the industry in which you need to find a vendor. For example, contact the National Association of Catering Executives (www.nace.net), International Caterers Association (internationalcaterers.org), or the National Speakers Association (www.nsaspeaker.org).

>> Search online for local vendors near your event. Be sure to read their reviews, ask for references, and thoroughly interview your choices.

After you have the names of several possible vendors, request a bid from each. Submit a detailed description of your event and exact information about what you need to each vendor. Be specific to ensure that the bid includes everything you need and that no extra charges are added later. Request that the vendor send a *written* bid by hardcopy or e-mail. Read all about requests for proposals (RFPs) in Chapter 11.

When you have your vendors' bids in hand, review them to make sure that they cover everything you requested. Eliminate any bids that don't meet your needs or vastly exceed your budget. You may have room to negotiate, so don't dismiss any bids that are only slightly over your budget.

Conducting interviews

When you have a short list of vendors to choose from, arrange an interview with each at their office or at the event location. During the interview, ask the following questions:

>> How long have you been in business? You don't have to dismiss a vendor who has been in business only a short while, but be sure that they have plenty of industry experience before starting their own business.

>> What is your background, education, and special training in the field? Do you have any professional affiliations? Have you won any awards or received any special recognition in your field?

>> Who will take your place if you're unable to work my event because of an emergency? If your equipment malfunctions right before or during the event, what back-up equipment do you have?

>> How can I contact you during *and* after regular business hours? If I have an emergency, how can I reach you quickly?

>> How long before the event may I cancel without penalty?

TIP

If the vendor is a multiperson firm rather than an individual, insist on meeting the person who will handle your account — the employee personally responsible for taking care of your needs.

Pay attention before and during the interview to how competently and professionally the vendor handles arrangements with you. Do they return your phone calls or text messages promptly? Are they thorough and helpful in their answers to your questions? Are they dressed neatly and appropriately? These personal habits will be reflected in their work on your event.

Checking references

Ask each vendor you interview for the names and contact information of three to five references. Request that the references be people who held events similar to yours.

Contact each reference and ask the following questions:

>> How was the vendor's level of service? Did the vendor respond quickly and effectively to your needs?

>> How easy was it to contact the vendor? Did they return phone calls and e-mails promptly?

- » Why did you choose this specific vendor over others you considered?

- » How satisfied were you with the vendor's overall performance and/or product?

- » What problems did you encounter with the vendor? If any, were they resolved quickly and to your satisfaction?

- » Would you use this vendor again? If not, why not?

Take notes during your interviews with both the vendor and references. When you're done, sit down with those notes and the bids from each of the vendors you interviewed, compare them, and make a decision. But make sure that you compare similar services and products.

Making the relationship work

After you've chosen your vendor, you can do several things to ensure that your business relationship is successful.

First, record all the details of your contract with the vendor in writing. These details include, but are not limited to, the following:

- » The services that are provided under your contract with the vendor and the services you will be charged extra for. Determine how taxes and gratuities are handled.

- » The vendor's arrival and departure time on the day of the event.

- » The vendor's attire and the attire of any additional staff the vendor will provide. For example, if you're hiring a caterer who is bringing wait staff that you want dressed in black pants and white dress shirts, specify that in writing.

- » Policies regarding contract cancellation. What are your obligations to the vendor if you cancel the event at the last minute? What if the vendor can't complete the work they were contracted to do? What if some outside force (such as an earthquake or fire) causes the cancellation of the event? See Chapter 11 for information on the legal aspects of your contracts.

If details of the event change as planning progresses, communicate the changes to the vendor in writing and ensure that they are placed in your file. Oral agreements often fall apart, sometimes because the person you talk with leaves the company before the event, and sometimes because the person simply forgets to record the change. Having everything in writing is an important safeguard for you.

Another important way to ensure a good working relationship with your vendor is to keep the lines of communication open. The vendor should know how to contact you during and after business hours, so remember to exchange detailed contact information.

TIP

Don't hold all of this information inside your head! Create a laminated page in your planning notebook with the contact information for all your vendors. In addition, maintain the information digitally to access through your tablet, computer, or phone. That way, you have the information readily available and easy to share whenever you need to reach a vendor quickly.

Working with Specific Types of Vendors

Information is a powerful tool that can help you choose a first-rate vendor who can successfully fill your needs. When hiring certain types of vendors, you need to ask a number of questions and deal with some industry-specific issues. The way different vendors answer these questions and handle these issues will help you make a sound decision when choosing from among them. Once you have selected and used a reliable vendor, you can add them to the network of tried-and-true help that makes your job much easier as you continue to plan events.

TIP

If you're pleased with the job a vendor does for you post your glowing review online, send a testimonial they can use on their website, and go "old-school" by sending a thank-you note on your company's letterhead. Vendors appreciate the gesture and may even reciprocate by promoting you as an ideal client!

Caterers

The way to your guests' hearts is definitely through their stomachs. Provide them with a good meal and you can be sure of a grateful response. But with so many caterers out there, finding one who can provide a good meal can be a challenge. Here are a few suggestions to help you engage a quality caterer:

» Make sure that your bids from caterers include a proposed menu, the number of meals, and the number of staff they will provide. Also ask them to specify the number of hours they will commit to the deal, including preparation and cleanup time.

» Arrange to attend an event being serviced by your potential caterer. Seeing caterers in action gives you a chance to taste their food and observe their level of service and professionalism. This is especially important if the caterer will also provide wait staff. At the very least, arrange a tasting of their food.

TIP

REMEMBER

TIP

>> Verify that potential caterers are licensed. Many city governments have a licensing office that you can check with, or you can contact your local health department.

Discuss with your vendor who is responsible for obtaining and paying for any necessary permits. Put your agreement in writing.

>> Ask potential caterers about their policy regarding guaranteed minimums (also called guaranteed numbers). Many caterers quote their prices based upon a certain number of meals, and they charge you an additional fee if fewer guests are fed. For example, if your caterer's original bid was based on meals for 100 guests, but only 75 guests show up, many caterers still charge for 100 meals.

>> Ask potential caterers whether they use any frozen or canned foods to prepare their meals. Many of the best chefs use only the freshest ingredients, and you can tell by the quality of their food.

>> Talk with potential caterers about making arrangements for your vegetarian guests and those with other dietary restrictions.

>> Determine whether the caterer will provide table linens, napkins, dishes, silverware, and glassware. Ask to see samples. If you don't like the tableware or linens the caterer offers or they don't pass your quality control standards, you can arrange to rent them from another supplier at an additional fee. Remember to discuss this issue with your caterer and amend your written agreement.

>> Work with your caterer to determine a good ratio of servers to guests. This number can vary, but a good general rule is 1 server per 12 to 15 guests. The more responsibilities the servers have, the smaller the ratio should be. For example, if the wait staff will refill wine and water glasses, pass out food, and clear plates, you want more servers to help keep up the pace. Keep in mind that additional servers increase your costs.

>> When you're researching potential caterers, ask them to provide a sample menu based on your budget and estimated head count.

>> Ask about specific training and experience of the wait staff. Also discuss appropriate attire for your function.

>> Describe exactly what you expect from the wait staff. Will they take and serve drink orders? Will they clear the tables?

>> Determine whether the caterer and their staff will be responsible for cleaning up, washing the dishes, and disposing leftovers and garbage. If they don't do this kind of thing, you need to find someone who will — such as a maid service.

Florists

Choose your florist as you would your other vendors: by getting recommendations from the venue, CVB, or other local experienced professionals. You're really buying the talent, style, and creativity of the florist who will be designing your arrangements. Check out their website and social media accounts to view their work and read their reviews. Ask yourself these questions:

>> Do the arrangements on display appeal to your taste? Do they reflect creativity and diversity?

>> Does the florist use a wide variety of flowers in different colors, shapes, and sizes?

>> Are the arrangements varied and creative, or do they all look the same? If all the pictures are from weddings and funerals, can the florist make the leap to arrangements for a business meeting?

TIP

Be clear about your vision and color scheme for your event and where the arrangements will be used. Ask the florist about their service the day of your event:

>> Who will deliver the arrangements? Is this service included in the quoted fee?

>> Are they familiar with your venue? If not, can they visit it to get an idea of how the arrangements will fit in?

>> What time will they deliver the flowers? Keep in mind that flowers dropped off too early can wilt and fade.

Destination management companies

Destination management companies (DMCs) can help you successfully plan an event in a distant city or another country. They are experts on their local territories and can help you with almost any aspect of your event planning.

If you give them the reins, most DMCs can plan your whole event for you. They procure a venue, hire caterers and other vendors, arrange transportation for you and your participants, and handle all the other details. In essence, they can do anything and everything. You can arrive at your event having done little more than oversee and approve their choices. At the very least, DMCs can recommend quality vendors and service providers in their area.

When you're holding your event in a remote location and can't be there to plan it or don't know much about the area, destination management services can be invaluable. Some DMCs are international (such as Ovation), others (like Nxt Event) are regional (Boston and New England), and some focus on just one particular city (such as PRA Nashville).

A quick search online will turn up a long list of these organizations. You can even simplify your search by going to DMCfinder.com and filling out a query form to have them connect you with an appropriate DMC within a matter of hours.

Destinations International (meetings.destinationsinternational.org) provides event planner resources and links to hundreds of CVBs and destination management organizations in North America. Additionally, www.cvent.com/meeting-event-planning provides extensive information about venues, CVBs, and city guides for hundreds of destinations globally.

Selecting promotional items

A giveaway item is a lot like a souvenir. People on vacation buy souvenirs to remind them of their time in a particular place. A favor or promotional item functions in much the same way: It reminds those who attended your event of their time with your company long after the event is over. Giving away a useless trinket that will be shoved in a desk drawer or passed on to a child will not work as effectively as something the attendee would find handy and use repeatedly.

Make sure it is lightweight and easily packable or plan to ship it directly to your long-distance travelers. Developing a dynamite giveaway takes thought and creativity. Check out companies such as Vistaprint (https://bit.ly/vistaprint-promo) or Land's End-Business (https://bit.ly/landsend-promo) for some good ideas at a variety of price points, and see Chapter 18 for more on giveaways.

REMEMBER

You may need to order some other incidental products too, including nametags, certificates of attendance, and awards. Order your items well before your event to ensure that you receive them in plenty of time to save yourself stress. You will usually pay a penalty for rush orders, so plan ahead.

PROFESSIONAL PLANNERS

When your workload gets too heavy or you need a little help ironing out the details of your event, why not call in a professional event planner? They'll work closely with you to develop the event you envision while taking a lot of the responsibility from your shoulders. They can handle whatever aspects of the event you'd like — or organize the *whole* event if you choose.

The professional planner knows the ins and outs of planning a successful business event and has access to a network of vendors and service providers previously used. Quite often, these contractors offer a discounted fee on their goods and services because of the planner's repeat business. The money you save on contractors' fees may even offset the cost of the planner.

To find a professional planner, search online for a "professional event planner" or "professional meeting planner".

Ground transportation providers

Unless you plan on using your car and time to shuttle meeting participants between the airport and the meeting site (hardly likely), you probably need to hire a ground transportation provider. Here are some important questions to ask potential candidates:

» How many vehicles do you own and operate?

» What kind of vehicles are they, and how old are they?

» What vehicles are available on the day of my event? (Specify in writing the type of cars you'll be renting.)

» Do you have back-up vehicles in case of breakdowns?

» What is the safety record of your company and drivers?

» Who are your drivers?

» How do they dress? Do they wear uniforms?

» How can they be reached for any last-minute changes of plans?

» What amenities are available in your vehicles? Bottled water? Snacks? Current newspapers and magazines?

» How will the individuals you're picking up locate your vehicle? Will your driver meet them at the baggage claim area with a sign, or will they have to walk out of the terminal?

» What type of accident insurance do you carry?

Audiovisual companies

Hiring a professional to manage the audiovisual needs of your event has obvious advantages. The fact that a professional can provide the equipment you require *and* the skilled labor to set it up and troubleshoot any problems means less work (and fewer headaches) for you.

A good audiovisual company can provide a quick replacement if something goes wrong with the projector, microphone, or other equipment you rent. This isn't the case with equipment you purchase yourself — if it breaks the day of the event, you could be in big trouble.

TECHNICAL STUFF

If you do purchase your own audiovisual equipment, check that it's suitable for the room you rent for your event. With an audiovisual company, you can choose any room and the company will provide the equipment appropriate for that environment. It will also help you determine what equipment works best for the types of presentations being given, ensuring a professional, high-quality production.

Some audiovisual companies can even help you develop a high-quality, cutting-edge video or slide presentation to use with the equipment they provide.

Be sure that your contract with the audiovisual company includes the following information:

» Exact setup and teardown times on the day of the event. The company may charge extra if it has to set up or tear down before or after regular business hours.

» Every ancillary component of the audiovisual system you're renting, including extension cords, power strips, cables, and more.

See Chapter 10 for more specific information about audiovisual equipment.

Chapter **13**

Drinking Champagne on a Beer Budget

Money makes the world go 'round. And when it comes to meeting planning, money can probably get you what you want. However, few event planners have the luxury of an unlimited budget. Your boss may caution you to spend less rather than more . . . and still expect miracles.

For most planners, preparing and managing a realistic budget is serious business. You need a budget to chart your way safely through the rough seas that invariably blow in when planning events. It definitely helps make you a better negotiator because you have a clear vision of your event and where and how the money is best invested to get the most bang for your buck.

With this chapter, I want to make budgeting smooth sailing for you. By discovering some fundamentals that can keep you out of harm's way, you can ride a relatively calm sea. In addition, I've stuck in some handy cost-cutting tips to help you do more with less.

Preparing a Budget

A budget is not an isolated tool, but rather one you prepare in line with your meeting objectives. And if your meeting has financial goals, your budget needs to also take those into consideration.

REMEMBER

When it comes to revenue generation, you always want to know your break-even point. This is when your revenue is sufficient to pay all your expenses. Anything over that amount is considered profit. What a wonderful word that is! Your meeting's financial goals should state whether your organization wants to break even or make a profit (and state how much), or if you're prepared to take a loss on the event and subsidize the difference when the outgoing monies exceed the incoming revenues.

Using my acute telepathic skills, I know exactly what question is going through your mind at this point . . .

What on earth do I include in the budget?

The answer's easy: *everything*. If you have historical data from a similar event, you're in luck. The data from a prior experience can give you an idea of previous expenses and revenues. If this is your first event, know that your work is cut out for you. I wouldn't recommend that you try to map out your budget all in one sitting, but rather plan a few sessions so that you do a thorough job. The more meticulous you are, the more accurate the end result. Your high level of precision will definitely please the bean counters.

REMEMBER

Any sound budget accounts for the following:

» **Fixed expenses:** These expenses remain constant no matter what — whether the event draws 1 or 1,001 participants. Fixed expenses include room rentals, marketing and promotion, speaker fees, signage, audiovisual equipment, insurance costs, and other services that you may need, such as interpretation and translation.

» **Variable expenses:** The number of participants attending your meeting or event affects variable expenses, which are calculated on a per-person basis. Food and beverage costs top the list, of course. Other items include transportation, on-site materials, gratuities, and currency exchange fees if you're working internationally.

When planning meetings outside of the United States pay attention to currency conversions. Be aware that exchange rates vary daily, and watch for when the dollar is strongest against the currency you're dealing with. When the dollar is strongest (valued more) against the local currency, that means you have more buying power. This can favorably impact your bottom line.

>> **Indirect expenses:** Often overlooked, indirect expenses comprise the administrative costs associated with your meeting: primarily staff salaries and equipment such as two-way radios for on-site communication.

>> **Hidden expenses:** However hard you try to figure out and account for every expense, hidden costs always seem to pop up. These may vary from event to event and can include such items as overnight shipping charges, rush charges for signage, taxes, labor union minimums, and overtime charges. The last two are common particularly in union cities such as Chicago, New York, and Philadelphia. Try hard to keep tabs on these unexpected or unplanned expenses so that you are prepared for the extras. They can mount up significantly.

>> **Revenues:** Many meetings have financial goals that include making some kind of profit. Revenues usually come from registration, exhibition, and advertising fees, as well as sponsorships, special functions that require an extra fee, and in-kind donations of products and/or services. For example, a transportation company may offer its services free of charge in exchange for advertising opportunities during your event. This saving then helps increase your revenue.

Categorizing your budget

The following budget categories can help you organize your revenue and expenses. List all the expenses, fixed and variable, or revenues, if appropriate, that fall under each of these categories:

>> Accommodations

>> Administrative

>> Audiovisual

>> Entertainment

>> Exhibition

>> Facility

>> Flowers and decorations

>> Food and beverages

- » Insurance
- » Internet connections
- » Labor charges
- » Marketing and promotion
- » Miscellaneous services (such as translation and interpretation)
- » Personnel
- » Postage
- » Programming
- » Registration and event technology
- » Revenue details
- » Shipping/freight charges
- » Signage
- » Speakers
- » Special functions
- » Travel and transportation

WARNING

Don't forget to include indirect expenses (see the previous section). The more thorough you are, the more accurate your final total.

Keeping costs under control

Because you probably have a limited budget to work with, keeping costs under control is a skill you need to develop — fast! Six important rules to remember are:

- » **Be flexible.** Remember to allow a certain amount of flexibility with your financial figures, because you'll probably experience some unexpected expenses or emergencies. Be prepared and build in a contingency of 10 percent of your total budget to take care of the unforeseen costs, such as overtime, speaker substitutions, overnight mailings, phone and computer hookups, and things you just overlooked.

- » **Check all invoices.** As soon as you receive an invoice, check it against the written quotation. Question anything that doesn't seem to compute. Make sure that you scrutinize your hotel invoice and food and beverage invoice while you are on-site. Ironing out discrepancies in person is much easier than over the phone. This is particularly true for any overseas events. Don't sign off on any bills until you are totally satisfied.

» **Consolidate.** One of the best gifts that you can give yourself for future events is to do a post-event consolidation report. Take all the budgetary data, notes, and tidbits of pertinent information and summarize them all into one document. A computer spreadsheet works wonders here. You'll love reviewing it when you plan your next meeting. Instead of having to plow through various file folders stuffed with scraps of paper, you have one wonderful information-rich document. In fact, consider formulating an organized note-taking form for each one of your supplier negotiations to keep accurate information.

» **Limit authorization.** Only a select few should have the authority to charge items to your master account at the hotel. Make sure the hotel has a list of these people, and instruct the hotel that under no circumstances can anyone else make charges. Refuse to pay for charges signed by unauthorized personnel. This definitely helps you keep control.

» **Review accounts daily.** To avoid any major surprises or heart failures when you see the final bill, consider reviewing your accounts with the facility on a daily basis. It's easier to spot errors or make necessary changes if costs are escalating in certain areas. For example, if you're using the hotel's business center for printing and find their charges are excessive, you may want to make alternative arrangements if you have a significant amount of printing to do.

» **Segregate accounts.** Work with the hotel to create a variety of *master accounts* (detailed accounts of all charges incurred during a specific meeting or event). Separating your bills makes it easier to review the individual bills for each event. Arrange copies of invoices, checks, and banquet event orders (BEOs) together with each master account. For example, if you are organizing two meetings at the same time at the same facility and want to keep the charges for each separate, you would have the facility create Master Account A and Master Account B.

WARNING

Don't forget to include taxes, gratuities, and service charges in your budget planning. These can add up to quite a substantial amount.

Looking for help?

You'll be pleased to know that you really don't have to undertake budgeting single-handedly. Help is definitely available and possibly more bountiful than you think. Here are a few suggestions to get you started:

» **Ask your accounting department.** Start with a visit to your friendly bean counters and find out how they can help you keep track of the expenses that you're going to incur with your event. Chances are that they'll introduce you to *line items.* These are titles of each account within a budget, which are usually identified by a code number — for example, "300 – Food and Beverage Items." All expenses related to food and beverages fall under the "300" column. By using line items, you can see what you've spent in that particular area and how much money you have left at any given time.

>> **Quiz Convention and Visitors Bureaus (CVBs).** You can find CVBs in almost every city, and they offer a wealth of information. Speak to them to get estimated costs for the services that you're looking for. (Of course, it goes without saying that you need to know what you want first.) Quiz them for suggestions of fun, unique things to see and do in their city or region. CVBs usually have extensive knowledge about their areas. At the minimum, they can refer you to worthwhile resources.

>> **Scan trade/industry publications.** Between the meeting planning industry and the incentive travel industry, several publications can give you ideas and resources to plan and price your event.

Check out `https://www.themeetingmagazines.com` for meeting planning publications and for conference and travel publications.

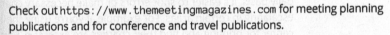

>> **Research meeting facilities.** Through your own research or with information from a CVB, assemble names of possible meeting facilities. Have them send you their costs for events similar to the one you're organizing. Obviously, at this point, you're really only talking about ballpark figures.

>> **Make inquiries with DMCs and individual suppliers.** You could make your life much easier if you hired a destination management company (DMC) because it could price your entire event — from soup to nuts. The question is then how to find one that's reliable and that you feel comfortable working with. The same applies to individual suppliers. Go directly to them and ask for quotations for the services you're interested in.

>> **Question industry colleagues.** Seek out colleagues in the industry who may share examples of budgets they've put together for similar events in the city or region that you're considering.

>> **Search online.** The web is every researcher's dream! All you need is time and patience to find all the information you ever wanted.

TIP

When gathering information, become a question-monger. Ask about anything and everything that you think may help you put together an accurate budget.

Making Money

Some events have financial goals that include making money or at least breaking even. Meeting planners rely primarily on seven conventional methods of achieving targeted revenue and profit. Of course, you may think of your own way. However, if you can't come up with anything new, use the following seven tried and true ways to increase your profitability:

>> **Registration fees:** Registration fees are the most common area where meetings can make money. The key is to price it right. The recognized formula meeting planners use to figure out the price to charge is:

Total fixed costs + per-person variable costs/number of attendees = registration fee

Because you probably don't know how many attendees to expect, your registration or conference fee is a tough one to come up with. You don't want to charge so much that people won't attend because it's too expensive. On the other hand, you don't want to make it so cheap that you don't make a profit (unless your goal is to increase attendance without regard to profit). Past performance records can definitely help, but if you don't have any, take a conservative guess. Consider doing some preliminary research to test the waters.

>> **Sponsorships and grants:** Sponsorships are often an easy way to raise money for meetings. If you represent an industry association, many of your corporate members may be interested in some special recognition — and willing to pay handsomely for it. If you want sponsorship ideas, look at what's being done in the sports arena. For more on sponsorship, see the nearby sidebar, "Sponsorship: A Meeting Planner's Delight".

You can also apply for a specific federal, state, local, or corporate grant to help hold the meeting. Finding the right grant and making the application can be time-consuming unless you know exactly what you're doing and how to do it. A good source of information is *Nonprofit Kit For Dummies,* 6th Edition, by Barbara B. Browning, Stan Hutton, and Frances N. Phillips (John Wiley & Sons, Inc., 2021).

>> **Exhibit booth sales:** If your meeting includes a trade show, you can make money selling exhibit space to suppliers interested in tantalizing your participants with their products or services. The size and design of the space you use dictates how many companies can exhibit. You need to design a floor plan that maximizes the space available.

>> **Special functions:** These are optional events. Participants can pay an extra fee to attend. Special functions may include an awards banquet, special tours, or a golf tournament.

>> **Advertising revenue:** Pick up some additional funding by selling ads on the mobile event app, signage, and also on the event website to encourage

connecting with specific vendors or speakers. If you produce a hard-copy publication specifically for the event, you have the opportunity to sell advertising space within its pages.

>> **Merchandise sales:** You may have the opportunity to organize a mini-store during the event and sell books that may interest participants, particularly those written by your speakers. You may also have specially designed logo merchandise for the event — T-shirts, sweatshirts, pins, and mugs are the most common.

>> **Digital replay sales:** Many conference-goers want to have access to the sessions they most enjoyed or those that, because of scheduling conflicts, they weren't able to attend. The files can be uploaded to a web page, stored on a video platform, or in a cloud service for selective access through a secure portal. You can offer to have your buyer select individual presentations, a small bundle, or the entire conference for a fee.

SPONSORSHIP: A MEETING PLANNER'S DELIGHT

If a business other than your own contributes financial or *in-kind* support (donating an item or service, such as floral arrangements or conference bags for participants) to your company's meeting or event, then you have sponsorship. When done well, sponsorship offers significant opportunities for the sponsor as well as for the sponsored. For example, a newly formed medical supply company that's seeking name recognition may contribute pens, large paper pads, and/or folios with its new company name printed on them to be set at each place setting for a meeting of hospital administrators. In exchange for supporting the event, the sponsoring company gets some great advertising.

You're more likely to win sponsorship when you can show that a company's participation can bring a return on the investment. A powerful complement to other marketing programs, sponsorship allows companies to reach specifically targeted niche markets without any waste, influence customer relations dramatically, and enhance the company's image.

Some of the most common promotional opportunities include the sponsorship of a speaker, an awards reception or banquet, educational programs, banners, badge holders, audiovisual equipment tote bags, shuttle buses, napkins, and drink cups. Remember, the more companies you find to contribute to your event, the less that you are bound to your own company's budget and the greater the possibility for a more splendid event!

Cost-Cutting Tips for the Savvy Planner

Instead of giving you one long list of cost-cutting tips, I've divided cost-cutting up into several different areas that I address in the following sections, so you can easily find suggestions that are applicable to your situation.

Locating a cost-effective meeting site

Consider a meeting space that is on your company premises, especially for smaller business meetings. If you decide on an off-site space, consider using local destinations or smaller cities that offer you more bang for your buck. If you find that you're booking meetings regularly, try to use the same chain hotels or properties, such as Marriott, Hilton, Hyatt, or IHG. You can then use your regular customer status to give you greater negotiating power.

Wherever you make it happen, various factors can come into play that can contribute to your financial gain or loss:

>> Schedule your meetings for low-usage times, low seasons, or days of the week when the facility is less busy. Booking near holidays such as Easter, Memorial Day, and Labor Day can often be advantageous. Check out Table 6-1 in Chapter 6 to identify these non-peak, good-value dates.

>> Ask for the best rates. Do your research. Check out the *rack rates* (the hotel's standard rates for guest rooms), corporate rates, AAA discounts, and so on, and compare them to the group rates that you're being offered. Call the toll-free reservation desk for the information.

>> Confirm and reconfirm your dates and event details. Overlooking a detail may cost you big bucks.

>> Insist on a site visit before making any final decisions. Have the local Convention and Visitors Bureau set up a visit for you.

>> Request a discount for on-site payments. On-site payments are made directly to the catering manager immediately after the event, or as the meeting is ending.

>> Be conservative with your room blocks. You may have to pay for unused rooms.

>> Negotiate comp rooms for speakers, discounted rates for your staff, and/or upgrades for VIPs.

Getting the details in writing

REMEMBER

Get everything, I mean *everything*, in writing. Make sure that all the agreements you make with suppliers come in written form. Make no verbal agreements — they're worthless in a court of law. You're probably not thinking of legal action as you plan, but covering a certain part of your anatomy is always the best course of action. Best yet — run all agreements by your legal department for approval.

WARNING

Don't sign anything you're not completely happy with. Be certain that your cancellation clause is reciprocal, so that both parties get the option to back out of the contract before a specified date, in case of any changes to the original agreement. You always want to protect yourself. Make sure that all complimentary concessions are written into your contract, that any changes to the original contract are initialed, and that you read every word in the contract before signing it.

Even before a contract is drawn up, the following negotiation tools could save you:

>> Make a list of everything you want for your event. Negotiating is easier when you know exactly what you want.

>> For smaller events, negotiate so that you pay a specified amount on food and beverages during your entire event, rather than a rate per person, per function.

>> Investigate the tax laws for your business location and the event location. You may be eligible for tax breaks that you're not claiming. A tax attorney can help you with this one.

For more on negotiating and contracts, see Chapter 11.

Keeping program expenses to a minimum

Keep your room setup simple. Theater-style (where only chairs are used) is less labor-intensive than classroom-style (which includes both tables and chairs), thus lowering setup costs. Wherever possible, keep setups the same from day to day. See Chapter 10 for more on setups.

Following are more tips for getting the program you want at a price you can afford:

>> Find out about the groups holding their meetings prior to and after yours and discuss staging needs. You may find that you can save on setup and teardown if you all have the same requirements.

>> Find sponsors to cover as many of your program expenses as possible, especially speaker fees, audiovisual equipment, and special meal functions.

- Arrange buffet luncheons in the same room as the meeting to save on having to rent a separate room. This is good for smaller committee meetings that may be held during a larger conference.

- Double-check speaker audiovisual needs to avoid renting equipment that isn't necessary.

- Keep your signage simple and reusable. Consider investing in a laminating machine to make your own signs.

- Use industry experts (who often work for companies that pay their travel expenses) as speakers, or book local speakers where appropriate to save on travel expenses.

- Discuss economical setups with your audiovisual supplier. For example, instead of renting special carts for equipment, skirting the cocktail tables can provide necessary storage space (underneath the tables).

- Limit the number of microphones needed. Find out if the hotel supplies a complimentary microphone in each meeting room.

- Look outside the hotel for a possible audiovisual supplier whose prices may be more competitive than those in-house. However, let the hotel know that you're thinking about using an outside supplier; the hotel may match the supplier's prices.

Traveling cheap

Make arrangements with a major airline carrier for discounted fares for your meeting attendees, and negotiate comp tickets based on the number of bookings.

Here are some additional ways to cut your travel expenses:

- Use airport shuttles instead of taxis. If you have a sizeable group attending your event, negotiate special discounts with the shuttle bus company.

- Check if the local taxicab or rideshare company can provide discount coupons to local restaurants, tourist attractions, and shows.

- Encourage your staff to double up and share rooms to cut hotel costs.

- Examine your staff's expense reports to avoid illegitimate expenses. Set limits on *per diem* expenses (for example: food, transportation, or client entertainment) and reward personnel who spend less than the limit.

Feeding the masses on a budget

Consider having attendees pay separately for meals and excluding the food and beverage cost from your registration fee. This gives participants more freedom to do their own thing if they choose.

If you decide to include cuisine, the following tips can save a bundle:

>> Negotiate paying for food based on consumption. You can then return food without having to pay for it.

>> Minimize portions. Serve mini-Danishes, muffins, and doughnuts, or cut larger servings in half. Many people only want half to start with.

>> Serve a continental breakfast instead of a full breakfast buffet.

>> Choose one menu when you have several different meetings being held at the same time, such as board and committee meetings.

>> Opt for a few choice hors d'oeuvres in larger quantities rather than a large selection in smaller quantities.

>> Have different companies sponsor meals and reception functions.

>> Organize a boxed lunch instead of a sit-down function.

>> Check restaurant prices versus an organized function. This may be particularly cost-effective for smaller groups.

>> Encourage your staff to eat at the event's organized meal times to avoid expensive room-service bills.

Serving alcohol without breaking the bank

Seek out a local winery, wine distributor, or microbrewery to sponsor your bar expenses. Offering to incorporate a wine tasting as a side event may pique the distributor's interest even more. If you don't have a sponsor for your event's drinks, consider having a *cash bar* (where people pay for their own drinks).

If your company decides to host, the following suggestions may spare you the shock of astronomical liquor charges:

>> Avoid salty foods during your receptions (salty food makes people thirsty and encourages them to drink, which drives up your cost and potentially your liability!).

» Waiter-passed drink service during receptions encourages guests to drink more because it's readily available. Stick to bar service.

» Ask the banquet captain to open wine bottles only as needed. You pay for every bottle that's been uncorked.

» Instruct the wait staff to refill wine glasses only as requested versus refilling automatically.

» Inquire if you can provide your own liquor and just pay a *corkage fee* (an amount the facility charges for allowing you to bring your own alcoholic beverages).

» Find out if the hotel can store opened bottles of liquor from one reception and use them for another reception during the same conference.

» Check if the hotel has *dead stock* wine available (such as wine that is no longer on the wine list). You may be able to negotiate a great price for some good-quality wine.

» Compare prices on a *per bottle* or *per drink* basis. Obviously opt for the best deal!

4

Building Bridges with Technology

In this age of rapid technological advances and more information than we know what to do with, meeting and event planners must stay on top of technology. More and more companies are looking for ways to maximize meeting time, and connecting virtually is often the best way to accomplish that.

My goal is to take the mystery out of using technology so that you feel totally comfortable with the various mediums available. Plus, I share some more of those wonderful practical tips and techniques to help you overcome any technology anxieties.

IN THIS CHAPTER

» **Discovering the benefits of modern meeting alternatives**

» **Exploring available technologies**

» **Choosing the best medium for your meeting**

Chapter **14**

Making Meeting Technology Work for You

Technology is booming, bringing people all over the world closer together through advanced systems of communication. Why not take advantage of this for your business? You can save time and travel costs by arranging meetings or presentations over the phone and online.

This chapter outlines the emerging role of technology in meetings and discusses some of the options available to you, including tips on selecting the appropriate technology to match your business event. I also introduce specific virtual meeting methods — how to host a successful conference call, video conference, or online conference, how to use the internet to your advantage, and how to use other available technologies to enhance both your in-person and virtual meetings.

Why Go Virtual?

Virtual meetings save time and money by eliminating the travel associated with the traditional business trip. Airfare, hotel, and other expenses evaporate when you meet via phone or online. People don't waste time waiting at the airport, sitting on an airplane, and then struggling to find their way around an unfamiliar city — just to attend a brief meeting and then turn around and go through the hassle all over again on the return trip. The lost productivity of time spent away from the office is drastically reduced.

Many virtual meeting technologies enable you to address important issues immediately, without the delay of extensive preparation and travel. In today's fast-moving marketplace, this benefit can be crucial because it allows you to tackle changing trends and consumer needs as they arise, enabling you to meet client expectations and demands instantly. You can make important decisions and act on them quickly, keeping ahead of the competition. You can also address a crisis as it begins, rather than allowing it to escalate while you struggle with the logistics of a business trip.

The technologies discussed in this chapter can be adapted and combined to support just about every kind of meeting. You can use them to effectively connect contacts in remote locations for weekly sales meetings, corporate training, project coordination, company addresses, board of directors' meetings, crisis management sessions, and much more.

Read on to find out what options might be the right fit for your next event.

Exploring What's Available

With the technology and communication systems that have been developed, you can choose from many alternatives to the traditional business meeting. People no longer have to travel for two days to attend a two-hour meeting. Now they can interact with contacts almost anywhere in the world from the comfort of their office, home, or favorite coffee shop. While a handshake and an in-person meeting are still valuable you can also build a real relationship with a potential client via technology, as the following options explore.

Conference calling

Conference calling involves much more than pushing a button on a phone to reach a colleague down the hall. You can partner with numerous communication companies to connect people all over the world via telephone, and those same companies provide additional services that can take the conference call to a whole new level of effectiveness.

Today's business world is moving at a faster pace than ever before. The ability to make quick decisions is crucial. With simply a phone, you can immediately connect the major decision-makers for discussion and quick action, despite the fact that they may be scattered across the country — or even around the world. Because of this, conference calling is ideal for crisis management. That is not the only application, however, as these phone conferences can also accommodate regularly scheduled meetings such as weekly sales meetings or board of directors' meetings.

Video conferencing

A video conference allows multiple participants to both hear *and* see each other, and many who use this meeting method say it's the next best thing to being in the same room as those you're meeting with. The video conference is an appropriate choice when you want to develop a relationship between participants, as the visual interaction it provides is more meaningful and concrete than just a voice on a phone.

Video conferencing technology can be adapted to suit a range of meeting sizes and types — from a meeting between only two individuals at two locations, to a meeting between small groups of people at numerous locations.

TIP

Video conferencing is available for free using tools such as Google Meet and Zoom and via subscriptions from online services. The free versions offer connectivity with restrictions on the number of people in attendance, the length of your meeting, and the options available for the conference leader.

Online conferencing

The major difference between online conferencing (or webinar) and video conferencing is that a video conference is a dialog while the online conference is a monologue. An online conference has a presenter who speaks to the audience with no visual input from the audience, no audible feedback, and no (or limited) text input unless it is requested. The presenter is focused on making their presentation and expects minimal audience input.

REMEMBER

Online conferences are great for putting out a message, providing training, or giving a presentation when you desire little or no interaction. The speaker can upload their presentation, provide the link to the invited guests, and just go for it. To connect with the audience, the speaker can ask for questions and input via a chat function and run polls to keep everyone engaged. This is a great advantage when presenting to large groups, especially in an educational or training function. Online conferencing can use the same platforms as video conferencing.

Other cool stuff

"Bah. Gadgets, gizmos, and toys." If that's your initial response to the mention of audience response systems, electronic whiteboards, and laser pointers, then you're missing out on some great new ways to enhance your in-person and hybrid meetings! Those gadgets, gizmos, and toys can help your meeting run smoother, and they can enhance the experience for everyone involved:

>> Audience response systems can tell you what's going on in the minds of meeting participants.

>> Electronic whiteboards can take notes for you.

>> Laser pointers let you control your presentation while interacting with your audience.

These aren't dream inventions for the future; they're commonplace tools in today's best meetings. Let's take a look at them in more detail.

Audience response systems

Audience response systems and apps are a great way to keep your finger on the pulse of a meeting. They provide immediate insight into what participants are thinking and feeling. You have instant access to their thoughts and opinions on what is being discussed. These systems also create a more enjoyable and interactive meeting for the participants.

You can use an audience response protocol before your meeting to gather demographic information about participants, to determine what they already know about the subject of the meeting, and so on. During the meeting, you can get their thoughts and opinions on the discussions. After the meeting, you can use the system to see what they've learned from the presentation and discussion and to gauge their level of understanding. You can even use the system to interject humor into a meeting — by taking a poll of everyone's favorite ice cream flavor, for example.

TECHNICAL
STUFF

You have the option of getting a dedicated handheld response system or asking your participants to download an app to their phones. With the handheld system you'll have the logistics of shipping, storing, distributing, and collecting the devices. With the phone app you may encounter signal issues, lack of a phone's capacity, or the ease of a participant's distraction to other phone apps.

Whichever protocol you select, the software creates a powerful and interactive system. You can pose questions with different types of answers — yes or no, true or false, multiple choices, a scaled range of answers, candidates' names, polling responses, and so on. The software determines how the participants' responses to the question are tabulated and shown to you. You can receive the outcome as a graph, a chart, or a list. You can also control whether the answers are anonymous or attributed to individual participants.

Whether you choose the handheld dedicated response system or a phone app you'll need to work with the response system designers to develop the questions specific to your presentation. Budget your time and funds accordingly. And remember, there is great value in the instantaneous and measurable feedback that you'll get from your engaged audience.

When researching the cost of an audience response system, ask the company what *exactly* is included in the proposed price and what are the charges for upgrades and customization. Do you have to pay a technician to set it up? Does the agency charge you for basic training on how to use the system? Also, what is the lead time for getting your questions programmed into the system?

Electronic whiteboards

Electronic and interactive whiteboards are much like your traditional whiteboard — on steroids. As their most basic function, electronic whiteboards create a carbon copy of what is written on them. The physical "board" is actually a screen that is sensitive to pressure. It tracks the location of a pen, finger, or eraser moving over it and translates that information into a computer document, effectively digitally re-creating the images or words that meeting participants have drawn or written on the screen.

These tools can act as stenographer, taking note of what is being written on them and storing it away as a computer file for later retrieval. With the help of an electronic whiteboard, you can create an accurate record of your meeting without tedious note taking, and without the possibility of note taker error or misinterpretation.

Projected whiteboards work with a computer interface through your digital projector to turn any wall into a whiteboard. The "magic" of the board happens through an electronic pen that is touch sensitive. This type of whiteboard enables you to pull up documents or presentations from your computer to share, highlight, or annotate in real time. There are also virtual whiteboards that allow remote teams to ideate and collaborate online. The whiteboard retains the information as a file and allows other team members to remotely contribute in a variety of ways. Each are excellent tools for building, sharing, and collaborating. Plus, you'll never have to hunt for a usable marker!

TECHNICAL STUFF

AN ELECTRONIC WHITEBOARD ALTERNATIVE

Some electronic whiteboards come as all-inclusive packages, complete with the touch-sensitive screen. An alternative to these whiteboards is mimio, a brand-name product (which, by the way, is not spelled with a capital *m*) that enables you to permeate that ordinary whiteboard you have hanging in your meeting room with *most* of the capabilities of an electronic one.

When mimio — a small, portable device — is attached to an ordinary whiteboard and you use special "pens" to write on that board, special hardware and software capture what is written or drawn in real time and can save it, print it, and/or transmit it online.

For more information on mimio's products and services, visit its website at www.mimio.com.

Laser pointers

Meeting leaders and speakers who rely heavily on their computers during presentations often resent being chained to their laptops, unable to move around and interact with other meeting participants. For them, a nifty hand-held laser pointer is a useful device. It gives presenters the freedom to move about the room and still control their computer. The laser pointer acts as a wireless mouse, plus the laser beam allows the presenter to bring attention to key information on the screen.

This very affordable tool makes every presenter look like a pro. But do remember to practice with it before you hit the stage! (Another benefit to the laser pointer is that you can use it to play with your cat the next time the little critter starts looking for your attention.)

TIP

When selecting a laser pointer, check its range, compatibility, and functionality. When trying out different pointers, your best bet is to hold it in your hand so you can see whether the feel is right for you and whether it's easy for you to control.

WARNING

Laser pointers have real lasers. Which means avoid pointing them at people, especially at their eyes!

Projectors

With whiteboards and the plethora of other new technologies available today, the good old projector may seem a bit outdated. Not true! The projector industry has benefited from the technological revolution, and manufacturers are making their products more powerful and more useful than ever. If you haven't shopped for a multimedia projector lately, it's a new world out there!

At one time, the video projector was a chunky expensive piece of equipment that was rolled from room to room with a tech servant to attend it. Now, permanently installed projectors are built-in or suspended from ceilings in many hotel meeting rooms, class rooms, and board rooms.

TIP

If you want to be sure that your presentation will hit the big screen, get yourself a portable projector. These marvels are compact, lightweight, and powerful enough to be used in a day-lit room. When choosing a projector, keep the following in mind:

>> **Resolution:** The resolution of a projector refers to the number of *pixels* — the individual dots of color — in the panel(s) or chip(s) it uses to display an image. The more pixels, the higher the resolution, and the sharper the image the projector displays.

>> **Brightness:** I can't stress enough how important the brightness of a projector is, especially if your meeting will take place in a relatively well-lit room. If your projector doesn't produce a bright enough image, your slide show will look washed out or, worse yet, attendees will be unable to see it altogether. The higher the *lumens* (brightness factor), the better.

>> **Contrast:** The contrast of a projected image refers to the difference between its light and dark areas. The better the contrast, the sharper and more realistic the image looks.

>> **Warranty:** When you're purchasing any piece of technology, computer, or projection equipment, look into what sort of warranty is available through both the manufacturer and the retailer.

REMEMBER

Practice with your projector! Be completely confident that you can connect your projector to your computer, retrieve the desired presentation, and get it to clearly project in a matter of minutes. When you are a smooth operator, your audience is captivated by your confidence.

AND TODAY'S CONTESTANTS ARE . . .

Why not add some excitement and friendly competition to your next meeting by incorporating a customized, television-style game show? *Gameshow Pro* is a software program by Learningware, Inc. that turns an ordinary meeting into what the manufacturer calls a "fun, interactive, total learning experience." Other resources are Kahoot! (a monthly subscription plan) and QuizXpress (which also provides game show type buzzers for a fee).

(continued)

(continued)

Many researchers believe that games reinforce learning. Participants enjoy the game show because it turns learning into a challenge and totally engages them. Wouldn't a game show be a welcome departure from a presenter droning endlessly on about a topic, trying to drill information into the heads of the audience?

With a game show format, you develop questions and answers on the topic of your choosing and import them into one of several game formats — formats that resemble Tic Tac Toe, *Family Feud, Jeopardy,* and *Who Wants To Be A Millionaire.* Using your mouse or keyboard, you become the show's host, controlling the action. The length of the game show, the subject matter, and the difficulty of the questions are entirely up to you!

A game show can reinforce information that has already been presented, and it can also present new information to players. You can add supplementary information to appear *after* a question to build on what's already been learned. Questions can include pictures, sounds, and movies, too.

You can import your company's logo and other personalized graphics or photographs into the program. When you're done with your meeting, you can post the game on a company's website for meeting participants who want to play again, or for people who weren't able to attend.

Selecting the Right Meeting Alternative

Selecting the right technology requires you to analyze your goals for the meeting you're planning and to determine what resources you can put into it. From there, decide which method can best help you reach those goals in a cost-effective manner. If speed and immediacy are important and you don't want to spend a lot of money, conference calling is a good option. If you want to present to a large audience with minimal feedback, online conferencing is the way to go. To get collaboration and interaction with a smaller group, consider a video conference.

TIP

Your answers to the following questions can help you make your decision:

>> **How many participants will be involved in the meeting?** If it is a large meeting (over 50 people) you may feel that an online conference will be the best way to get your message out with interaction via a chat function or polling features within the system. When you have smaller numbers, you can break attendees off into groups and let them have audio and video input in real time through a video conference. Of course, for quick decisions a conference call might be the best selection.

>> **How important is it to impress meeting participants?** Your answer can help determine the quality of the broadcast that you want to invest in. If it's an internal meeting between employees whom you don't particularly need to impress, a high-quality video conference may not be worth the price. If, however, you need your audience to be wowed, then go for the best!

>> **What resources do you have available?** Consider your financial resources, facilities, equipment, staff, and so on. The prices of the systems and services discussed in this chapter differ substantially, and the amount of investment you're willing to make will help guide your decision. You can save costs if you already have in-house technical staff who can help set up the event. Also note whether you have on-site facilities that can be reworked into video conferencing rooms.

>> **How much time do you have available to plan the meeting?** Aside from an agenda, an online or video conference requires visuals to support your message. A conference call can be put together much more quickly.

>> **What do you hope to accomplish with the meeting?** Are you looking for a quick decision on a time-sensitive topic? Do you want to demonstrate a process or show samples to a client? Do you want a one-way transfer of information from a single source to a large audience? Is it important that participants be able to interact with each other?

>> **What special needs do you have for the meeting?** Do you want the ability to work on a document collaboratively? Would you like to share a presentation? Or do you have some other specifics for the meeting?

REMEMBER

You can combine different technologies to create the ideal environment for your meeting. For example, consider an interactive whiteboard used during a teleconference.

Chapter **15**

This Phone's for You: Conference Calling

onference calling, also known as teleconferencing, is the act of meeting via a phone call, and is one of the simplest and most cost-effective forms of meeting. You can use your mobile phone, landline, or an app on your computer to have a conversation with a group spread out anywhere in the world.

Conference calling has been a preferred method of meeting for legal and financial concerns as it can provide a secured line and a recording of the proceedings. A conference call has an advantage over a video call since it uses far less bandwidth.

REMEMBER

Conference calls enable participants to make decisions quickly, handle problems immediately, and address needs and changing markets faster. Participants can join the meeting from anywhere through their phone and, when using a service, via their digital device.

Modern technology has taken this type of meeting to new heights, allowing you to enhance your conference calls with secured lines, dial-in or dial-out systems, and professional facilitation. These extra services are available to turn any phone into a powerful meeting tool.

TIP

Even though a conference call conjures up the original ideal of multiple people meeting through phone lines, current technology and apps such as Google Meet and Zoom makes it easy to connect through your computer or tablet. `FreeConferenceCall.com` is one of the services you can access to utilize a speaker phone in a conference room. Alternatively, you can connect through their app on your computer to reach your cohorts working at other sites.

Although conference calling has many advantages, you need to be aware of a few possible drawbacks. Because participants can't see each other, there is no way to read facial expressions or body language, so communication can sometimes be difficult. Some people are easily distracted from phone conversations. Other people find it hard talking in a vacuum and may refrain from participating, whereas in a face-to-face situation, they may be more engaged. A well-planned conference call can minimize these concerns. This chapter presents all you need to know to plan a successful conference call.

REMEMBER

As with all technology, conference calls have advantages and disadvantages. Think about your goals for the meeting and consult Chapter 14 before you decide on any method.

WARNING

INTERNATIONAL RELATIONS

Conference calls involving international participants have pitfalls that can be avoided by following a few basic rules. Keep the following in mind:

- Speak slowly and clearly. Americans usually speak quickly, making it even more difficult for participants with a language barrier to keep up with the discussion.

- Stop occasionally to ask international participants if they understand what is being said and offer any clarification they may need.

- Avoid using slang, colloquialisms, jargon, and metaphors, especially sporting ones that Americans love to use, such as "in the ball park" or "this deal is a slam dunk."

- Watch your humor and sarcasm. International participants may misunderstand and think you are speaking literally, or they may take offense at something said in jest.

- Use a simultaneous captioning system to ensure clear communication. Companies such as Worldly (www.worldly.ai) can integrate with your selected online conference system. Some platforms have integrated captioning/translation as part of their system. For instance, Google Meet supports English meetings translated into Spanish, French, Portuguese and German.

- Consider providing handouts in the various native languages.

Exploring Service Options

You don't need to be a computer guru or a technical genius to plan a conference call. A quick search online will turn up many companies that provide conference calling services. They can walk you through your first few conference calls, and they can do much of the technical work during your meeting, freeing you up to focus on the meeting agenda. For example, conference call services can supply representatives to greet guests that call in for your meeting, connect individual participants to the call, troubleshoot any technical problems that arise, and facilitate in other related ways to ensure a smooth call.

TIP

If you plan on hosting a lot of conference calls, or if you plan to use them for spur-of-the-moment or emergency meetings, consider purchasing a permanent phone number that will be available to you at all times. This enables you to arrange calls much quicker, as you won't have to distribute a new phone number and access code to participants before each call. You can purchase such a number, sometimes called a *bridgeline,* through the conference call service provider of your choice.

The following sections present some general options you can choose from as you set up your conference call. Not all companies offer each service.

Dial-in

Using the dial-in method means that prior to the conference call, the chairperson advises all participants of the date and time of the meeting and provides them with the dial-in phone number and access code for the call. Each participant is then responsible for calling that phone number at the appointed time. Participants are greeted by the chairperson (or operator, if requested) and connected to the call.

TIP

If you choose to use the dial-in method, remind participants of the telephone number and access code the day before and a half hour prior to the conference call to ensure maximum participation.

Dial-out

Under this option, the chairperson (or operator, if requested) dials participants and connects them to the call. If you don't have a dedicated phone number that you have purchased and you need to put a conference call together quickly, this option is preferable to dial-in because it eliminates the need to get phone number and access code information to the participants before the call can take place. Each participant simply answers the phone and is immediately connected to the call.

Many conference call service providers can assist you in putting together a last-minute dial-out call in under 15 minutes. (However, the number of people you want to involve in the call, and the time of day you want to hold it, can have an impact on the time it takes to put the conference call together.) Simply call the service provider of your choice and ask for assistance.

Operator-assisted

If you purchase this option, an operator greets participants when they call in, and that operator usually performs the roll call of attendance. (Otherwise, the chairperson is responsible for roll call.) The operator also remains available throughout the call, sometimes staying on the line and monitoring the call through its entirety, and other times simply remaining accessible through a button on the keypad.

Lecture/broadcast

This feature allows a single person to speak or lecture for part or all of the conference without interruption. All other participants are placed in listen-only mode, their lines muted so there is no background noise or interruption from them. This type of conference call works best for a one-way transfer of information from one party to many parties, such as a speech by a company executive to their employees.

Question-and-answer

This feature is analogous to raising your hand. During the conference, each participant other than the presenter is placed in listen-only mode. A participant who has a question indicates it by pressing a key on the phone, such as #. The chairperson can then place the person into speak mode. The chairperson usually has the ability to field questions before they are addressed to the group, cutting down on unnecessary interruptions and keeping the conference call running smoothly.

Subconferencing

This feature allows participants to break into small groups for discussion and then rejoin the main conference. Say, for instance, that new information is presented to a group of conference call participants from several different departments or teams (such as research and development, legal, marketing, and so on).

Subconferencing makes it possible for the participants to break into groups by department or area of expertise and discuss the ramifications of the information among themselves, and to then rejoin the main group to present their conclusions and recommendations to the other departments.

Polling

This feature allows participants to respond to, or vote on, questions. Polling is a feature offered by some conference call services as an upgrade. Be sure to check with your conference call provider to determine if polling is available and the fees that are involved.

Secured line

This feature keeps unwanted listeners out of calls by blocking all entrances once the call has begun. Distinct from this optional feature is the level of security the conference call service offers on all its calls. If you will be discussing a confidential topic, ask the service what method it uses to ensure privacy.

Recording/rebroadcast

Conference calls can be recorded to be rebroadcast later, either to clarify what was said during the call or to reach those who missed the original call completely. To make it easy for interested parties to hear a recording of your meeting, you can arrange for it to be available on demand whenever they call in. To accomplish this, you often have to establish an account name and password that allows them access to the recording. Discuss this option with your service provider.

WARNING

When you decide to record a conference call for posterity, clarity, or playback be sure to notify all participants at the beginning of the meeting that the call is being recorded. It is a Federal legal requirement and state laws may differ — so check the requirements and notify everyone just to be sure.

TECHNICAL STUFF

DO-IT-YOURSELF CONFERENCE CALLING

As technology continues to evolve, new ways to merge conference calling and personal computers are being developed. Conference calling companies allow you to view all sorts of information regarding your call by using your computer desktop or a phone app. You can see a list of the people currently connected to the call, along with their phone numbers and locations. The current speaker is highlighted, making it much easier to track who is contributing.

This technology also gives you greater control over the call, as it enables you to disconnect or mute certain callers and call on participants who have questions. It eliminates the need for an operator and reduces cost. I suggest, however, that you get used to running a conference call with the assistance of an operator before you take on more technical responsibility for the call.

Tips for a Successful Conference Call

Although the service provider you choose handles the technical aspects of the call, you need more than luck to help the other aspects of the conference call run smoothly. A successful conference call does require some planning, and the more you organize it, the more seamless it will be. You can't possibly plan all the details of a conference call when it's a last-minute or emergency meeting, but the following sections address some things to keep in mind when you do have the time to plan.

Preparing for the call

These seven steps help you organize your conference call in the weeks and days leading up to the meeting:

>> Make a list of all attendees and check their availability on the date and time planned.

>> If the service provider you choose requires a reservation, check to see if the date and time you want is available.

>> Decide on what options you will use for your call. Will it be dial-in or dial-out? Do you want it recorded? Refer to the descriptions earlier in this chapter for the most popular options available.

>> Contact all participants and give them the date and time of the conference call. Specify which time zone you're referring to — a critical point that is often overlooked!

>> If you opt for a dial-in conference call, provide participants with the telephone number and access code for the call, as well as your name and contact information in case any problems arise.

>> Create an agenda for the conference call. See Chapter 3 for more about planning agendas.

>> If you're going to provide handouts and supplementary material to participants, send it early enough so that it arrives before the conference call begins, giving participants time to read it and prepare for the meeting. Include a written agenda. Short biographical information on the participants is a nice addition, especially when people aren't familiar with each other.

YOUR AGENDA: DON'T CONFERENCE CALL WITHOUT IT!

Creating an agenda for your conference call ensures that you cover all important topics, and it helps the meeting run smoothly and on time. It also keeps participants focused on the subject at hand and helps prevent them from drifting off during the discussion. If, during the course of the conference call, a question or topic arises that isn't scheduled on the agenda, suggest that it be discussed after all topics that *are* on the agenda have been covered.

When creating your agenda, include not only the topics you want to cover but also the amount of time you want to spend on each one. Including this information keeps the call from running over the assigned period.

TIP

Because they have no speaker to look at during a conference call, participants focus more intently on any handouts you provide. This is a perfect opportunity to create handouts that make an impact! Pay close attention to detail and use strict quality-control standards when creating your handouts. Check closely for spelling errors, grammatical problems, and typos, and use attractive, easy-to-read fonts. Pictures or illustrations can enhance your handouts, but make sure they're not too distracting.

Running the meeting

Regardless of whether you're the chairperson or not, your primary function as the meeting's planner is to make sure everything runs smoothly. Here are a few guidelines to help you or the chairperson accomplish this:

>> Always take a roll call at the beginning of the conference so that everyone knows who is involved and listening. If participants don't know each other, briefly introduce each one. You might also include biographical information on participants (such as their position in the company and specific area of expertise) with any handouts you send.

>> Begin with enthusiasm, setting the tone for an upbeat and positive meeting. This tone determines, in part, how engaged and attentive your audience is.

>> Outline the objectives and the agenda of the meeting. Consider giving participants printed copies of the agenda ahead of time so that they can follow along.

>> Give participants the basic rules and guidelines for the call. Cover speaking time limits, instruct them to pause occasionally so that others have a chance to get a word in, and quickly go over the most important etiquette points outlined in the section "Minding Your Manners: Conference Calling Etiquette," later in this chapter.

>> Organize your presentation and discussion into clear, concise points. Doing so helps participants follow what is being said, as they may lose their place in the conversation during a lengthy discussion without visual clues.

>> Keep an eye on the clock to make sure that you follow your agenda.

>> Keep track of who contributes to the discussion and who doesn't. To engage those who are too quiet, ask them questions or ask for their opinions on the subject being discussed. Calling on them encourages them to keep up with the conversation, much like when you were back in school and knew you might be called on in class.

>> Pause periodically throughout the conference call to get feedback and take questions from the other participants.

>> On long conference calls, schedule a 5- to 10-minute break every hour. The longest call without a break should be around 90 minutes.

>> Before ending the meeting, go around the virtual room and address each person by name, asking for any questions or comments they might have as a result of the discussion.

>> Make it clear when the conference call is over. Briefly go over what was discussed, clarify any action the participants need to take, and, finally, instruct them to hang up.

Soliciting feedback

Giving participants a chance to offer feedback on the conference call is a good practice. Immediately after the call, e-mail them an *after-action report* that lists a brief outcome of the meeting, the assigned tasks (if any), and a request for their feedback. The minutes for the meeting can be included if ready, but are not required if you're after a quick response.

Your feedback request should include the following inquiries:

>> What additional questions or comments do you have about what was discussed?

>> What topics didn't we discuss that you would like to see addressed?

>> What suggestions do you have to make future conference calls more effective?

SPICING UP YOUR CALLS

TIP

A few simple things can keep your teleconference from becoming boring for participants. As you can imagine, listening to person after person drone on without interruption or variety can get tedious, and it can encourage participants to tune out what is being said.

Facilitate your conference call to keep your participants engaged. Establish and enforce a time limit for responses and questions. Be ready to call on participants that have not contributed to ensure that they are still on the line and that they feel their input is valuable.

And begin and end on time!

Minding Your Manners: Conference Calling Etiquette

TIP

In order for a conference call to run smoothly, participants must follow certain rules of etiquette while on the call. Follow the guidelines I present in this section whenever you're involved in a conference call, and consider distributing them to the participants of any conference calls you plan, especially for first timers:

>> **Be on time, and stress the importance of being on time to other participants.** When someone *does* arrive late, don't immediately cut into the conversation to introduce the latecomer. Wait until there is a pause, and then simply say, "Sorry for the interruption, but it appears that Jane Doe from New York has joined us."

However, you show respect to other participants by letting them know that the CEO of your company has stopped by and is eavesdropping on the conversation using your speakerphone. You can handle this tactfully with a simple, "It appears that our company's CEO has joined us. Please continue."

>> **Choose a location with little background noise or learn how to mute your phone.** If some background noise is unavoidable, use the mute button on your phone when you're not speaking. Simply turn off the mute feature when you want to contribute to the conversation.

>> **Use a headset.** Whether you are on your mobile phone, calling in through your desktop, or using an actual landline, a headset adds clarity to your voice and provides better audio. Avoid speaker phones as they pick up all the background noise and diminish the privacy of the call.

>> **Turn off all your ancillary functions.** You do not want to be interrupted by incoming notifications.

>> **Identify yourself before speaking.** The lack of visual cues makes this practice essential.

>> **Address people by name when you speak to them.** Again, because there are no visual cues, if you simply ask a question or make a remark without indicating to whom you are speaking, other participants may have trouble determining who is being addressed.

>> **Direct questions to a specific person, instead of posing them to the audience at large.** Doing so helps prevent confusion and chaos and helps ensure that your question is met with an answer rather than just silence as everyone tries to figure out who is going to respond.

>> **Never, ever put your phone on hold during a conference call.** Doing so forces the participants left on the call to listen to the music your telephone system plays to those on hold, effectively ruining the discussion. If you absolutely must step away from the call, put the phone on mute and set it on your desk instead. Do your best to avoid stepping away from the call, as it creates a problem when people try to address you without realizing that you're not there. The politest thing to do is to let the other participants know that you need to leave the call momentarily. However, you should leave only in an absolute emergency.

TIP

Take detailed notes on the topics discussed, including who said what. Consider having your service provider record the call, in case you need to go back and clarify something that was said. (But see my warning earlier in this chapter about informing participants that you're doing so.)

Chapter **16**

Holding Meetings Online

M eeting online is no longer reserved for high-level executive pow-wows. Since 2020, nearly everyone from grade school kids to grandparents has experienced online conferencing. Our need to connect during the COVID-19 pandemic encouraged approximately 200 online conference platforms to emerge, many with very powerful capabilities. The online meeting is now as prevalent and necessary as the mobile phone. Use this to your advantage when planning a meeting!

What you need to decide is which type of online conference will best suit your needs. You have a choice of a *video conference* (that allows attendees to participate with both audio and video), a *hybrid conference* (where you are sharing a live presentation with a broader online audience), and finally you can offer a *webinar* or *online conference* (where you are the main attraction and there is limited interaction from your attendees).

REMEMBER

Video conferences allow participants in remote locations to see and hear each other through video and audio connections. Video conferencing adds an important visual dimension to ordinary conference call and enables participants to communicate with facial expressions and body language. Participants can relate to each other much better when they're more than just disembodied voices. online conferences or webinars are live or pre-recorded sessions that bring your message to many with little feedback. The webinar audience can see and hear you, but the participants are not visible and may only be audible when and if the host chooses to let them speak. Hybrid conferences are a combination of a live in-person event with an online audience. You can choose to have the online participants connect through a video conference (communicating visually and audibly) or an online conference (without the visual and with selective audio input.)

Video conferences have participants. Online conferences or webinars have viewers. Hybrid events can utilize whichever platform works best for the online audience without detracting from the live audience.

Meeting online is a powerful communication tool. It may seem daunting to the technical novices among you, but fear not! Plenty of help is available, and if you plan well, you'll find that meeting online is an effective and efficient way to connect people all over the world. This chapter is here to help you get started.

The Pros and Cons of Meeting Online

Because so many meeting alternatives are available, you need to know both the advantages and disadvantages of using this particular medium in order to make an informed decision. Chapter 17 also provides details you'll find helpful when making that decision.

Considering the positives

TIP

Some of the advantages of online meetings include:

>> It's the next best thing to being in the same room. You're not just a voice on the phone, but someone the other participants can see and relate to.

>> This visual medium allows for demonstration. The maxim "a picture is worth a thousand words" certainly rings true here. You can show participants samples or demonstrate a solution to a problem.

>> Videoconferencing enables participants to put a face with the name of a person they may know only as a voice on the phone or the sender of an e-mail message. As a result, videoconferencing may help to build a stronger relationship.

>> Webinars allow you to quickly connect to a larger audience by recording your live session for playback at the viewers' convenience.

>> Hybrid meetings allow conference planners to include participants that may otherwise miss out on hearing a speaker, learning a skill, or being introduced to a new product.

Weighing the negatives

WARNING

As with every new meeting technology, online meetings also have limitations and drawbacks:

>> As with anything new, participants may not feel comfortable at first. It may take some time and effort to put all participants at ease with the idea of seeing themselves on the screen.

>> A lot of careful planning is necessary for a successful online meeting.

>> Technology can sometimes fail you.

>> Each platform has a learning curve and you need to be proficient before you go live.

Determining Your Needs

As you begin to develop your online meeting, you must accurately determine your needs and resources. Ask yourself the following questions to guide you in your planning:

>> What does the meeting chairperson hope to accomplish with this meeting? Does the meeting chairperson want a collaborative event, or a one-way transfer of information from one party to another?

>> Is it possible to accomplish the goal through an online meeting?

>> Is an online presentation compatible with the meeting chairperson's personality and presentation style, or would a meeting done in person or through another medium be more effective?

>> Do I need an online meeting facility? If so, do I have the resources to create or rent one?

>> Do other potential participants have online access?

>> How many participants will be involved, and at how many sites?

>> Do I need to hire technicians and site facilitators, or will I be able to do it alone or use existing staff?

I tackle these questions in this chapter and also in Chapter 17.

Choosing the Right Format

The type of online platform you choose depends on the nature of the meeting you're planning and the resources available to you.

Are you looking to provide a collaborative, interactive meeting in which all participants can share their thoughts in real time, or do you prefer a meeting more similar to a lecture, with information being transmitted from one party to the others with little need for interaction or feedback? Will multiple sites participate, or only two? How many people will be at each site?

When you select an online platform to help host your virtual conference, you have to pick and choose among the various features it offers. Before making any decisions, familiarize yourself with the features in the following list. As you do so, think about what you're trying to accomplish with your meeting and the message you want to communicate to participants:

>> **Application sharing:** The host can run any computer application while conference participants watch. In a video conference, the control of the application can be passed around to conference participants, making the meeting even more interactive. This hands-on approach is particularly useful and effective for demonstrating software and for training attendees on computer applications without installing the app on each participant's computer.

>> **Document sharing:** All conference attendees can view the same document or graphic on their screen. In a videoconference, they can also work collaboratively to annotate and edit the document. If the host chooses, each participant can have the ability to make notes and changes to the text or image. This feature is great for involving remote participants in the creation and evolution of text documents such as important letters and other communications, marketing and promotional materials, and company policies. Document sharing is quicker and more effective, as the conference also acts as a brainstorming session and allows remote participants to play off each other and provide valuable input as it comes to mind.

>> **Interactive chat:** Audience members can type private messages to any other participant or to the entire group. This feature can be used in addition to, or in place of, voice communication.

>> **Real-time polling:** In both videoconferences and webinars, the host can ask participants a question, have their answers tabulated, and the response is published almost instantaneously for all to see.

>> **Recording and archiving:** The conference can be recorded and archived for later review.

>> **Visual presentation:** Online conferencing at its most basic consists of a slide presentation and then providing the link to the meeting participants. From there you have two options: You can choose to have an interactive videoconference or a speaker-led webinar.

>> **Online browser sharing:** The host can surf the web . . . and take conference attendees along for the ride. The online browsers of all participants are synchronized, so they follow along as the leader jumps between websites.

TECHNICAL STUFF

The video and audio you capture during your videoconference can be transmitted between sites using the open internet or through a VPN (Virtual Private Network) which utilizes the internet but limits access to only the intended recipients. When you are looking to maintain the security or confidentiality of your information, VPN is recommended.

Aside from a platform's features, the number of people participating in your meeting also determines whether room-based or desktop videoconferencing is right for you:

>> **Room-based videoconferencing.** As its name implies, this involves a whole room — whether there are two or twelve people in it. The camera takes in the whole area, tabletop microphones enable attendees to interact with participants at other sites, and large monitors show what's happening at the remote locations.

Creating your own room for videoconferencing may be a good investment if you plan to host this type of meeting often. Setting up a videoconferencing room involves the purchase of video cameras, microphones, and monitors. You can easily purchase an all-inclusive room-based videoconferencing package rather than the individual components, making your job much easier and eliminating compatibility issues between the different parts of the system.

If this cost doesn't fit your budget, you can also rent a public videoconferencing room. Many hotels, conference centers, business centers, and colleges offer videoconferencing facilities. The audio and video you capture with your equipment can be transmitted over the open internet, through a closed intranet, or through a secured internet connection.

>> **Desktop videoconferencing.** Although room-based videoconferencing works well for groups of people, desktop videoconferencing is less expensive and ideal for conferences with one or two participants per site.

Your computer or mobile phone is all you need to use apps such as Zoom, Google Meet, or Microsoft Teams for your video conference.

Many desktop conferencing programs also give you the ability to share documents and use an interactive whiteboard, which I discuss in Chapter 14.

Staging a Successful Videoconference

When it comes to running a smooth video conference, you can't be too organized or too detailed. For your first conference, you need to begin planning at least several weeks in advance. As you become familiar with how the equipment and systems work, subsequent conferences may take less work and less time to plan. The following sections outline some basic steps to get ready for the big day.

Early planning

You can do a lot in the weeks and months before your videoconference to ensure its success. By starting early, thinking ahead, and staying on top of things, you can reduce the stress of last-minute preparations in the days right before your event.

Here's a list of tasks you can complete starting several weeks (or more) before your videoconference:

>> Schedule a date and time for the videoconference. Keep in mind that participants may be in different time zones. Planning a videoconference too early or too late in the day may pose a problem for remote sites.

» Reserve the room and equipment you need. Be sure the room you choose for the videoconference is temperature-controlled. Nothing is worse than suffering through a meeting — videoconference or otherwise — in a hot, stuffy room. Because of the way light and noise affect the cameras and microphones used in a videoconference, you may not be able to open a window to cool the room off.

» Become familiar with and practice using the equipment.

» Appoint and communicate with facilitators at each site, guest speakers, technical support, and so on.

» Distribute the necessary information to the site facilitator at each location. Include your plans and goals for the conference, contact numbers, technical information, and so on.

» Run through a practice session with all sites. You want to ensure the compatibility of systems and a seamless performance the day of the conference.

» E-mail handouts to participants well in advance of the event.

» Decide how you will set up the room. This includes seating, lighting, cameras, microphones, monitors, and so on.

» Work out the conference length and agenda. This includes speeches, question-and-answer periods, breaks, and so on. Videoconferencing can be intensive, so a good general rule is a 10- to 15-minute break every hour or so.

» Develop a plan of action in case technical problems arise. I discuss this in the section "Planning for disaster," later in the chapter.

Final preparations

A week or two before your meeting, complete the following tasks:

» Make sure that each remote site has the necessary materials, including equipment, contact numbers, handouts, and so on.

» Order refreshments for the event if you're hosting a room-based meeting.

» Send a goodie box of snacks and swag for the desktop participants to help them feel included.

When your videoconference is only a day away, it's time to:

» Confirm all details with the site facilitators and technicians who will be handling the videoconference.

>> Do a final test run to double-check the equipment. Check camera angles, the sound system, and so on.

As the day of your videoconference dawns, complete these last-minute tasks:

>> Arrange the room. (See the next section, "Springing into Action," for tips.)

>> Make sure that you have all the information you will need available in the room with you, including the contact numbers for each site facilitator and technician.

>> Connect with the remote sites 15 to 30 minutes before the beginning of the meeting to allow time to address any last-minute technical issues and to let participants get used to the technology before the meeting begins.

Springing into Action

The big day is finally here! Your online meeting is due to start in just a few hours. Are you ready to shine?

Creating your presentation

If you (or a participant in a meeting you're planning) opt to use visuals during your online meeting, follow these basic guidelines to develop an effective presentation:

>> Keep the slides simple, making sure that they're easy to read and understand. A couple good general rules are to express only one concept per slide and to limit each bullet point to six to eight words.

>> Make the text of the slides blue or black and then add accents with small amounts of color and simple pictures.

>> Use at least a 24-point font for the text.

>> Stick to basic fonts such as Times New Roman and Arial which are easy to read.

>> Use graphs, charts, and pictures. As the saying goes, a picture is worth a thousand words. Often times, a properly chosen graphic can convey an emotion or idea better than any number of words can.

>> Keep it simple. The purpose of the presentation is to support the conversation, not be the main attraction. Think billboard — six to eight words! For more information look through *PowerPoint For Dummies, Office 2021 Edition* by Doug Lowe (John Wiley & Sons, Inc., 2021).

REMEMBER

When planning or participating in an online meeting, remind those attending to close all computer applications that they aren't using. Doing so allows computers to work faster and lessens the risk of computer errors. Also, they should mute and put down their phones.

Staying out of trouble

WARNING

When planning a presentation for an online meeting, be aware of these potential trouble spots:

>> Remember that some transitions and animations used in PowerPoint slides and other presentations don't work on all browsers.

>> Test your links to videos before you go live to ensure they are still viable and functional.

>> Keep transitions between slides simple to prevent lag and pixelation.

>> Get a presentation partner to keep an eye on your chat. They can watch for questions and comments that may be pertinent, while you focus on delivering your message.

Even if you're not an internet aficionado, you can still host a successful online meeting. Conference platforms offer hands-on training so that you can get familiar and comfortable with the process.

Connecting with speed

Your connection to the internet determines how quickly information is transmitted to and from your computer during an online meeting. Ensure that you have access to high-speed internet.

TECHNICAL STUFF

Do an internet speed test to learn your upload and download speeds and determine if you need to improve those results. If your connection is too slow, check with your IT department or your internet service provider for available options to guarantee you'll have the best connection speed.

DRESSING THE PART

Although a videoconference or webinar doesn't require the wardrobe department of a major movie studio, you may want to offer a few guidelines to participants to help them look their best by wearing clothes that flatter them the most in front of the camera.

Clothing colors to avoid include red, white, and black. Red tends to "bleed" and blur on monitors, large expanses of white create a distracting glare, and all-black outfits can make people look washed out. Advise participants to choose pastels or combinations of light and dark pieces.

Avoid large checks, patterns, and extravagant prints, as they're distracting to viewers. Participants also should steer clear of large, shiny jewelry — they want the audience to listen to their message, not be mesmerized by their swinging earrings!

In the event you lose the feed, ensure that you can contact your other sites via your phone with a call, text, or e-mail. And be sure to have contact information for your technicians and service provider if you have outsourced your meeting.

Preparing the room

Unfortunately, your meeting room will not automatically arrange itself for your online meeting. You have to organize the tables, chairs, lighting, and audiovisual equipment to make the room conducive to your event. As you do this, keep the information in the following sections in mind.

Seating

Depending on the size and style of your meeting, there are several different ways to arrange seating in the room. In a U- or V-shaped setup, tables are placed in a U or V shape, with the camera and viewing monitors at the open end of the U or V. This versatile arrangement is ideal for conferences with a limited number of attendees. However, if the tables are too long, participants at the far end may not be able to see the monitors.

For larger meetings, consider a classroom-style arrangement in which participants sit in rows with a writing surface in front of them. If participants don't need to take notes or write anything down, consider removing the writing surfaces to focus the viewers' attention on the speaker.

No matter what seating arrangement you choose, *everyone* should be able to see the monitors displaying the remote sites. Sit in various seats around the room before the conference begins to make sure that you don't have to strain your eyes to see the screen. In interactive meetings, participants should also have ready access to a microphone so that they can easily contribute and participate. Read on to find out more about monitors and microphones.

TIP

Rooms with carpeted floors are better than rooms with tile, wood, or other hard flooring because the carpet muffles extraneous sounds such as footsteps, moving chairs, and dropped objects.

Monitors

Because the monitor is the visual link between participants at different sites, everyone must be able to see the screen clearly, without straining. It is suggested to mount the monitor about one-third the distance from the screen to the farthest seat in the room. For example, if the farthest seat were 12 feet away from the screen, the optimal height for the monitor would be about 4 feet high.

The size of the monitor should be based on the size of the room. Start with a 65-inch (diagonal) monitor for a 15–16-foot room. If your room is larger than 22 feet deep, consider a video wall so that everyone can see the screen.

Lights

People who already feel uncomfortable on camera may become even more anxious under bright, direct lighting. Avoid *can lights* (those little lights that look like soup cans recessed into the ceiling), which have a spotlight effect that causes unflattering shadows on the face.

Indirect lighting (light bouncing off the ceiling or walls) is highly preferable. If necessary, you can often redirect lights to produce this effect.

If participants will be taking notes during the meeting, be sure that the lights are bright enough for them to see to write. If possible, turn off the lights directly in front of the monitor or projection screen to avoid glare.

Running the meeting

You've planned and prepared; now it's time to perform!

When the cameras start rolling, the following information will help you and your participants navigate your online meeting with ease.

Communicating with participants

Taking part in an online meeting for the first time can be an intimidating experience for several reasons:

>> Participants may not understand the technology being used.

>> They may not know what is expected of them.

>> They may be reluctant to actively contribute because they don't have a good grasp of what is happening around them.

TIP

Put participants at ease by having each site facilitator briefly go over the basics of how the meeting will run and how the online platform works. Site facilitators don't have to get technical; they should simply point out the main components, such as the camera, microphone, and monitor. An explanation of the equipment is especially important when participants at remote sites will be actively participating in the conference, using the camera and microphone to communicate with participants at other sites.

Begin the meeting by introducing each site and the facilitator at each site. ("We also have with us today several people from our office in Los Angeles, where this meeting is being facilitated by Leslie Martin.")

Ask participants to introduce themselves before they begin to speak to avoid confusion. ("This is Evelyn Small from Los Angeles. I was wondering. . .")

Participants may notice a lag of several seconds between the remarks of a speaker at one site and the response from the other sites. Don't jump into pauses too quickly or you may cut off someone's response or final thought. Encourage everyone to wait a few seconds before speaking.

Even though a speaker may not be in the room with their audience, they should be extended the same courtesy they would receive at a traditional meeting. Participants shouldn't be wandering around, whispering, having side conversations, or distracted by their phones.

As the conference coordinator, you must direct the action. If the meeting is interactive, make sure that people at each site have an opportunity to speak. You can do this by saying something like, "Let's hear from Los Angeles for a few minutes now."

Working with the camera

When people see themselves on camera, the experience can be both exhilarating and terrifying. Encourage participants to act naturally and try not to get too mesmerized by their own images on the screen.

Here are some other tips to pass along to your participants:

» Sit in one place or stand still as you speak, but if you must move, do so slowly and fluidly. This allows the camera to remain focused on you and eliminates jerkiness in the video image caused by rapid movements.

» Smile, be confident, and lean slightly forward as you look into the camera.

» Don't pace as you talk, but if you do plan to move around, know the parameters of the camera range so that you don't wander out of view.

» Be aware of your quirks and avoid fiddling with your glasses, tapping your feet, shuffling your papers, or making any other repetitive movements that can quickly become distracting on camera.

TIP

Consider putting markings on the floor so that presenters who do walk around know the parameters of the camera range.

Using the microphone

Microphones often pick up more than you want them to — the squeaking of a chair, the crinkling of a candy wrapper, the sniffling of your co-worker with a cold. Although some extraneous noise is inevitable, remind participants not to tap pencils or cough near the microphones. Consider muting certain microphones when appropriate, such as when someone is giving a speech and there's no need for interjection from the other sites.

TIP

If you provide snacks for participants to munch on during the meeting, avoid individually wrapped candies and other similar items. The crinkling of the wrappers as participants try to open them quickly becomes distracting and annoying. Also avoid overly crunchy foods — unless you want to hear Joe from accounting munching a pretzel while you try to concentrate on what is being said. Dried or fresh fruit makes a great snack for videoconferences and meetings in general!

Planning for disaster

Into each life a little rain must fall, and at each online meeting a technical glitch that can foul things up is always a possibility. Planning for this possibility isn't pessimistic — it's realistic. Contingency plans also keep an otherwise well-organized online meeting from falling apart when the unexpected happens. So what do you do when you look up and see a frozen image on the screen? Or when you lose the connection to your remote sites?

PROMOTING ONLINE EVENTS

You have a very powerful tool to manage your online meeting. It's called the internet! Once you've chosen your topic and selected your target audience, start encouraging participation with a website specifically designed for your event.

Ensure that the page has clever graphics and copy to attract attention and then add the important basics: the date and time, the topic, registration information, speaker(s), outcomes, and a link to learn more. Your event page can be part of your company website or a stand-alone page with invitation-only access.

There are sites that offer event management for you which includes a dedicated URL for the event, e-commerce, attendee management, and communication. These powerful tools make you more efficient and put a professional polish on your event.

The following suggestions help keep the situation from becoming unproductive and chaotic:

>> Develop a contingency plan for each site and communicate it clearly to the site facilitators. Make sure that they know how to inform you that they have a problem and that they know whom to contact to fix it.

>> Designate a troubleshooter for each site who can work on fixing the problem while the site facilitator continues to run the meeting.

>> Have an alternative activity that the remote site can conduct to maintain productivity while the problem is being fixed. For example, hold a brainstorming session or discussion on a predetermined topic.

Special Considerations for Webinars

Much of what this chapter describes for videoconferences will transfer well for webinars or online conferences. The major difference is that a webinar is one presenter speaking to many with limited input from the audience.

You will still need an online platform to deliver your message. Things to consider for your webinar include the size of your audience, the length of your presentation, and whether you wish to record it. The length of your webinar presentation and the size of your expected audience should be determined long before you send out the invitations or start promoting your event.

TIP

When calculating the duration of your webinar include 10–15 minutes for gathering people online plus the length of your presentation, plus breaks, activities, and any questions and answer sessions you may want to include. If you are doing a brief 30-minute presentation, you may be able to get it all in within an hour from when you open the "doors" to your last "Thank you for coming."

Many online platforms offer a free service with limited accessories for webinars that are under an hour and have a small group of attendees (for example, Google Meet, Zoom, and Free Conference Call). Once you pass their time or attendance thresholds you will need to subscribe to their premium service.

A webinar presenter requires very basic equipment. You'll need a quiet room without interruptions from humans and pets, a computer, a video camera, good lighting, a microphone, and headphones or earbuds. Before you get started:

>> **Check your camera.** Check the quality of the camera on your computer and consider upgrading to a stand-alone web camera.

>> **Consider lighting.** Ring lights are an inexpensive way to bring good lighting into your space and make you look fantastic.

>> **Think about your audio output.** The microphone on your headset may be okay, but for a minimal investment you can purchase high-quality mics that make you sound like a pro. Headphone or earbuds are helpful to ensure that you are hearing what your audience is hearing.

Your live webinar audience can be just a couple of people to hundreds depending on your online platform and the intention of your presentation. For instance, free online training sessions frequently have a large viewership as the attendees determine if the paid version will be right for them. And if they do invest, that paid version may have five or ten people who have made the commitment to attend the live sessions.

REMEMBER

Because webinars have limited interaction with the audience, you can record your presentation and offer it as a playback for anyone who may have missed it or who would like to share it, or see it again. Check to ensure the online platform you choose has an option for recording your webinar.

One of the advantages of a webinar is that the speaker is the focus of attention. Webinars offer the same advantages as a video conference for utilizing a presentation, sharing your screen, or pulling up a whiteboard, but it is for the speaker's use only. With a webinar, the speaker controls the input from the audience. They may request viewers to put comments and questions in the chat area, but there is no need to mute and unmute individuals. Also, the viewers are not on camera and may find that participating in a webinar is more comfortable for them.

TIP

A webinar is easily managed by two people. It is best to have a moderator to support the speaker. The moderator can keep an eye on the chat to monitor how the audience is responding to the content, handle the technical tricks of launching presentations, linking to videos, and watching the clock while the speaker focuses on their message.

Running Hybrid Meetings

Imagine you have created the most fabulous sold-out live multi-day conference in an exotic locale and you just wish there was some way to get all those folks on the waiting list to participate. There is! It's called a hybrid meeting.

With the hybrid meeting you take your live content and provide access to people around the world who couldn't be there in person, allowing them to watch the proceedings live. Because it's a hybrid meeting, people unable to attend the full conference are able to virtually participate in the entire event (or just the selected areas of interest).

TIP

An online or remote viewing audience has a shorter attention span and expects high-quality production values, similar to those they see on TV! In many cases, the hybrid meeting can double the cost and complexity of managing the overall event. The costs can be justified by the higher number of paid participants that an online audience may bring in. However, analyze the cost versus the benefit of such a meeting before moving forward. The way to monetize these valuable hybrid events is by selling virtual access. You can create packages allowing people to select full access to all the sessions, or a lower price-point ticket for particular days of the conference (or for the key speakers or sessions).

If your meeting is just a small gathering, you can do it as an interactive videoconference and allow the online audience full video and audio participation. This means everyone, live and online, can fully participate with each other through audio and video. For a large live group consider conducting a webinar as your hybrid option. The presenter will be able to handle the questions and input from the live audience. Meanwhile a moderator keeps track of the online audience's comments and questions submitted via chat, and feeds them back to the presenter for their response. Having the moderator as a liaison keeps the online audience as engaged as fully as the live participants.

Chapter **17**

Expanding Your Reach with Virtual Events

V irtual events are not the stuff of science fiction; they are very much our daily reality. So, if you are technologically shy, crush your fears and know that reading this chapter helps you look like a pro!

These events are no longer reserved for major corporations with huge budgets. Just about anyone anywhere with a decent internet connection can now host a video conference, webinar, or hybrid event to capture their audience and send a message worldwide (and if you don't understand those terms, read on as I explain them later in this chapter!). You need to jump on the bandwagon and take advantage of this technology without reservation. In this chapter, I talk about the many advantages of virtual meetings and how to get help when you need it.

TIP

Each virtual meeting platform has its own special setup. Most of them offer online tutorials so that you can be a whiz when it is your turn to host a virtual meeting.

Understanding Virtual Events

Aside from bringing the world to your doorstep, virtual and hybrid meetings support inclusivity, are cost-effective and efficient; and provide key data about your audience. Smart event planners are utilizing virtual and hybrid models to expand their connection to a worldwide market while making it convenient for anyone in their ideal audience to connect to their message.

Virtual events can be as simple as a quick video chat with a colleague to a multiday live event (often known as *virtual summits*) with tens or hundreds of people all connected through the internet. Both types of event involve a digital connection and the internet. Both events require planning and forethought. And both events, because of their virtual nature, enable people from just about anywhere to connect and communicate with relative ease.

REMEMBER

By going virtual, event planners have found that they have increased their event participation. Without the concerns of travel or time away from other priorities, participants can more easily commit to a virtual event and still fulfill their other obligations. Virtual events are also budget-friendly for the event planner. The costs of travel, lodging, and shipping are either eliminated or optimized by utilizing a virtual connection. For instance, a hybrid event may only be able to host 500 people on-site, but the virtual audience can be many multiples of that live audience, which stretches your Return on Investment (ROI) to the maximum.

Virtual events give you the most flexibility for meeting planning since you no longer have to gather everyone in one spot. Your attendees participate from their ideal location. Guest speakers can drop into the meeting for their spotlight and then go back to their business. Since the internet is 24/7 you can easily gather people across time zones to share information.

REMEMBER

Your camera is your best friend for virtual meetings, so treat it that way. Prepare yourself to be on camera just as you would for a visit from a highly valued friend. Use a good-quality webcam placed no lower than eye-level. Lighting is crucial; use a ring light and avoid sitting in front of a window to make sure you are not backlit. Tidy up your background, wear appropriate attire, and be animated and engaged as you listen and confer with the other attendees. Select a quiet location as your meeting site, and put up the "Do Not Disturb" sign to keep other life forms from intruding on your event!

Types of Virtual Events

Virtual meetings range from one-on-one conversations to hybrid meetings with thousands in attendance. These events all need solid internet connections and a digital platform; from there, the sky is the limit. Let's look at your options. (Chapter 16 looks at some of these events in more detail.)

Video calls

You can connect through any digital device with a camera. The advantage of the video call is that it makes a stronger connection between a handful of participants as you can see and hear each other. It is also an extremely efficient way to meet since there is minimal prep work and most phones and computers have an app ready to make that rapid connection. These video calls are best used for quick check-ins, introductions, and brief conversations or urgent problem-solving on the fly.

Video conferences

Video conferences are interactive and a wonderful tool for brainstorming, problem-solving, and strategizing. Many digital platforms are designed for these interactive group meetings, and allow for video and audio exchanges, screen sharing, whiteboards, polling, chat, and other features that make it seem like you are all in the same room. Plus, many platforms offer breakout rooms for small group meetings within the larger event.

REMEMBER

A video conference needs an agenda and someone to keep the meeting rolling along.

Webinar/online conferences

These live or pre-recorded events are an excellent choice when you need to deliver a message quickly or repeatedly without feedback from your audience.

Webinars have viewers rather than participants. When the webinar is presented live, viewers may have the opportunity to participate in polls or submit questions via the platform's chat feature, but there is no give-and-take as you would have in a video conference.

REMEMBER

Once a webinar has aired, most platforms offer a playback option so that viewers can either watch it again or view it for the first time at their convenience. Webinar content tends to be *evergreen* (meaning that it has longevity and remains valuable over time).

Virtual summits are a type of online conference featuring multiple presenters speaking individually on one specific topic. These experts are brought together to discuss different aspects of the chosen subject and a host coordinates the event. These sessions may be live or pre-recorded.

Hybrid conferences

Hybrid combines the best of both worlds — a live event with an online option. Offering a hybrid event means that while you are presenting to a live audience, such as in an event hall or a boardroom, you also have a virtual connection to reach out to other valuable participants. You can choose to make your hybrid a cross between an in-the-room live presentation and a video conference.

When planning live conferences, the hybrid model gives access to a much larger audience. Teams can stretch their budgets by sending the key people to the full conference and allowing other members to participate virtually.

TIP

Virtual meetings are a great way to develop another income stream for your company by offering training sessions for consumers (B2C) or other businesses (B2B) directly from your site to theirs.

Doing it Yourself or Getting it Done for You

For a simple video call you can take a DIY (Do It Yourself) approach using an app on your phone or computer (such as Duo, Facetime, Zoom, or Google Meet.) However, once you get into meetings with multiple sites, speakers, events, and time zones you may want to consider a DFY (Done For You) option and bring in an expert to manage the details for you. To find your expert, search online for "event management platforms."

DIY options usually offer training to give you the confidence to control the platform on your own, while the DFY platforms let you select how they can serve you to create a polished presentation. Each platform can serve you at different times; you don't have to commit to just using one or the other. Determine your goals and your budget for your event and then choose the option that works best for you.

You can rent video conference rooms that are fully equipped with the necessary internet connection, monitors, cameras, and digital interface. Plus, they may also include technical assistance, for a fee, if you need it.

There are DFY online platforms with real people who will build your event portal, support your marketing and registration, control your attendees' access, connect your participants through a secured and closed internet feed, and offer unbiased facilitation for your meeting as part of their menu of services. Examples include Cvent (https://www.cvent.com) and Big Marker (https://www.bigmarker.com).

REMEMBER

For larger events, DFY platforms can manage your hybrid events, provide crucial data on the event participants, and also set up virtual trade show booths where you can meet with qualified leads. (For more on qualified leads, check out Chapter 19.)

Making Your Event Run Well

Virtual events have three crucial components:

>> An internet connection

>> An online platform

>> A digital interface

As outlined in Chapter 16, your internet connection can be open or a secured line, depending on your needs. The online platforms offer a dashboard of tools to help you run your meeting and manage your attendees. And the digital interface is the computer, camera, and microphone that you'll need to be seen and heard.

But there's more than just these three components to consider, if you want to run an event smoothly. The following sections offer up further considerations and benefits.

Understanding the features of virtual event platforms

Every virtual event platform offers a slew of bells and whistles to make your online meetings interesting, productive, and engaging.

TIP

Before you select your virtual platform, establish what you need to accomplish during your meeting. If you need cooperative input, you should find a platform that allows screen sharing and collaborative whiteboards (such as Microsoft Teams or Zoom.)

If you are hosting a hybrid event, determine how your selected platform can serve the in-person event as well as the virtual online audience. You'll want to keep both audiences engaged and excited about your event.

Determine what you need for your event, and the outcome you want to achieve, so that you can be clear when you make your platform selection.

Fine-tuning the details

While you have been diligent about arranging the best platform, either DIY or DFY, and selected the functions you require, you also have to prepare your digital deliverables!

Digital deliverables are product sell sheets, press kits, promotional materials, charts, graphs, whitepapers, and any other key information that you want to share with your attendees. Printed documents are no longer necessary, nor are they desirable for meetings. You'll save trees and physical file space by creating digital handouts and presentations to share with your attendees.

To keep your participants on track, you can choose to share documents during the presentation as needed rather than sending docs or decks to them in advance. Some companies offer separate web "vaults" to hold your presentation content for easy access during your live online event. By holding onto your documents and decks until needed you can be sure that all participants are simultaneously working from the same information and that the content hasn't been lost in an e-mail spam folder.

Consider setting up special URL addresses that lead to access-only web pages for qualified prospective clients. That special access allows them to learn more about your products or services and snag bonus content, if offered.

However, e-mail is still a powerful marketing tool for any major event. Use it to promote the event, confirm registrations, and share important information, such as your agenda and event reminders. You can also send personalized e-vites to key contacts to attend special sessions and invitation-only networking opportunities.

After the event, you can use e-mail to send out links to surveys or event documents, thank-you notes, or follow-up reminders for event-related opportunities.

Enjoying the benefits

By hosting a virtual event you not only gain efficiency and expediency, but you also get extremely valuable data. The digital nature of your event provides you with demographic information, quantifies your audience's level of interest, and easily follows their path through your marketing funnel. With that information, you can tweak your message to better match your market.

Here are some examples of the collectible data you may be able to gather:

>> Content downloads

>> Digital networking connections

>> In-session poll responses

>> Length of time your participants stayed

>> Questions asked

>> Visits to the exhibitor virtual booth

>> Sessions attended

>> Social media engagement and mentions

>> Speaker reviews

>> Survey leads captured and qualified

If you are going to DIY your data gathering, you'll need to review and assess each report to develop a clear picture of your participants' journey through your event.

DFY platforms offer unified data gathering tools to capture, manage, and interpret the data from your meetings. It comes at a cost, but it does save you the time and effort of analyzing the data.

REMEMBER

Hybrid events give you opportunities to make more on your meeting investment by offering access to individuals who can't attend the live event.

You also have additional opportunities for virtual event sponsorship that mirrors the live event (see Chapter 13 for more on sponsorship).

5

Exhibiting at Trade Shows

Trade shows and exhibitions are very special kinds of events that make up a subsection of the meetings industry.

Many conferences and conventions include a small or large trade show, featuring industry suppliers, as a value-added benefit to meeting participants. In this part, I introduce you to the dynamic and complex world of exhibiting.

Whether you're an exhibitor or a show organizer, I guide you through the process to help you maximize your exhibiting investment before, during, and after the show.

Chapter **18**

Planning for Gold: Exhibiting 101

W hether you promote your products and services at a trade show or a conference, exhibiting is a powerful extension of your company's marketing, advertising, public relations, and sales functions. Customers, prospects, and the general public see a broad view of exhibiting companies — their staff, products, services, and activities. Yet, I am continually amazed at companies that invest thousands of dollars exhibiting at trade and consumer shows, conferences, expositions, and mall shows — both in the United States and overseas — but don't take seriously this extremely powerful marketing tool.

Even though shows last only a few days, they interfere with the year-round normal selling routine, and many employees consider them a hindrance or nuisance. However, when exhibits are taken seriously and given top management's total support and commitment (plus forethought and planning), companies can profit nicely from their exhibiting efforts. It's important to realize that exhibiting is a business event — a big, important one.

Exhibiting consists of three distinct phases — activities that take place before, during, and after the show. To simplify the exhibit marketing process, think of it in terms of the four Ps:

> » **Step 1: Planning.** Planning lays the groundwork for exhibiting, focusing on the purpose and positioning of your marketing efforts.

>> **Step 2: Promotion.** Promotion examines opportunities to attract business and communicate a consistent message in line with your image in the marketplace.

>> **Step 3: People.** The people representing you at the event must develop certain skills that are critical to their effectiveness and overall success.

>> **Step 4: Productivity.** Productivity explores appropriate after-show follow-up to ensure productive results and benchmarks to evaluate your show efforts.

In this chapter, I discuss the first two Ps – Planning and Promotion. Chapter 19 considers People and Productivity.

REMEMBER

Every aspect of your exhibit marketing plan — including your promotions, your booth, and your people — should be aimed at making an impact and creating curiosity.

Planning a Successful Exhibit

From choosing the right show to participate in to developing and executing a thorough exhibit marketing program, planning is the key to your exhibiting success. From start to finish, adequate planning normally takes 6 to 9 months and sometimes even 12 months, so take time to go through the tips in the following sections to avoid blunders.

Choosing the right show

Thousands of shows are held every year both in the United States and overseas. Your choices include the following:

>> **International shows:** These major events within a specific industry attract exhibitors and attendees from all corners of the globe. These shows offer a forum for launching new products and services and discussing industry issues. Historically, in the United States, these events have typically attracted 10 to 20 percent of their participants from overseas.

>> **National shows:** These shows are primarily targeted at buyers and sellers in a specialized industry and are promoted to attract visitors nationwide. Frequently, a majority of attendees come from a 200- to 400-mile radius of the show site.

>> **Regional shows:** Organized in a particular area of the country, these shows attract visitors from a 100- to 200-mile radius. State shows are included in this category. Many of these events are open to the public.

>> **Local shows:** These shows draw attendees from the immediate vicinity and are often open to the trade and the general public. They include consumer events such as home shows and hobby or boating shows, which attract many local attendees.

Choosing the right show for your purposes requires some serious thought. The following questions can help you match the type of show with your meeting goals and objectives:

>> How well does this show fit your company's marketing needs?

>> How convenient are the show dates?

>> What other events are scheduled on those dates?

>> How convenient is the show location?

>> What percentage of attendees falls into your company's target market?

>> What percentage of attendees comes from your company's major service areas?

>> What does show management do to promote the show?

>> What is the show's past success rate?

>> Which of your company's competitors also exhibit at this show?

>> What return on investment can your company expect from the show?

TIP

Whenever possible, visit the show before making a decision to invest. You can then determine firsthand whether it's right for you.

Having a proper exhibit marketing plan

To make trade shows a powerful dimension of your company's overall marketing operation, make sure that total alignment exists between the strategic marketing and your exhibit marketing plan. Trade shows should not be a stand-alone venture, but rather a key component of your company's marketing communications mix, designed to contribute to specific goals for both long- and short-term objectives.

Answers to the following questions make up the foundation on which to build your exhibit marketing plan. I highly recommend that you ask these questions before each event you participate in.

Where do trade shows fit into your marketing strategy?

Examine your present marketing plan and determine how you can best use trade shows to enhance your strategy. Look at what you want to accomplish. Do you want to

>> Increase existing products/services in existing markets?

>> Introduce existing products/services into new markets?

>> Introduce new products/services into existing markets?

>> Introduce new products/services into new markets?

Why is your company exhibiting?

As with any project you undertake, you need to know the reason why you are doing it. Begin with the end in mind and ask yourself what you want to achieve. Goals, or the purposes for exhibiting, make up the essence of the whole trade show experience. Knowing what you want to accomplish at a show helps you plan every other aspect — your theme, the booth design and layout, graphics, product displays, premiums, literature, and so on. Exhibiting goals should complement your corporate marketing objectives and help in accomplishing them.

Set specific measurable goals for each show so that you're totally clear on the results you expect, but remember to be realistic. Your specific goals are the yardstick for measuring your results. Companies participate in shows in order to

>> Increase sales

>> Write orders

>> Introduce new products/services

>> Project an image

>> Provide target audience education

>> Educate customers

>> Recruit dealers or distributors

>> Conduct market research

TIP

When setting goals, make sure they're quantifiable so that you can measure your effectiveness at the end of the show. Here's an example of a quantifiable goal: Collect 100 quality leads and sell $100,000 worth of products or services within three months after the show.

READY, SET, GO: THE FIVE-SECOND TEST

In five seconds or less, visitors walking by your display should know

- Who you are
- What you sell
- The benefit of your product or service to *them*

If they don't see anything of interest, they're just going to walk on by and not even notice you.

What does your company want to exhibit?

Your goals determine the products or services your company needs to exhibit. For example, if you plan to launch a new product or service, your exhibit needs to focus on the new product.

Companies with several product lines often think they must display their complete range of products. Doing so not only demonstrates your lack of planning any specific goals but also overwhelms and confuses anyone visiting your exhibit, who probably has little or no clue as to what you're selling.

Who is your target market?

A critical element of your trade show marketing is knowing which of the following groups are most interested in your products or services:

>> **Present customers or clients:** People you're already doing business with.

>> **Technical personnel:** People interested in the technical aspects of your products/services.

>> **Manufacturers:** People who produce products and who may benefit from what you have to offer.

>> **Specifiers:** People who instruct others to use specific products/services to produce another product. For example, an interior designer might specify using a specific brand of carpeting for a project.

>> **Suppliers:** People who might provide you with products/services.

>> **Consumers:** People who use the products/services you sell.

>> **Influencers:** People who sway others to buy.

>> **Consultants:** People who advise others about specific products/services.

Definitely take time to think through the group or groups you want to target because doing so will help direct your promotional effort.

What is your exhibiting budget?

What would you do without a good old budget? Establishing a trade show budget can be tough, especially if you have no past performance information to refer to. Your budget for each show will vary because requirements differ from show to show.

TECHNICAL STUFF

According to Vispronet.com (who supply and design customized trade show displays and signage), your trade show budget should be three times the cost of what you will spend on your exhibit space. Using an average of $138 per square foot, a 10-foot x 10-foot booth would be $13,800. Multiply that by three and your exhibiting budget should be $41,400. And *EXHIBITOR Magazine*, the leader in trade show and corporate event marketing education, recommends in their 2019 (pre-COVID 19) Economic Outlook Survey that your trade show budget spending should break out like this:

>> Floor space: 32 percent

>> Graphic design & production: 9 percent

>> Exhibit design & construction: 5 percent

>> Show services: 14 percent

>> Staff travel/lodging: 14 percent

>> Shipping: 12 percent

>> Advertising, promotion, and special activities: 7 percent

>> Other (such as tips, dry-cleaning, repairs, or rush services): 7 percent

Reading the exhibition bible

The exhibitor manual or show service kit is show management's bible — a complete reference guide to every aspect of the show — so it's critical that you read it. You normally receive a copy after signing up for floor space. This manual recommends essential information for your show survival. In addition, it saves you tons of aggravation, stress, and money. What a bargain! Your job is to read it cover to cover, digest it, and act on the information. I guarantee it will pay you dividends.

Unfortunately, every show you participate in will have a different set of rules, regulations, and guidelines presented in a different format. Some manuals are easier to read than others. However, everything you need to know about the show appears in the manual — show schedules, contractor information, registration, service order forms, electrical service, floor plans, exhibit specifications, shipping and freight services, housing information, advertising, and promotion. To simplify the process, many show management companies now post order forms and other materials on their websites.

REMEMBER

When reading the exhibition manual, take deadlines very seriously and adhere to them because pricing for any services you order while you're at the show normally runs 10 to 20 percent higher than if you request them in advance. Examples of deadlines you'll come across include your orders for show services, such as electricity or carpeting for your display.

Determining your space and display needs

A very important part of your exhibit planning is knowing how much space you want on the trade show floor for your display. It's very much like buying a piece of land and then building a house. The difference here is that your display is a very temporary structure.

Figuring out your space requirements

When determining how much space you need, refer back to your goals and, more importantly, your budget. Some organizations want to make a statement about their size in the market and buy exhibition space accordingly.

In the United States space is normally sold in multiples of 10 square feet, with the smallest space being 10 feet x 10 feet. Pricing is based on a square foot rate. The larger and more prestigious the show, the higher the price for square footage.

What you plan to exhibit also affects the amount of space you need. If you intend to demonstrate a large piece of equipment, allow enough extra space for your presenters and the booth visitors. A general rule is to allow 55 to 65 square feet per person. Add to this the size of the equipment and then some extra space for visitors, and you'll have a good idea how much space you need.

Choosing the location of your space

Every company wants the ideal location on the trade show floor. However, every show is different, and the perfect spot varies from company to company. A standard guiding principle is to position your display to the right of the entrance or the central area on the show floor. Research shows that people tend to gravitate to the right or to the center most frequently. If the show you plan to attend is in the same location every year, study the traffic patterns and then choose your space for next year accordingly.

Before making any final decisions, discuss the floor layout with show management to determine where the main attractions, industry leaders, and your competitors are situated. Then decide how close you want to be to them. Avoid companies that demonstrate noisy equipment or have crowd-drawing attractions (known as *live marketing*) — they may draw crowds away from your space. Also, stay away from dark, poorly lit areas and dead-end aisles. Finally, avoid situating your exhibit near restrooms — people have other things on their mind when they visit these spots on the show floor.

TIP

Request a floor plan of the exhibition room. Use a magnifying glass and question every mark on the show floor plan. A small black spot, which may look like a speck of dust, may indicate a column, and a dash could mean a low ceiling. You need to know about everything on the floor plan before booking space. Don't leave anything to chance.

Considering your display options

A plethora of display choices is on the market today, but they broadly fit into two main categories: portable systems and custom-built displays. Standard portable systems include the following:

>> **Tabletops:** Designed for display on top of a 6- or 8-foot table, these systems are easy to transport and are usually the least expensive type of display.

>> **Modular systems:** The modules are designed to be interchangeable. For example, an entire display might consist of six modules that can be arranged in various formations on the show floor to fit your allotted space or to achieve different looks.

>> **Panel systems:** A system of interlocking, heavy-duty panels is used to display merchandise.

>> **Graphic panel displays:** This type of system is like a panel display, but the panels are large graphics and typically do not hold merchandise.

>> **Pop-up systems:** Designed to come out of a shipping container, these displays just "pop up" for easy setup.

Custom-built displays are designed and constructed to showcase your products and services in a more sensational manner than portable displays, and as such they require a much larger budget. Estimate that 50 percent of your exhibit design budget covers display hardware (structure and accessories) and 50 percent covers graphics.

On the show floor, your exhibit makes a strong statement about who your company is, what you do, and how you do it. The purpose of your exhibit is to attract visitors so that you can achieve your marketing objectives. In addition to designing an open, welcoming, and friendly space, you need a focal point and a strong key message that tells people why they should consider doing business with you. People want to know what's in it for them.

Another important element to think about is the image you want to display. For example, do you want people to think of you as high-tech, contemporary/ trendy, traditional, or sporty? Or would you prefer to just be seen as an established, quality operation? Your booth design can make any of these images happen. The color and quality of your carpeting/flooring should complement your image. Use lighting to accentuate product displays and create moods, and use special effects such as moving objects, videos, magicians, robots, mannequins, banners, flags, or live entertainment to grab the visitors' attention. Just remember to watch your image!

REMEMBER

If your booth has lighting, you'll need electricity! If you want to have access to the internet, you'll need to sign up for Wi-Fi. These two necessary elements are examples of add-ons that you'll want to secure when you fill out your booth application.

As for your graphics, make them interesting, even life-size or larger than life to really grab attention. Keep any copy to an absolute minimum, as very few visitors take the time to read in this environment. However, if the boss insists on having some copy, make sure that it focuses on the buyer, stresses one benefit only, is concise, and uses action words. Use your company logo to establish your branding identity.

REMEMBER

Don't leave graphics to the last minute. Rush orders, changes, and overtime charges add significantly to your bottom line. Planning your graphics in plenty of time — at least six to eight weeks before show time — is less stressful for everyone concerned and can help prevent many blunders that occur under time pressures.

When selecting furniture, use just enough to create a homey and welcoming atmosphere. Place tables for literature and other materials on the sides of your area and not at the front so you don't create a barrier between the display and the aisle. Use chairs for visitors only; if the exhibit hosts start getting too comfortable in chairs, they'll never get up to speak to prospects.

Flowers and plants are a fun and interesting way to liven up a dull or drab display. Use them to accentuate graphics, hide electrical wiring, and add natural life to the environment. Consider using silk rather than live plants because you can reuse them.

Concerning yourself with details

Exhibiting is like assembling a jigsaw puzzle — both activities involve many different pieces. In the space available, I can't cover every little detail of trade show planning. I do, however, want you to be aware of some other general areas that you must research.

One concern is making the right transportation decisions for shipping your exhibit display, materials, products, and so on. The other involves working with union labor.

Take time to learn the essentials so you save yourself lots of frustration and save your company money. Trade show management should offer guidance — all you have to do is ask.

Promoting Your Exhibit

Trade show management is responsible only for promoting the show to the right target audience. They are accountable to exhibitors for delivering quality traffic to the show. What visitors do and where they go once they're at the show is not under show management's control. You, the exhibitor, are responsible for informing your target audience about what you are exhibiting, where your display is located in the show hall, and why they should visit you.

According to trade show research, 76 percent of show attendees come to a show with a fixed agenda. If they don't know you're exhibiting, the chances are slim that they will find you, especially at large shows. So promotion is a key ingredient to your exhibiting success.

Here are three basic questions you need to ask to develop a high-impact promotional program:

>> How can you create a program so that people will remember your company, your corporate message, and your products and services?

>> What strategies will produce successful, measurable results?

>> How can you best allocate your budget?

REMEMBER

It's not what you spend but how you spend it that's critical. Your promotion should accomplish the following:

>> Attract quality prospects into your exhibit

>> Engage visitors in interesting activities that encourage interpersonal interaction

>> Enhance positive memorability for your products, services, and messages

Defining your promotional plan

A significant part of your marketing includes promotion — before, during, and after the show. Most exhibitors fail to have a plan that encompasses all three areas. Of course, your budget plays a major role in deciding what and how much promotional activity is possible.

The key to successful preshow promotion is targeting those people whom you really want to walk into your exhibit, find out more about you, and do business with you. The best preshow promotions are multiple, distinct programs aimed at various target visitors. Most companies target the following mixture of visitors:

>> **Key customers:** This extremely important group of existing customers provides most of your business. The good old 80/20 rule usually applies here: 80 percent of your business comes from this 20 percent of your customers.

>> **Other customers:** This group already buys from you, but they don't give you all their business, which means you have the opportunity to gain more of their business.

>> **Prospects:** This group of people is on your priority list, and it is just a matter of time (you hope) before they decide to buy from you.

>> **Other good prospects:** You would dearly love to sell to these people if only you had the time to devote to them.

Realize that a one-size-fits-all marketing plan won't work. You have to look at each target group and decide how best to communicate your message to them.

REMEMBER

The key ingredient to the success of your promotional program is understanding what your audience is looking for. The number one reason people go into a retail store — and the number one reason they will walk into your exhibition space — is that the store is selling something they want to buy. Prospects are looking for IDEAS, as defined in this list:

>> **Information:** The major reason people go to trade shows and conferences is to discover what's new. They're eager to learn about the latest technologies, new applications, or anything that will help save them time and/or money. So tell them! Even if you don't have a new product or service to introduce, think about a new angle to promote what you're offering.

>> **Direction:** Prospects are looking for guidance, suggestions, and recommendations. This is where you can excel and show your knowledge of the industry and specific products/services, particularly yours, that will help steer prospects toward doing business with you.

>> **Education:** Most people visit trade shows for personal development, and most of those are interested in bettering their job performance. Wherever possible, educate your target audience. Doing so enhances your credibility in your given industry and shows that you're interested in more than just selling your products or services.

>> **Assistance:** People need help with the various challenges they face in their working environments. They come to trade shows and conferences to find people and companies that understand and empathize with their situations and can help them.

>> **Solutions:** Visitors are looking for solutions to their work problems or challenges. Ideally, they want to leave a show with concrete answers and solutions to various issues. If you've done a good job, your products or services will be just what they want and need.

Creating a memorable message

As you think about creating your promotional campaign, you want to have a unique message that helps to differentiate you in the marketplace. To help design this message, ask yourself the following questions:

>> What is your company presenting that is so compelling, so hot, so different, that visitors will flock to your exhibit, dying to do business with you?

>> What does your company do better than your competition?

>> What does your company offer to buyers that's of real value? For example, do you have a better guarantee, offer faster delivery, boast the lowest price, or feature the largest selection?

Choosing your promotional tools carefully

Promotional tools are the means by which you communicate with the people you want to visit your exhibit. The following sections present the main tools that exhibitors use to generate traffic to their exhibits and also to create name and brand awareness. Make sure your promotional tools reflect your message and the image that best symbolizes your company.

Personal invitations

Use personal invitations when you want to reach a select, special group — for example, key customers or prospects. Invitations definitely carry more clout when top management issues them.

Trade show management often provides complimentary VIP or discounted tickets that you can distribute together with your personal invitations.

Telemarketing

Use this approach before the show to set specific appointments for prospects to visit your display. People are more likely to visit when they have previously agreed to meet at a precise time. You can use telemarketing by itself or in conjunction with issuing personal invitations.

Direct mail

Direct mail is still one of the most popular and versatile promotional vehicles that exhibitors use. Postcards, multi-piece mailings, and e-mails are among your direct mail options. Be sure that your direct mail campaign has a specific purpose based on your show goals and objectives. Give visitors a good reason to come and visit you. With a hall overflowing with fascinating products and services, combined with time constraints, people need an incentive to visit *your* exhibition space. For example, should they come to your display to participate in a contest, collect a gift, or see a demonstration?

Advertising

Advertising is an important aspect of the promotional marketing mix that lets attendees know your company will be at the show. Your promotional budget and your show goals dictate your advertising campaign. Your budget determines the media format you can afford to use, and your show goals dictate specific advertising objectives. Table 18-1 offers some pre- and at-show places to advertise. For more on advertising, see *Advertising For Dummies*, 2nd Edition, by Gary A. Dahl (John Wiley & Sons, Inc., 2006).

Public relations

Public relations is one of the most important opportunities for the trade show exhibitor. It is one of the most cost-effective and successful methods for generating large volumes of direct inquiries and sales. Savvy show organizers know the importance of maximizing publicity before, during, and after their event. They usually have established mutually beneficial working relationships with people in the industry, business, and local media.

REMEMBER

Traditional media still has the power to influence your trade show efforts, whether on television, on radio, or in print. Social media is a very cost-effective and targeted way to promote your trade show exhibit, plus you have complete control of the message and when and how it is delivered. Your job is to target your endeavors to create a positive company image and brand awareness of your products or services. The following sections address how to do that.

TABLE 18-1

Advertising Possibilities

Preshow Suggestions	At-Show Suggestions
Trade/industry publications	Show programs
Association newsletters	Daily show publications
Local publications	City billboards
Billboards	Taxicabs
Local radio/television	Balloons
Transit advertising	Hotel — on/under room door promotion
The trade show website (banner ads, for example)	Hotel TV
Your website	Convention TV
Airport billboards/electronic message boards	Kiosks/billboards/electronic message boards in show hall

BEFORE THE SHOW

Ask show management for a comprehensive media list complete with contact names, addresses, and phone numbers of all trade, business, and local media. Also ask about show management's media plan for the show. Find out which publications are planning a show edition and their deadline for press releases. Realize that many trade journals work several months in advance.

When you have your media list, send them a *digital press kit* that includes press releases, photos and graphics, and your contact information so they can connect directly with you. Realize that editors are interested in timely, newsworthy information; industry trends; statistics; new technology or product information; interesting material such as do-it-yourself tips, techniques, or strategies; useful advice; and human-interest stories, including celebrities who may be coming to the show.

Reserve press conferences for major announcements, new product introductions (but only if they are truly new or improved), or general industry trends — what's hot and what's not. Media representatives get upset if they attend a press conference that is poorly organized and offers nothing newsworthy.

DURING THE SHOW

Make sure that you have a media spokesperson in your booth at all times, even over the lunch hour. Be prepared to explain your product and its importance in easy-to-understand, nontechnical terms.

Keep your press kit on your phone, tablet, and computer so that you can easily send it to media representatives you meet. Also, use a *QR code* (those mysterious digitized black and white squares you see popping up on signage, that link through to websites when they're scanned) at the booth to quickly link to your press kit.

Ask show management about opportunities to conduct presentations, seminars, or workshops. Find someone in your organization who speaks well and can present an industry topic clearly and concisely. Both the speaker and your company will then be perceived as industry experts. Some conferences request proposals to be submitted many months prior to the event. Have a digital handout for your presentation with company contact information and a link to the company website. During your session, offer something for free — a copy of the presentation, special industry report, checklist, or tip sheet — and ask participants to come to the booth to collect it. Again, this can be a digital document linked to a QR code, which participants can access when they submit their contact information.

AFTER THE SHOW

Send postshow press releases reporting trends, statistics, or information on significant newsworthy information or orders that resulted from the show.

Create a state-of-the-industry report based on your observations at the show and send it out or offer it free to prospects or customers responding to a postshow mailing.

Sponsorship

Sponsorship leaves the door open for savvy marketers to capitalize on unique promotional possibilities. Some of the most frequent trade show promotional opportunities include sponsorship of the press room, exhibitors lounge, speaker or VIP room, awards reception, educational programs, banners, badge holders, audiovisual equipment, Wi-Fi connection, display computers, tote bags, shuttle buses, napkins, and drink cups.

The internet

Many show organizers now offer their exhibitors the opportunity to participate in a virtual trade show — a replica of the show online. Visitors to the actual show have the opportunity to preview it and map out where they want to go and which booths they want to visit, before they even set foot on the show floor, saving them time and energy. For the many people who can't attend the show itself but wish they could, the virtual show allows them to "attend" the show in their own time and with no registration and associated travel costs.

To make the most of this promotional tool, investigate advertising and sponsorship opportunities with the virtual show — you'll reach a highly targeted and greatly expanded audience. Also explore the possibility of establishing links from the virtual show to your company's website, giving you more opportunities to sell your products and services.

Using giveaways effectively

Tied into giving visitors an incentive to visit your booth is the opportunity to offer a premium item to entice them, known as a *giveaway.* Your giveaway items should be designed to increase memorability, communicate, motivate, promote, or increase recognition of your company. Developing a dynamite giveaway takes thought and creativity. For example, you could put together a booklet of industry-specific websites, or create a special report on a particular industry concern, such as safety in the workplace. The visitors get access to these documents in exchange for their contact information (specifically, their e-mail address).

Consider what your target audience wants, what will help them do their jobs better, what they can't get elsewhere, and what is product- or service-related and educational. Think about having different gifts for different types of visitors. Use your website to make an offer for visitors to collect important information, such as an executive report, when they visit your booth. You can use giveaways in two ways: as a reward or token of appreciation for visitors participating in a demonstration, presentation, or contest; and as a thank-you to the visitors who give you specific information about their particular needs.

Of course, a trade show wouldn't be any fun without a handy memorable little branded something (aside from candy) as a thank-you for stopping by. Ideas for trade show giveaways range from web camera covers emblazoned with your logo (costing less than $1.50 each) to actual webcams (at about $50 a gift).

TIP

Keep in mind that you should have levels for the gifts you give. The show vultures who are just hovering for whatever is laid out deserve the candy and maybe a pen. The folks who provide you with information and seem genuinely interested in your product or service can go to the next level gift. And then for the hot prospects, offer to send them the bigger gift, rather than having them tote it with them in their suitcase.

Selecting marketing collateral

Picture visitors at a trade show trudging down the aisles laden with bags overflowing with pamphlets and materials, known in the trade show industry as *collateral material.* At these events, people have a psychological urge to take whatever is handed to them and whatever is available to be taken, whether or not they will actually go through it all later.

According to trade show research, over 66 percent of all literature gathered at shows is discarded before attendees leave the show site. To avoid wasting money on filling the trash cans, follow these simple guidelines for managing your collateral material:

>> **Offer to digitally send the information.** Many prospects appreciate the offer to send them literature. This gesture frees them from lugging around extraneous material and finding room for it in their baggage. However, if you promise to mail your information, do so promptly. If you don't, your competition will. If you can send it while your visitor is still in front of you, you'll be assured they have received it and you can follow up later to get their feedback. Having QR codes strategically placed in your booth provides visitors easy access to product information and allows you to capture their information.

>> **Give only to qualified prospects.** Unless your goal is to get information into as many hands as possible, hand out or offer to send material only to qualified prospects (those people who express a positive interest in your products or services). This way, you're not giving your valuable information to people who are likely to pass it on to the competition.

>> **Remember that literature does not sell — people do.** Exhibit staff often feel uncomfortable in the trade show environment or talking to strangers, so they may end up just grabbing e-mail addresses, thinking that they're doing something productive. However, randomly collecting visitor information is a barrier to having a meaningful conversation with a visitor. The truth is that your people do the selling; your literature acts purely as a backup.

TIP

Consider sharing a private link to your website for exclusive information and a thank-you gift. Links are weightless, and easy to carry on a phone or tablet!

Chapter **19**

Strutting Your Stuff: Exhibiting 201

A s described in Chapter 18, exhibiting consists of three distinct phases — activities that take place before, during, and after the show. This can be simplified to the four Ps: Planning, Promotion, People, and Productivity. In this chapter I'll give you the lowdown on the last two steps: People and Productivity.

REMEMBER

People is about ensuring that the people representing you at the event develop certain skills critical to their effectiveness and overall success. *Productivity* explores appropriate after-show follow-up to ensure productive results and benchmarks to evaluate your show efforts.

Counting on People for Exhibit Success

The most crucial aspect of any exhibit is the people who staff it. Your image doesn't stop with an elaborate booth, fancy advertising, or impressive literature. These things certainly help, but your people actually sell your company and its products and services. The team members you choose to represent you are your ambassadors, and they have the awesome responsibility of making or breaking future relationships with attendees, prospects, and customers. Their attitude, body language, appearance, and knowledge help to create positive or negative perceptions in the minds of visitors.

REMEMBER

As much as 85 percent of a visitor's impression about your exhibit is determined by the attitude and behavior of the people staffing your exhibit, and roughly 80 percent of a final decision can be influenced by the booth interaction. These figures reinforce the critical role that people play on the show floor.

TIP

Because people are at the heart of your exhibiting success, take the time and spend the resources necessary to develop and train your exhibit staff — certain skills are critical to their effectiveness.

Selecting the right team

Because your people play such a major role, selecting the right team to represent you requires forethought and plenty of attention. Choose your team carefully based on their excellent knowledge of your company's products and services. My PEOPLE formula is an easy way to help you make the best decisions:

» **P** is for **people-oriented** employees. They generally enjoy interacting with diverse groups. They are outgoing and friendly, like building relationships, and are team players.

» **E** stands for the **eager** and **enthusiastic** people you want to represent your organization. They need to have a positive attitude about themselves and what they stand for. Their excitement and enthusiasm are contagious and help the selling process.

» **O** represents the **observant** people you need. With all the activity on the trade show floor, your staffers need to be capable of picking up on many different actions and nonverbal behavior.

» **P** is for the excellent **product knowledge** that your personnel should have. They need the ability to match appropriate product or service features and benefits to the prospect's stated criteria. Staffers have, on average, three to five minutes to make an impact on each visitor. The booth is no place for rookies — people who are new to the company and don't really know what they're talking about.

» **L** stands for the skilled **listeners** that you must have in the booth. In conversation, booth visitors often give away important clues about their buying interests. Your people need to focus 100 percent of their attention on the visitor, ask smart questions, and be attentive to the answers.

» **E** is for the **empathetic** nature required of exhibit staffers. They need the ability to relate well to a visitor's situation, to be understanding and appreciative, and to respond to the needs and concerns visitors express.

Preparing your team for the job

Preparing your staff for the demanding time they'll spend on the show floor is essential. Before the show, organize a preshow meeting and go through the points outlined in the following sections.

REMEMBER

Successful people aren't born — they're trained. To this end, there are business courses for trade show staff training as well as multiple online videos you can find by searching the internet for "trade show training."

Review the reasons why you are exhibiting

Explain the purpose for your organization's involvement in the show and what you expect to achieve through your participation. Use this time to also share the company's exhibiting goals and objectives.

Brush up on what you are exhibiting

Let your exhibit team know about the specific products and services you plan to exhibit. For example, if your team expects to demonstrate your Mark II model, don't display your Mark III model. The team may or may not be familiar with this particular one. Also, if you're hosting any kind of hospitality activity, sponsoring an event, or doing any other promotional activity, let your staff know.

Let your team know what you expect from them

Encourage your staff to set their own individual goals for the show based on the established overall exhibiting goals. Each staff member should have at least one personal goal. Goals increase accountability, change unproductive habits, increase productivity, and build motivation.

Your exhibit team members also need to know what you want them to do on a daily basis. For example, they need to know how many visitors you expect them to interact with and what kind of information you're interested in capturing.

Stress that you want them to leave negative attitudes behind. When employees have a negative attitude about being at a show, their body language lets everyone around know that they're thinking: "This is a futile and unimportant exercise." Remind them that everyone representing the company is an ambassador. By being helpful and courteous and having a professional demeanor, they can strengthen the company's image and gain new customers.

It never hurts to remind staff that they shouldn't eat, drink, chew gum, sit, read, chat with colleagues, or use their phones in the booth.

ARE YOU REALLY LISTENING?

Here are six habits that really upset visitors to your booth. They all let visitors know that the company representative isn't really listening to them:

- Doing all the talking.
- Interrupting when another person is talking.
- Never looking at the person talking.
- Focusing on your phone.
- Keeping a poker face so visitors don't know whether you understand them.
- Being too serious and never smiling.

Tell them how to meet your expectations

Your representatives may need specific areas of training to help them be more effective on the show floor. For example, maybe they need to know how to demonstrate the products on display or qualify prospects effectively. Just because they're your best salespeople in the field doesn't mean that they can be as effective on the show floor. The skills are very different.

Creating a strong presence at the show

During your preshow meeting with your exhibit staff, review the four stages of exhibit selling with them.

Stage 1: Engaging your visitors

Welcome and thank each visitor for coming to your booth. Smile, and maintain eye contact. You want to create rapport and a positive impression right from the start. Ask questions — beginning with who, what, where, when, why, or how. Relate those questions to the industry, your products or services, their benefits, or a specific situation.

Stage 2: Qualifying your prospects

Qualifying your prospects means finding out if your visitor really makes the grade. Continue to ask open-ended questions to uncover the prospects' level of interest in or need for your products or services, to inquire into their decision-making process (that is, their influence and/or authority), and to explore their time and budget parameters.

TIP

Remind your team to observe the 80/20 rule — listen to prospects for 80 percent of the time and talk for only 20 percent. Remember that you're trying to uncover *their* needs so that you can better present *your* solutions.

Stage 3: Presenting or demonstrating your goods

Armed with the information you gain in Stage 2, you can now present solutions to prospects' problems. Show existing customers new product lines or new applications they don't know about. Never assume that prospects know everything.

Stage 4: Closing the encounter

Throughout your conversation, make notes on a lead card or app (designed to record pertinent information about your visitors for follow-up after the show). Answer all of your visitors' questions and then get a commitment or basically an okay that they are interested enough in your products or services for an after-show follow-up. (For example, have a sales rep call, or send a quotation.)

Finalize the interaction by shaking hands, thanking the prospect for stopping by, and, if you have a gift, presenting it as a thank-you-for-stopping token. After you've finished with one prospect, make any additional notes on your lead system and get ready for the next visitor. For additional information on lead management, see Chapter 19.

QUALIFYING PROSPECTS WITH DYNAMITE QUESTIONS

Asking questions to reveal needs is a powerful way to let prospects know that you're interested in gaining information to help them solve their problems. Following are some questions you can use throughout your visitor conversation.

Opening questions

Find out immediately who you are talking to and where they're from. You don't want to spend unnecessary time with visitors you can't help.

- What are your main objectives for attending this show, and what specific products or services are you looking for?
- What project are you presently working on?
- What are some of the major challenges you're experiencing?

(continued)

(continued)

Investigating questions

Move on to more probing, business-specific questions to create the fuel for your ultimate sale.

- What do you like most about the product or service you presently use, and what would you like to change?
- What are your top three criteria for buying?
- Are you part of a buying team and, if so, what specific information are you looking for?

Demonstrating questions

During your demonstration, keep the prospect involved and interested.

- What do you think of this product's performance, and how does it compare with what you presently use?
- What specific concerns do you have regarding our products or services or about doing business with us?

Closing questions

Using well-prepared closing questions can help produce appropriate follow-up action.

- How does your company decide which vendors to work with?
- What else would be important for you to know, and what would you like to see as the next step?

Not every visitor to your booth is going to be a hot prospect, ready to place an order on the spot or immediately after the show. Use the information you gather from these questions to help you rank your prospects. For example, 1 = immediate need; 2 = interested in buying within the next six months; 3 = partial interest. Such a system helps to create a more efficient follow-up process.

Keeping your exhibit staff motivated

Staffing your company's exhibit at a show is hard work. Keeping your team motivated can often be a real challenge, especially at the end of a day or during the final hours of the show when traffic is slow (a prime time for serious buyers to swoop). Here are a few tips to energize the troops:

>> **Select people who want to be there.** The key ingredient for anyone to be motivated to work a show is simple: They need to want to be there. All too often employees are told by management to just show up to work a particular show. Given a choice, they would often prefer to stay home.

>> **Get top management support.** When top management supports the company's trade show activities and demonstrates that support by attending the show, helping in the booth, and taking part in training programs and preshow and postshow activities, their enthusiasm is contagious.

>> **Create a positive, fun, and reinforcing environment.** This job is management's responsibility. Management can create such an environment by using a variety of rewards to recognize trade show accomplishments such as reaching exhibiting goals, placing new orders, and getting quality qualified leads. Rewards can range from personal thank-yous to gift certificates for local stores or restaurants. The power of recognition and appreciation creates a more positive, productive, and enjoyable environment while working a show.

TIP

Consider creating an MVBSP (Most Valued Booth Staff Person) award. Ask the team members to select a deserving person, based on performance. This can be a daily award, if you want.

>> **Build team spirit.** Everyone in the exhibit should work together as a team, helping each other out whenever and wherever necessary. If a large group of staffers is working, split them up into teams, with technical people working alongside salespeople. Encourage them to establish their own action plans for working the show, which also promotes a certain amount of autonomy within the groups. As a team, they need to have time before the show to get acquainted, develop a level of trust, and get to know and understand each other's strengths and areas of specialty.

Consider hiring an outside consultant to act as a catalyst to help bring a new and refreshing approach to the team spirit. You could have the consultant conduct a training program prior to the show so that everyone knows specifically what to do to make the most of your trade show efforts.

>> **Review performance.** At the end of each day, conduct debriefing sessions to review performance. Encourage all team members to participate. The purpose is to look for ways to improve past performance and make each day better than the previous one. Managers must remember that individual achievement is worth group recognition.

Ensuring a Productive Exhibit

What happens at the trade show is obviously important to your success, but equally important is what happens after the show ends. If you want your company to truly benefit from all the hard work that went into exhibiting, you must ensure that appropriate follow-up activities take place.

Making your show leads pay off

Too often, sales departments give a lukewarm response to leads gathered at trade shows because show leads have a reputation for having no substance — they're either just cold business cards or similar basic information in the lead system. For salespeople to view leads as being worthwhile for follow-up, they need quality information.

One of the biggest after-show frustrations that companies experience is quantifying and managing the leads gathered at trade shows. More often than not, leads are distributed to the sales force, and little if anything is seen or heard of the outcome. Show performance and return on investment is then difficult, if not impossible, to measure.

To turn your leads into sales, you have to start with the end in mind. Begin the process of maximizing the benefit of trade show participation by knowing exactly what results you want to achieve at the various trade shows you attend. Set specific goals for each show and be totally clear on the results you expect, but remember to be realistic. Make sure that your goals are in line with your company's overall marketing objectives.

Consider involving your exhibit staff in the goal-setting process. Doing so increases their accountability for your company's show results and raises their enthusiasm for participating. Your specific goals are the yardstick for measuring your results. When I say specific, I mean it. Your goals must be quantifiable — a dollar amount, percentage, or number of leads — in order to measure your level of success.

Before the show, you must spend time going over the lead collecting process. Explain the importance of the information you're gathering and dissuade possessive salespeople from pocketing leads. Make sure that everyone knows exactly how to use the lead collecting apps. These apps allow you to capture leads by scanning the barcode or QR code on an attendee's badge with your phone camera. Some suitable apps include Cvent Lead Capture (https://www.cvent.com/en/onsite-solutions/lead-capture), Validar vCapture (https://www.validar.com/vcapture-lead-retrieval-suite), and CompuSystems CompuLead (https://www.compusystems.com/events).

At the end of each show day, hold a debriefing session. Have staffers share hot leads with the team. This gives team members the opportunity to add further information that may help in the follow-up.

Developing a follow-up system

The best time to plan for follow-up is before the show. Effective follow-up is too valuable a tool to misuse. If you don't plan to use the information gathered at a trade show effectively, why bother participating in the first place? Develop an organized, systematic approach to follow-up. You may even want to establish different methods for different categories of leads according to your ranking system. Remember that one-size marketing does not fit all!

Consider selecting a team member at the show to take responsibility for identifying all hot leads at the end of each day and alerting the team back at your office to immediately connect. Assign someone at the office as a follow-up manager. This person, who does not attend the show, takes charge of carrying out the follow-up system that was established before the show.

REMEMBER

Send something — a letter or e-mail— to everyone who came by your booth. Such a gesture is a way to thank them and let them know when they can expect to hear from your company again. Whatever system you use, send some kind of follow-up in a timely manner, such as within three to five days after the show. If you don't follow up, your competitors will.

Tracking your leads

Whatever system you use for lead collection must synchronize with your company's customer relationship management system (CRM). Your CRM is the database that stores your customer's contact and company information, their interests in your products and services, and a record of every contact that has been made with the customer. Your CRM is the vault holding everything there is to know about your customer that will help you to better serve them!

In addition to each prospect's basic information, load all the additional detailed information gathered on the lead card and track which sales representative was assigned the lead. Encourage your salespeople to intensely review the information gathered at the trade show so that they know what the various prospects are interested in.

WARNING

Salespeople should not go through the same information that was given at the show when they meet with a prospect after the show. Such a sales pitch definitely shows a lack of communication and organization. Prospects are likely to think, "If they can't pass on relevant information, what would they be like to deal with once I actually placed an order?"

TIME WAITS FOR NO ONE!

Here's a true story. A few years ago my husband, Alec, wanted to upgrade his computer. As I was attending a local business-to-business show, I thought it would be nice to give someone this hot lead. With a computer dealer on every aisle, I had a hard choice deciding which one to pick. Eventually I made my choice (I'll call it the ABC Company — how original) and proudly presented the sales rep with the lead, not mentioning that the interested party was my husband.

Two weeks later Alec came home with the news that he was comparing a couple of computer options. I asked the inevitable question: Was the ABC Company the supplier? He told me that ABC hadn't yet contacted him. Another two weeks passed, and Alec proudly announced that he'd made his decision on a particular computer. Once again, I asked whether my contact had been in touch. Still nothing. A week later, now five weeks out from the show, the ABC Company finally made contact. Eureka! The ABC Company was still alive and kicking, but not hard enough.

Did the ABC Company stand a chance of a sale? Once upon a time it did. However, Alec was certainly not going to wait around for them to call. He needed to upgrade his computer system pronto!

The moral of this story needs very little explanation: Follow up quickly or else you'll miss the boat and instead watch as the competition sails by.

If you have a high volume of show leads and don't have the capability to manage them effectively in-house, consider using an outside resource.

Holding sales representatives accountable

Leads are very valuable commodities. Staff members expend a great deal of effort and expense to gather them, and you can't afford to waste a single one. You never know which lead will become the pot of gold at the end of the rainbow. Because of this, sales representatives who receive show leads must be held accountable for each lead they are given.

Consider requiring a written progress report from each salesperson on show leads at regular, predetermined intervals. Then enter this information into the CRM so that at any time you can track performance, count the sales made, and so on. The CRM also provides an excellent method for evaluating the return on your show investment.

Measuring Results

Keeping track of your leads (see the previous section) allows you to measure sales directly attributable to your trade show participation. Recorded data enables you to calculate the return on investment and demonstrate to management the effect that trade show participation has on the bottom line. Other important information can include types of prospects who visited the booth, dates and times of their visits, products and services of interest, buying intent, results of any preshow promotional activity, and so on.

To measure the cost per trade show lead, simply divide your total show expenditure by the number of leads gathered. To measure the cost per sale, divide the total show expenditure by the number of sales.

The key to trade show success is wrapped up in the lead management process. You must know at the outset what you want to achieve, establish a strategy that is user-friendly, and, finally, implement a follow-up operation that leads to bottom-line profitability. With a little forethought and planning, the results will speak for themselves.

Evaluating your efforts

Realize that each show you attend is not a destination. Rather, it's a continual marketing journey. You always want to be looking at ways to improve your efforts. Because every show you attend differs in one way or another, there's no panacea or accurate formula that you can plug in time and time again to guarantee success. Each show attracts a different population and is held in a different city at a different time of the year. Plus, the economic climate varies from year to year. This all adds up to each show being a unique experience.

To make the most of future trade shows, constantly look for ways to improve your past performance. Evaluate what has gone well and what you know needs to be changed for the next show. Keep accurate notes so that you don't make the same mistake year after year. Solicit feedback from your team members. Ask for their suggestions and implement them. The next section gives you a comprehensive list of questions to help improve future exhibiting efforts.

Rating your performance

How worthwhile are the shows in which you exhibit? What can you do to improve and fine-tune your present performance? There is always room for improvement, however small.

Invest time with your exhibit booth staff *immediately* after each show to evaluate your performance. Doing so will pay enormous dividends. Ask the following questions:

>> Overall, how did we perform in relation to our goals?

>> What can we do differently to improve our performance the next time we exhibit?

>> What were our major challenges at the show?

>> What happened that we did not expect, or for which we were unprepared?

>> What areas do we need to address with exposition management?

>> Should we exhibit at this show again? If no, why not?

>> What changes can we make to improve our exhibit?

>> Which of our products or services attracted the most attention? The least attention?

>> What response did we get to our preshow promotion?

>> What improvements can we make to future preshow promotional campaigns?

>> What response did we get to our at-show promotions?

>> What was the response to the virtual options?

>> What improvements can we make to future at-show promotions?

>> How can we improve our lead system to get more effective information?

>> How many leads did we gather? Who is following up and how?

>> How did we classify our leads? Do we have a dollar value?

>> How effective was the staff?

>> What attention-getting activities did our competitors use?

Chapter **20**

Presenting the Floor Show: Exhibiting 301

This chapter focuses on helping you get the most out of your trade show participation — from collecting quality information for your salespeople to gathering insightful data on your competition. You're learning how to be a savvy exhibitor as well as a creative sleuth. The more you know about your competition (and what your customers want), the more you can differentiate your products and services from them. To sharpen your competitive edge, employ the tips in this chapter.

Honing in on Leads

As discussed in Chapter 19, a lead is a connection you've made that could "lead" to potential business. Technology has been a boon to capturing leads and it starts when participants register. At registration, visitors receive their nametag or event bracelet encoded with their contact data. A quick scan with your phone's data capture app of the attendee's name badge or bracelet, allows you to qualify, rate, and take notes on each lead.

TECHNICAL STUFF

At larger events, encoded data is often collected during the registration process. This could include name, company, e-mail, phone numbers, and general demographic data. The information is then embedded in the attendee's name badge as a QR or barcode.

The process of determining which prospects are ready and willing to purchase is called *lead qualification*. Not everyone who expresses interest in a product or service can be considered a potential customer, so it's important for exhibitors to have an effective way of screening out unqualified leads before they waste time on them!

REMEMBER

The key to getting more specific details relative to your product or service is to customize your lead collection details. Add custom questions for better sales qualification for effective after-show follow-up (see Chapter 19), as well as providing additional marketing data, such as product interest, purchasing influence, budget, and delivery time frames. Work with your sales team to understand the key information they need to turn a lead into a prospect.

Most show organizers provide rental opportunities for lead management solutions to capture, qualify, and connect with the right attendees. By working with the show management's registration service provider you can customize your output. Depending on the service provider, customization can take a few weeks or can be done at the show. Do your research — take time to talk to the supplier to find out what they can do for you.

Giving Visitors a Touch of Show Biz

According to trade show research, live presentations are the third most important reason why people remember an exhibit (after display size and product interest). Any form of live presentation, such as a staged product demonstration, theatrical skit, magician, game show, choreography, video, audio, robot, or singer, can attract a throng of visitors to your exhibit. Also consider using virtual reality to have your visitors "walk through" your demonstration.

The key to success is using this powerful promotional tool as an integral part of your exhibit marketing plan to appropriately communicate your company or product message — you don't want just a dog and pony show. Some keys to successful presentations include the following:

>> Identify how the presentation helps to achieve your goals for the event.

>> Think about the audience you want to attract and what impressions you want to make on them.

>> Come up with some promotional activities to ensure that you'll have an audience for your presentation.

>> Focus on how to involve your staff in the presentation, perhaps using them to gather the crowd or to capture and monitor pertinent information from the audience during the presentation.

>> Evaluate success. Before the show, plan how you will measure the success of the presentation. For example, will you gauge your success based on the number of people attending or the number of leads collected?

Feed Them and They Will Come: Using Hospitality Suites

Feeding people seems to have a magnetic effect. They gravitate toward food, which is another way to get people interested in your products and services. Using hospitality suites as an extension of your exhibiting activity on the show floor provides an opportunity for your company to spend more quality time with key prospects, customers, distributors, and the media, away from the prying eyes and ears of competitors. Hospitality suites can create more business and leave a favorable impression with your target audience.

The guidelines in the following sections can help you use this powerful marketing tool more effectively.

Managing the logistics

To maximize results, set specific hospitality suite objectives based on your overall exhibiting objectives, such as launching new products, giving in-depth demonstrations, or educating target audiences on new processes or applications. Print special invitations. Send them out before the show and/or distribute them at the booth. Exclusivity increases the importance of the function to the guest. Requesting a response will enable you to better plan the event.

Reserve adequate space in the convention center, a nearby hotel, or another conveniently located off-site facility for the number of people you expect to attend. Consider hiring transportation if the facility is away from regular activities. Regardless of your hospitality suite's location, make sure that your company and products or services are properly displayed. Have literature or other promotional material and premiums necessary to strengthen your exhibiting message available for the taking.

TIP

Plan a menu to fit the image you wish to portray — for example, finger food with or without servers, or a buffet. Consider serving only soft drinks, beer, and wine to keep budgets reasonable. Hard liquor is often an unnecessary extra expense.

Decide whether tables and chairs are necessary. People mingle better when they stand. If you plan to include lengthy or formal presentations, however, seating is advisable.

To create a congenial atmosphere, provide background music, either live or recorded. Providing name tags for each visitor that include the name of their company also helps encourage congeniality. You want visitors to feel relaxed and welcome.

Staffing your hospitality suite

Staff your hospitality suite with employees who are energetic and enthusiastic, have a positive attitude, and enjoy socializing. Remind them of the overall purpose of the function and let them know what is expected of them.

TIP

Recommend a dress code to help ensure that your staff doesn't show up in inappropriate clothing. They should be dressed to match the event and even if you are hosting a casual event, establish a "team uniform" of slacks and company polo shirt so your team is easily identified.

Encourage employees to practice a confident handshake and a brief self-introduction that includes their name and position at the company. Ask employees to mingle with as many visitors as possible, spending no more than eight to ten minutes with a visitor or group. Alternatively, assign various employees to host specific guests while they're attending your hospitality suite. The purpose of this strategy is to gain greater insight, learn new information, and improve relationships. Suggest that employees prepare a list of small-talk topics in case conversation runs dry.

Review positive nonverbal communication with employees. Remind them to make eye contact, smile, and use open and receptive body language — no crossed arms, for example. Instruct employees on proper etiquette for introductions — introduce a younger person to an older person, a peer in your company to a peer in another company, a fellow executive to a customer.

WARNING

Caution employees about sitting and talking with co-workers, telling inappropriate jokes, drinking too much alcohol, smoking, monopolizing someone's time, and complaining.

Arrange a debriefing and evaluation immediately following the function.

Getting into Uniform

During my "How to Exhibit Successfully" workshops, participants inevitably ask whether they should have uniforms for the trade show. The answer is yes. If a uniform ties into your theme or image you want to portray, and you have the budget, definitely provide uniforms for your exhibit staff. They help to give your team a cohesive look and also make it easy for a visitor to spot the right person to talk to.

REMEMBER

If you supply uniforms, the staff needs to realize the extra responsibility they carry. They now become a walking billboard for your company, and wherever they go, people know where they're from. Consequently, the only privacy they'll have, away from prying eyes and ears, is in the confines of their hotel rooms. They have to watch what they do and say all the time as they'll never know who's spying or eavesdropping. The trade show environment is a very public forum.

If you don't supply a uniform, specify exactly what you want people to wear. For example, maybe you prefer navy suits with white shirts or blouses and red ties or scarves. You can't leave anything to chance because you have no clue what people have in their closets — they may turn up in anything.

Uniform or not, your employees are like actors on a stage. When the show is on, the curtain is up, and they need to play the appropriate role — company ambassador. This same advice applies to outside restaurants and clubs.

WARNING

Getting drunk and being rowdy and unruly reflects negatively on the company. Emphasize that the trade show isn't a vacation, but rather work in another setting, so all the same rules apply. Sorry, team, but you have to behave!

Dealing with Snoops

Just by their nature, trade shows foster an overt espionage environment. Where else can you walk right into your competition's enclave, freely talk to them, and pick up literature at the same time? And, if you're particularly lucky, the company will have a rookie working the exhibit who's eager to tell you everything you want to know about the company and its products and services. Believe me, this happens frequently.

Remind the staff in your exhibit booth to beware of the competition. If they're observant and good listeners, they'll find that competitors easily give themselves away by either knowing far more than the average customer or by asking precise, probing questions. Make sure that your staff does more questioning than talking, so that you lessen the chances of divulging valuable, proprietary information.

TIP

If someone asks a suspicious question, respond with, "That's interesting you should ask that question. Help me understand why specifically this information would be helpful to you." Get into the habit of answering a question with a question. Then you're less likely to say something you shouldn't.

Outfoxing the Competition

At the same as time you're trying to avoid giving your competitors too much information, you should be gathering information about those competitors as aggressively as you can. While this type of research is an ongoing process for any company, trade shows are an excellent forum to fill in gaps of information about your competitors' practices.

TIP

Before the show, check out your competition online to learn as much as you can about the company and their team. You're on a reconnaissance mission!

Researching general information

Use the following list of questions to uncover general information about your competition:

>> Who are our direct and indirect competitors? Include current market participants, potential market entrants, and providers of substitute products/services.

- » Which competitors pose a threat to us?
- » What are important differences among our competitors?
- » Where are they located, and is their location a competitive advantage?
- » How long have they been in business, and what is their reputation/image in the marketplace?
- » What is their market share?
- » What is their corporate and business philosophy, and how is it implemented?
- » What important acquisitions have competitors made in the past year, and how has this given them a competitive advantage?

Finding product and service information

With the next group of questions you're looking to get more specific info about the competition's products and services:

- » What is the depth and breadth of our competitors' products or services?
- » What are the features or specifications of their products or services?
- » What are their most recent product or service introductions?
- » How well do competitors deliver orders on schedule?
- » What changes are taking place in competitors' make or buy strategies?
- » What new materials are being used in the industry? Do they provide a cost advantage?
- » How have competitors incorporated cost savings?
- » Who are our competitors' suppliers?
- » How easy are their products to install or maintain?
- » What are the competitors' strengths and weaknesses in quality and service?

Gathering sales and marketing information

This set of questions focuses on your competition's sales and marketing activities:

- » What are our competitors' marketing and sales strategies?
- » Are their sales forces organized by product line, geographic market, or end user?

- >> Who are their largest and most important customers?

- >> What group of customers does our competition sell to that we don't, and why have they been successful in this market?

- >> Which group of customers is least satisfied and why?

- >> Why are customers switching to competitors' products or services?

- >> What new distribution channels have they developed?

- >> What medium other than trade shows do they use to market their products or services?

- >> Which products or services are they pushing?

- >> Which features are they emphasizing?

- >> What are their pricing strategies — in the commercial, nonprofit, government, and foreign sales categories?

- >> What special pricing policies — such as credit, discounts, incentives, and consignments — do they offer?

Once you are at the show, you can slyly glean more information about your competition by visiting their booth and chatting up their team. You may find more details than were available on their website, plus you might find someone you'd like to recruit for your team!

Compiling customer information

This final set of questions turns the focus onto the customers to find out about their preferences:

- >> What do customers consider most valuable about our competitors' products or services?

- >> Why are they satisfied with their current supplier?

- >> What might induce them to switch to another vendor?

- >> What are their principal complaints?

- >> Which companies do they see as the market leaders in the industry?

- >> Which of their needs are going unfulfilled?

- >> What do they see as the key factors in purchasing decisions?

- >> How are changes in the industry affecting them?

6
The Part of Tens

These chapters provide a rapid-fire set of ideas to help you polish your meeting and event planning skills.

Use them as simple references that keep you focused on the essence of what makes an effective, efficient, and — most of all — successful meeting and event planner.

Chapter **21**

Ten Creative Ways to Meet

Meetings, because of their often-lengthy time commitments, can take away from your ability to be as productive, effective, and efficient as you'd like to be. And meeting in the same room at the same time with the same group of people every week eventually saps your creativity. But what choice do you have if you need to share information with your co-workers or get the troops together to do some brainstorming or problem-solving?

This chapter shows you some "meeting of the mind" options worth considering if the thought of scheduling one more meeting seems too tedious to bear.

Being a Sport

Does your team enjoy a game of golf or some other sport? Try organizing a sporting activity that brings everyone together and allows you to mix some business with pleasure. Add some good food and drinks to the mix, and the creativity could soar exponentially. Encourage team members to use the gaming activity as an analogy to help solve a particular business challenge your department may be experiencing.

Starting a Thread

Digital tools allow you to start a thread in your virtual networks, e-mails, text messages, and group platforms. Ask a question or make a statement to request answers and feedback within the thread. This saves your team from being locked down in an hour-long (or more) meeting to get the information and discussion that you need. It also allows the introverts of your group to speak up when they may not take the opportunity in person.

Getting on the Phone

Hello! This might be the most obvious alternative to a meeting that is easily overlooked. Rather than tying up your cohort and yourself for a meeting, make a quick phone call. Holding individual discussions with particular staff members can help you get their personal points of view, which they may be reluctant to share in a larger meeting environment. One-on-one discussions also allow you to build a better working relationship, especially when you're an empathetic listener and give your team members the opportunity to talk.

Making It a Game

Most people love playing games — it's probably a legacy from childhood. If your staff members loathe meetings, set up a competition for them to find creative ways to disseminate necessary information without having meetings. Meaningful prizes or rewards are mandatory because staff members will want to know what's in it for them before putting time and energy into this project. You may be surprised by the wonderfully creative ideas they dream up!

Recording a Message

Consider putting out a weekly company or department update using audio or video. Your team can witness all your pearls of wisdom as they sip their morning beverage. This works well for one-way communication; however, if you need feedback, your team can always add comments or reply directly to you.

Sharing the Knowledge

When you have a problem to solve, instead of holding a brainstorming meeting, consider using one of the most popular solutions — FAQs (Frequently Asked Questions) stored on your website with access to the general public or securely set up for insiders only.

Answering these FAQs in advance enables you to locate in-house experts — people who have built up stores of knowledge in a specific area — and retain their expertise. Sharing information through FAQs is an effective way to tap into existing resources and, as information and the questions change, you can easily update the content.

Writing an E-Mail

E-mail is an integral part of our lives. An e-mail is a quick and easy way to connect with people around the globe, around the corner, and in the office next to yours to send or receive key information.

Keep your body content brief and include necessary links or attach vital documents before you press "Send." Be clear when you are requesting a response either directly to the e-mail or confirmation that an action will be taken.

Tapping Productivity Apps

To move projects along without meeting in-person or virtually, consider using a productivity app such as Microsoft Teams, Trello, Basecamp, or Asana. These provide a workspace for real-time collaboration and communication.

Whiteboard Brain Storm

Set up a whiteboard with markers in a high-traffic area of your workplace and post a question or an idea on the board. (You can also use a virtual whiteboard if you are using a productivity app as mentioned above.) Then encourage your team to answer the question or determine how the idea might be implemented . . . and the benefits of the concept.

If you are going old school with a literal whiteboard, use sticky notes so that later on the comments and ideas can easily be categorized. An online whiteboard usually allows you to organize the comments. Remember to put a start and end time on your request for submissions!

Sending out a Survey

Many great digital options are available for surveying your team. This virtual show of hands goes beyond a "yay or nay" answer and can include everything from judgment scales to long-form answers. Be sure to put a deadline on the survey response and remember to post the results for the participants to see.

Chapter **22**

Ten Common Meeting Mistakes to Avoid

W ith the umpteen details meeting and event planners need to handle, mistakes are bound to be made, and sometimes heads will roll as a result. To make certain that yours isn't one of them, I've tackled ten of the most common meeting blunders in this chapter to help you rise above your counterparts.

Forgetting to Check Dates

Before finalizing any dates for your meetings or events, check that they don't overlap with any religious, public, state, or federal holidays. Also, consider avoiding an overlap with any major sporting events. At the beginning of the calendar year, generate a checklist of all the upcoming holidays and events so you don't let one slip by you. It's too easy to do!

Booking a Site Before Making a Visit

Often when you're organizing an event at a destination many miles from home, there's not enough time or money in the budget to make a site visit. Big mistake! Even if you've seen their website and taken a virtual tour make the effort to do a live visit. Why take the risk that everything won't be fine on the day of the event or rely on someone else's judgment? Make a point of seeing and determining for yourself whether everything is the way you need it. This is particularly critical for larger meetings and events. In addition, checking out the scene beforehand allows you the opportunity to meet and build a rapport with the staff you'll be working very closely with on the day of the event.

Failing to Market Your Event

It's really quite simple: In order to get people to attend your event, you need to let them know about it in plenty of time. It's all about marketing and communication, which is part and parcel of your planning and organizing process. The longer you wait to inform potential attendees, the stronger the chance that they'll have made alternative plans for your meeting dates. Communicate your message well in advance so that your event is their number one priority.

Signing Contracts That Lack Specifics

I know of a meeting planner who had her day in court when she cancelled a meeting because the hotel she booked had not made, in her opinion, sufficient progress on its planned renovation. The hotel argued differently and, in fact, won the case. The written contract had specified that "substantial progress" would be made prior to the meeting date. Being such a subjective phrase, it was open to different interpretations. Make sure that your contracts are ironclad with undisputable details. Avoid phrases like "to be negotiated" or "to be determined at a later date."

Failing to Plan

Throughout this book, I preach the importance of planning in all aspects of your event. Fail to plan, and you're laying yourself open for disaster. Far too many pieces of the puzzle need to be put together for you to just wing it or pay lip service to a plan. Vow to be as thorough and meticulous as possible. Check and recheck the details. Discuss your event with people not involved in the business to get outsider opinions. Create checklists and checklists of checklists (check out this book's Appendix!) Cover all your bases. The more thorough you are, the less chance of failure and more probability of success.

Neglecting to Check References

Having a gut feeling about someone is great, but always check to make sure they are as good as they say they are. Yes, it will take some extra time to check references, but it's well worth the effort. Why take the chance of spoiling your important event with a supplier who lets you down at the last minute or supplies you with second-rate equipment or poor-quality service? A key question to ask the reference is, "Would you use this supplier again for your next function?" You know what to do if the answer is negative!

Leaving Important Details to the Last Minute

Putting your meeting together takes time, and the more you have, the better the chances of making fewer mistakes. The more rushed and panicked you are, the more likely you are to forget some of the essential (and sometimes most obvious) things. Use your checklists religiously, and handle details in the early planning stages. Leaving the basics to the last minute will undoubtedly cost more money, as you'll probably incur rush charges, and it will definitely add unnecessary stress to your life!

Letting Someone Else Do the Planning

So you want to take the easy way out, and you find yourself a professional planner to handle all the details. Can you afford to just sit back in the hope that this wonderful person performs magic? I don't think so! Just because you hire some assistance doesn't mean you're out of the picture. On the contrary, you now take on the role of steward, which makes you responsible for directing all the operations. Yes, let others do the running around on your behalf, but always have a visible presence in the background making sure that everything runs smoothly. Remember, in the final analysis, the buck stops with you!

Neglecting Contingencies

Another aspect of your planning process involves developing contingency plans. Unfortunately, the chances are pretty high that something you planned for won't necessarily go as arranged. So what's your backup? If you don't have one, all your original plans could be destroyed in an instant, and you'll be scrambling to put a second strategy into operation. Have a Plan B ready "in the wings" just in case you need it.

Trying to Save Money

With tight budgets and a boss breathing down your neck and expecting you to do more with less, the temptation to make vendor decisions based solely on price is strong. Yes, you'll always find someone who's prepared to underprice services just to get the business. But how good and reliable are they? Cheap prices and good quality usually don't correlate. So the next time you're tempted to make a buying decision based entirely on price, think again!

Chapter **23**

Ten Top Negotiating Tactics

Master the art of negotiating and you master the ability to get almost everything you want!

Negotiating is considered the number one business skill, and it's one that people use daily. However, some do it better than others. What does it take to become a negotiating whiz? The ten tactics in this chapter can definitely catapult you in the right direction to negotiate the best deals for your meeting or event.

Knowing What You Want

Skilled negotiators start with a detailed plan of exactly what they want from their negotiations. Why defy what works? Take plenty of time to thoroughly understand what you want and need from the potential supplier. Formulate lists of items that you're willing to compromise and concede if necessary. Know your budgetary constraints and how they can affect your discussions.

Doing Your Research

Doing research is a key strategy in your negotiating arsenal. Find out as much as you possibly can about your potential supplier. Know what your business is worth to them. Understand their business — the peaks and valleys. The more they want your business during a slow period, the greater your negotiating clout.

Rehearsing Your Opening

Your opening words set the tone for the discussions that follow. Just like an actor's opening lines, the first words out of your mouth set the stage for the rest of the performance. Make certain that you know exactly what you want to say. Craft the words so that your message is clear and concise, and spend time rehearsing your lines. You want your opening to be perfect.

Asking Powerful Questions

Asking powerful questions is an essential skill for every negotiator. It not only provides you with strong information on which to build your case, it also creates opportunities for breakthroughs in your discussions.

Questions are the most powerful search engine to help you tap into critical information, evaluate the strengths and weaknesses of a supplier, and make decisions. But, like everything else, they need planning. Each question you ask directs the action that follows it. For example, "Can you match the best price I've received? If not, what price can you offer me?" Take the time to map out what questions you need to ask to get the results you want from your negotiations.

Becoming an Information Monger

Even though you're asking powerful questions to get some heavy-duty information from your supplier, you want to continually probe for more. Listen to what's being offered and, at every opportunity, ask for clarification and more information. Become an information monger, never being satisfied until you have exactly what you want from the discussions.

Being a Champion Listener

So much of successful negotiating comes as a result of great listening. Listen to what people do and don't say. People often tell you plenty about themselves.

The problem is that the supposed listeners just don't hear them because they're so caught up in their own thoughts. When you take time to listen to people, they tell you about their positions, problems, qualities, likes, and dislikes — chances are that you won't even have to ask. Listen for any sense of urgency to close the deal. Perhaps a vendor wants your business because they have quotas to fill. You were given two ears and one mouth — use them in that ratio to help make the best deal!

Creating a Positive Mood

Negotiating in a congenial atmosphere helps create a more receptive mood. Set the stage with some getting-to-know-you talk. Make direct eye contact as you speak to your potential supplier. If your supplier has a tough time making eye contact, either they aren't being totally honest with you or their people skills need work: You make the decision.

Tell the supplier one or two personal stories that they may relate to. Your goal is to establish an atmosphere of trust and honesty. Don't just jump straight into your negotiating babble. Rather, take time to develop a friendly rapport so that the person with whom you want to do business feels comfortable speaking with you. You'll both work together more productively in a relaxed environment.

Being Prepared to Walk Away

This incredibly potent strategy is possibly one of the hardest for negotiators to actually implement. How it works is that when you really want something badly enough, and you aren't happy with the supplier's offer, you simply walk away from the negotiating table. One of two things can happen:

>> The supplier will concede to your wishes.

>> The supplier will let you go your own way.

Remember that if you want to use this strategy, you need to have a second potential supplier in the wings. Otherwise, you may be left out in the cold fending for yourself.

Knowing Negotiating Styles

Read any book on negotiating, and you quickly discover that there are many different styles and techniques to help you through the negotiating minefield. Make a point of familiarizing yourself with ones that fit your style of doing business.

In addition, find out about the different behavioral styles you may encounter in a supplier — what kind of information different types of people need, and how they approach negotiating. For example, an analytical type needs tons of data to help in the decision-making process, whereas a more controlling, dominant type wants only the facts. Recognize people's differences and use them to your advantage — it's all part of the game!

Exercising Silence

The old saying "Silence is golden" is particularly true around the negotiating table. Negotiating mavens know that when discussing a deal, the first one who speaks often loses.

To be successful, dominating the conversation is not wise. In fact, the more you talk, the more information you're supplying a potential vendor. And the sharing of information, though seemingly trivial, could lessen your chances of getting a bargain. So exercising silence can help prevent you from spewing out unnecessary stuff. Your silence can also help create the perception that you are a thoughtful and methodical decision-maker.

Chapter **24**

Ten Strategies For Exhibiting Overseas

G oing global isn't optional anymore — it's essential. Survival in today's price-sensitive and intensely competitive marketplace means that U.S. companies need to abandon their marketing myopia for a more global approach.

Exhibiting at overseas exhibitions is one of the fastest and most cost-effective ways to identify the best foreign markets for your products and services. It not only allows you to test your products' export suitability but also helps you evaluate your competition and potential partners within a particular country (including suppliers, distributors, and customers) before making any sizable financial commitment.

Doing Your Homework

Thoroughly research overseas shows to find the ones that attract your target market. Unfortunately, there is no complete reference that lists international events. However, information and statistics are available from a number of different sources.

A good starting point is the U.S. Department of Commerce International Trade Administration (USDC-ITA, https://www.trade.gov). This office publishes several resources with information on international shows. Each year it organizes a variety of exhibitions to promote U.S. products with high export potential. It also has industry and country specialists who can help you with specific information.

Starting Early

Start your planning 12 to 18 months before an international event. Because space allocations are usually on a first-come, first-served basis, it is recommended that you reserve space at least 12 months ahead. Work closely and meticulously with the show organizer to avoid blunders. Many larger overseas shows have offices in the United States.

TIP

Plan to arrive at your international destination at least two days early to take care of possible logistics, and don't underestimate jet lag!

Budgeting Carefully

Establish a realistic budget. Costs of overseas shows vary widely, depending on a host of variables such as location, exchange rates, and time of year.

In addition to your display, shipping, promotional, and staff costs, also consider import duties and export regulations. As a safety net, add 25 percent to your budget to cover unexpected costs, tipping, and exchange-rate fluctuations.

Designing Your Overseas Exhibit Space

In most countries, an exhibit booth is referred to as a *stand*. The smallest version is approximately a 10 x 10-foot space with a three-sided prefabricated whitewashed shell that houses your display.

Elaborate custom exhibits, particularly prevalent at large European trade fairs, are more expansive and might include a conference area, lounge, kitchen, and bar (especially where hospitality is expected). Light snacks and drinks are the norm, so plan on including a conference or lounge area in your exhibition space. Often, the size of these exhibits far exceeds anything you might see in the United States.

REMEMBER

Remember that measurements overseas are metric.

Constructing Your Exhibit

Exhibiting stands come in all shapes and sizes, from a whitewashed shell to elaborate pavilions with several floors. What you decide to use depends on the type of exhibition, and of course, your budget.

Consider these four options when deciding on your construction:

» Design and build in the United States and ship it pre-built to the show site.

» Design in the United States and build overseas.

» Design and build overseas.

» Rent a prefabricated exhibit from an exhibit house located in the country you are exhibiting in, but supply your own graphics and signage.

Dealing with Customs Issues

WARNING

Customs issues are a necessary evil when exhibiting internationally, and having the right paperwork is critical.

Your most important document is an ATA Carnet — an international customs document that simplifies customs procedures for the temporary importation of commercial samples, professional equipment, and goods for exhibitions and fairs. It serves as a "merchandise passport" that saves you time and money, as well as helping avoid extensive customs procedures, eliminating payment of duties and value-added taxes. It also eliminates the need to purchase temporary import bonds. Don't leave home without one!

You can obtain this document through the U.S. Council for International Business (www.uscib.org).

Providing Hospitality

Frequently, hospitality and entertainment are an expected way of doing business overseas. Consider a conference or lounge area where you can serve food during your discussions.

Plan a menu to fit the image you wish to portray. For example, consider whether you want staff to serve finger food or whether you want a buffet-style arrangement. At some German trade fairs, full meals are served on real china with metal utensils. Plastic and paper are not acceptable because of the country's "green" policies. In Middle Eastern countries, businessmen bring their entire family to the show and expect them to be entertained.

Consider serving soft drinks, beer, and wine to keep budgets reasonable. Hard liquor is unnecessary except when exhibiting in Russia, where vodka is expected.

Exhibiting Sensitivity to the Host Culture

Doing business internationally means knowing that cultural differences exist. Understanding what you should and shouldn't do definitely helps you avoid unnecessary blunders.

WARNING

Be mindful of cultural dietary restrictions. Understand that colors and numbers have specific meanings in different countries. If your company's literature, product, or packaging is the wrong color, you will lose sales. Do your homework to avoid costly mistakes.

Using Native Speakers for Translations

To avoid costly mistakes and embarrassments, always use a professional translator — a native speaker — when translating copy, crafting business communications, or designing packaging to be used at an overseas trade fair.

Humiliating gaffes occur when a translation is done by a non-professional with limited knowledge of a language or culture and little or no understanding of slang and colloquialisms. A native speaker who also possesses technical knowledge of your products/services or industry is worth their weight in gold!

Having a professional interpreter at your exhibit helps translate business buzz-words, acronyms, and slang which cause misunderstandings that cost time and money when you're trying to do business. By keeping written and spoken communication basic, it is far easier to understand one another.

Being Patient

Americans seem to be constantly rushing! Time is money. Consequently, the people representing your company may think that time with visitors is at a premium, so they want to get straight to the point and then flush out the details later.

However, most other cultures don't feel the same way. They think this approach is blunt and crude. At overseas shows, foreign buyers often spend several hours discussing all relevant details connected with future business transactions. They rarely complete a deal on the spot. Remind your exhibit staff that doing business overseas demands time, patience, and most of all it's about building long-term relationships.

Appendix

Checklist Heaven

Checklists are a meeting and event planner's best friends. They alert you to tasks that might otherwise be overlooked, force you to think about your budget during every step of the planning process, and keep you organized and focused. This appendix contains just a few of the many checklists you might want to have on hand as you begin planning your meeting or event.

Small Meeting Checklist

Running a successful small meeting is almost as challenging as organizing a larger event. Use this checklist, along with the information in Chapter 3, to stay on top of the details.

» Decide on the purpose of the meeting (the meeting objective).

» Know exactly what the meeting needs to accomplish.

» Determine if the meeting is really necessary.

» Outline specific agenda items.

» Decide what messages(s) need to be communicated.

» Decide how you want people to feel when they leave.

» Choose the right meeting location.

» Find out how long the meeting will last.

- ❯❯ Invite only the people who need to be there.

- ❯❯ Assign participants specific roles during the meeting.

- ❯❯ Let participants know what they need to bring.

- ❯❯ Put together a written agenda.

- ❯❯ Set a date for when the agenda should be sent out to participants.

- ❯❯ Organize, if necessary, how attendees get to the meeting location.

- ❯❯ Find out about any special needs.

- ❯❯ Check on what specific materials and equipment are needed.

- ❯❯ Choose what refreshments and snacks are necessary.

- ❯❯ Stick to the agenda during the meeting.

- ❯❯ Evaluate the meeting after it is over.

Site Selection Checklist

When determining which facility would best suit your purposes, use the following checklist (provided courtesy of Diane Silberstein, CMP) as well as the tips in Chapter 5.

Planning

- ❯❯ Make sure that your meeting objectives (educational, social, business) are clear and concise.

- ❯❯ Know your meeting format (the flow of events).

- ❯❯ List preferred dates/times and have a few alternatives in case your first choice isn't available.

- ❯❯ Have a realistic figure of the number of guests you're expecting.

- ❯❯ Know your guest expectations.

Function space

- ❯❯ Identify the number, size, and shape of the meeting rooms you need.

- ❯❯ Look for an easily visible registration area with room for multiple guests as they wait to sign in.

- » Observe any room obstructions and note ceiling heights.
- » Question in detail all venue costs (rental, utilities, elevator, insurance, and so on).
- » Ask about storage area location and access.
- » Be familiar with the kitchen location and access.
- » Find out about delivery access.
- » Check the location of freight/passenger elevators (particularly important in exhibition halls).
- » Locate and inspect the condition of restrooms.
- » Ask about overlapping functions.
- » Know rules, regulations, and policies for installation and dismantle.

Transportation

- » Know the distance and travel time from the airport.
- » Familiarize yourself with directions from major roads.
- » Know distances/drive times for guests.
- » Find out the approximate taxi/rideshare fare for guests.
- » Check on taxi/rideshare availability after hours.
- » Ask about parking facilities/cost for cars and buses.

Policies

- » Ask about the booking policy.
- » Understand the cancellation policy.
- » Find out about the deposit and payment policy.
- » Ask whether gratuities are mandatory or optional.
- » Discuss insurance requirements.
- » Find out about any restrictions on time, décor, food and beverages, and entertainment.

Services

>> Know and understand all the services provided by the facility.

>> Find out how many employees will be available during each of your functions.

>> Get a list of preferred suppliers the facility uses.

>> Verify Wi-Fi availability and access for your event and participants. Ask about bandwidth, the number of access points, and be sure to mention your anticipated usage patterns.

Miscellaneous

>> Get exact contact information for everyone involved during the event development stage and the event itself.

>> Find out if the facility is compliant with the Americans with Disabilities Act (ADA).

>> Discuss any renovation plans, completion dates, and what happens if renovation is going on during your event.

>> Get references for three similar groups that recently held events at the venue.

Food and Beverage Functions Checklist

In Chapter 7, I provide lots of advice for making sure the food and beverages you offer your guests will make an impression (at the right price). The following checklist will help you handle your food and beverage needs.

Food

>> Decide on food functions needed:

- Breakfast (full or continental)
- Brunch
- Refreshment breaks (morning and afternoon)
- Lunch
- Dinner

- Receptions
- Parties
- Banquets

» Arrange a meeting with the catering manager and chef to choose menus for the various food functions.

» Decide what kind of hors d'oeuvres to serve at your receptions.

» Check on special meal requirements among your guests.

» Determine what type of food service will be used:

- American
- French
- Butler/Russian
- Buffet (including individually packaged food option)

» Arrange who will sign off on the individual food functions.

» Check the deadline for guaranteed numbers.

» Verify that all details on the BEO (Banquet Event Order) are correct.

Beverages

» Decide what beverages will be served.

» Establish how costs for drinks will be calculated:

- By the person
- By the drink
- By the bottle

» Arrange how drinks will be served:

- Open or hosted bar
- Cash bar
- Limited drinks using tickets
- Waiter-served drinks

» Investigate state liquor laws and on-site policies.

Miscellaneous

>> Ascertain whether to use a theme for the function and what decorations are needed.

>> Determine if a head table is needed and who will sit there.

>> Check whether reserved seating is necessary.

>> Check on the need for printed menus and place cards.

>> Organize music/entertainment.

>> Arrange necessary audiovisual equipment such as microphones, staging, lights, projectors, and screens.

>> Arrange table centerpieces.

>> Check on the need for a photographer.

>> Organize an alternative location (in case of inclement weather) if the function is held outdoors.

Accessibility Considerations Checklist

Use the following checklists, along with my tips in Chapter 3, to ensure that all your participants have full access to your meeting or event.

For deaf & hard-of-hearing participants

>> Arrange for sign language interpretation of all events.

>> Prepare a confidentiality agreement for the interpreter(s) to sign.

>> Make sure the hotel rooms have telephones with volume control and with lights that flash to indicate incoming calls.

>> Arrange for the hotel room(s) to have a visual indicator that someone is at the door.

>> Provide TDD machines (Telecommunications Devices for the Deaf).

>> Ask the hotel to provide televisions with closed-captioning capability.

>> Arrange for hotel staff to personally alert these guests in the event of an emergency.

For visually-impaired participants

>> Have Braille translations of all handouts and other written meeting material.

>> Make sure there is Braille signage throughout the hotel.

>> Ask hotel staff to take the guest(s) on a tour of the hotel upon arrival.

>> Let the hotel know if your guest will be accompanied by a guide dog, and ask the participant what supplies the guide dog will need.

For mobility-impaired participants

>> Check if the main entrance of the meeting venue is wheelchair-accessible. If not, find out if there is an accessible entrance.

>> Check how deep the carpeting is in the meeting room and throughout the venue.

>> Check how heavy the doors are throughout the venue. For heavy doors, arrange for someone to escort the guest(s) in and out of the heavy door areas.

>> Make certain that the meeting rooms are wheelchair-accessible.

>> Be aware of stairs and narrow doors.

>> Make sure aisles in the meeting rooms are wide enough for a wheelchair to fit down.

>> For mobility impaired speakers or presenters, arrange ramps or lifts to access the stage.

>> Find out if the hotel restaurant and other on-site facilities are accessible.

>> Ask about the number and availability of accessible guest rooms.

Audiovisual Equipment Checklist

Part of your job as planner is to provide each presenter scheduled to speak at your meeting or event with the types of audiovisual equipment they need. Following are some of the most likely possibilities; see Chapters 3 and 10 for details.

>> Staging

>> Lighting requirements

- **Microphone**
  - Handheld (with or without a cord)
  - Lavaliere/lapel (wireless, with or without a cord)
- Screen (sized to room and group size)
- Flip chart, easel, and markers
- LCD projector (minimum 2,000–3,000 lumens output)
- Wi-Fi connection
- Sound system
- AC power outlet with multi-plug surge suppressor
- A/V rolling cart
- Laser pointer
- Lectern
- Duct tape
- Spare bulbs and batteries

Staging Checklist

Setting up the room(s) for your meeting or event may involve more details than you expect. Use the following checklist, along with the information in Chapter 10, to make sure you're prepared.

- Check ceiling clearance.
- Check for rigging points for hanging heavy items from the ceiling.
- Check for visual obstructions (low-hanging chandeliers, columns).
- Find out the space dimensions available for a stage.
- Find out if a runway or ramps are needed.
- Decide on the staging décor.
- Check for light sources or reflective surfaces (windows, mirrors).
- Locate the house lighting controls.
- Find out if there are any follow spotlights available.

- >> Familiarize yourself with entrances and exits.

- >> Check to see if doors squeak or don't close completely.

- >> Look at ways to decorate the stage (skirt, carpet, light).

- >> Put up a backdrop that ties into the theme of your event.

- >> Determine whether to include any special effects:

  - laser lights

  - pyrotechnics

  - confetti

  - fog machines

  - fiber optics

  - revolving stage

RFP (Request for Proposal) Checklist

Use the following checklist of information that should be included in an RFP, as well as the advice in Chapter 11, as you prepare to request proposals from potential vendors.

- >> Company name

- >> Meeting name (if you have one)

- >> Your contact information

- >> Meeting location

- >> Meeting budget (optional)

- >> Meeting dates (offer alternative dates wherever possible)

- >> Meeting goals and objectives

- >> Estimated number of participants

- >> Participant profile

- >> Previous meeting locations (city and facility used)

- >> Previous meeting history

- » RFP deadline and a decision date (allow a minimum of 10 days from the time you send out the requests)
- » Specific areas for which you need pricing

Meeting Contract Checklist

When negotiating with a hotel or other facility, use the following checklist, along with the information in Chapter 11, to ensure you get all the essentials in writing.

- » Name and dates of meeting
- » Sleeping room block
  - • Types of rooms
  - • Total number of room nights
  - • Guarantee on rooms to be filled
- » Check-in/check-out times
- » Reservation cutoff dates
- » Room rates
- » Complimentary rooms and upgrade arrangements
- » Specially arranged services (such as health club use, parking)
- » Reservation procedures
- » Exhibit space
- » Food and beverage arrangements
- » Liquor liability
- » Audiovisual equipment needs & Wi-Fi access
- » Master accounts (billing and credit arrangements)
- » Deposit arrangements
- » Service gratuities
- » Cancellation and termination policy
- » Change of ownership/management policy
- » Americans with Disabilities Act (ADA) compliance

>> Safety and security issues

>> Insurance issues

>> Facility construction/renovation

Trade Show Budgeting Checklist

Trade shows are a terrific way to enhance your company's promotional efforts. See the chapters in Part 5 for details about exhibiting at trade shows, and keep the following checklist on hand as you prepare your trade show budget.

Expense	Estimated Cost $	Actual Cost $
1. Space		
Booth		
Hotel suite		
2. Exhibit Display		
Design & construction		
Graphics refurbishing		
Products for display		
Booth rental		
Used booth purchase		
Literature holders		
Easels		
Tool kit		
Lighting fixtures		
3. Booth Furnishings		
Tables		
Chairs		
Garbage cans		
Carpeting		
Floral arrangements		

Expense	Estimated Cost $	Actual Cost $
Computer rental		
Credit card processing		
Audiovisual equipment rental		
4. Show Services		
Setup/teardown labor		
Electricity		
Water, gas		
Booth cleaning		
Photography		
Security		
Overnight services		
5. Shipping and Storage		
Freight		
Drayage (moving your booth containers from the dock to the show floor and storing the containers for repackaging)		
Exhibit storage		
Insurance		
6. Advertising and Promotion		
Preshow promotion		
On-site promotion		
Postshow promotion		
Direct mail		
Public relations activities		
Premiums		
Special show literature		
Telemarketing activity		

Expense	Estimated Cost $	Actual Cost $
7. Personnel		
Travel expenses		
Hotel accommodations		
Show registrations		
Meals		
Out-of-pocket expenses		
Special uniforms		
Special activities		
Guest entertainment		
Receptions		
Sales meetings		
Speaker expenses		
Presenters/live talent		
Training expenses		
8. Hospitality		
Meeting room		
Food/drink		
Gifts		
Audiovisual equipment rental		
Other		
Total Show Budget		

Exhibitor Toolkit Checklist

In addition to a solid budget, a successful trade show exhibitor comes prepared with the tools to do the job right. Technology has made your toolkit much lighter since most of what used to be printed is now digitally rendered.

However, remember to bring a hardcopy of your *event documents* as well as keep a digital copy for universal access. Keep this list on hand as you prepare to strut your company's stuff, and turn to the chapters in Part 5 for more information.

Office supplies

- Lead collection protocol
- Order forms and contracts
- Price lists
- Business cards
- Computer and necessary cables/wires
- Printer with cables and ink
- Ballpoint and marker pens, pencils and erasers
- Clipboards and digital tablets
- Staplers, staples, and staple remover, paper clips
- Scissors and pocket knife
- Calendar/appointment book
- Tape (duct, masking, transparent, double-sided)
- Cleaning supplies
- Rubber bands and string
- Keys or combination lock numbers
- Sticky notes
- Calculator
- Flashlight, beyond the one on your phone

Specific show items

- Exhibitor kit, contract, and order forms
- Supplier phone and fax numbers
- Exhibit furnishings not rented, such as trash cans, floral arrangements
- Setup tools

- >> Bill of lading
- >> Copies of submitted advance orders
- >> Company/product literature/specification sheets
- >> QR codes or URLs to collateral
- >> Links for press releases and press kits
- >> Giveaways and other promotional items, contest prizes
- >> Extra uniform items, such as ties, scarves, sweaters
- >> List of all staff members and mobile phone numbers
- >> Exhibit duty schedule
- >> List of invited guests for hospitality functions

General items

- >> Airline/travel tickets
- >> Credit cards and cash for on-site payments
- >> Hotel and rental car confirmation numbers and phone numbers
- >> First-aid kit
- >> Sewing kit with safety pins
- >> Computer, tablet, and mobile phone, with their necessary chargers and relevant preloaded apps

Post-Event Evaluation Checklist

The book isn't closed on any meeting or event until you take some time to consider what worked, what didn't, and what you can do better the next time. Use the following questions as you evaluate your planning performance.

- >> Overall, how did we perform in relation to our goals?
- >> What could we do differently to improve our performance the next time we plan an event?
- >> What were our major challenges?

>> What happened that we did not expect, or for which we were unprepared?

>> In what areas do we need more preparation?

>> What areas do we need to address with facility management?

>> Should we use this facility again? If no, why?

>> How effective was our programming?

>> What changes could be made to improve our program for future events?

>> Which of our presenters got the best evaluations and the most attention? The worst evaluations?

>> How effective was our message/theme?

>> How satisfactory were our transportation arrangements?

>> How satisfactory were the food and beverage arrangements?

>> How effective was our event marketing?

>> How did our staff perform?

>> What changes, if any, need to be made for the next event?

Index

A

AC (air conditioning), 40, 107, 130

accessibility considerations, 36–39

  checklist, 296–297

  hard-of-hearing participants, 37, 87

  transportation, 87

accidents, 61–62, 160

ACT (attrition, cancellation, termination) clauses, 157

active participation, 58

ADA. *See* Americans with Disabilities Act

advertising

  exhibiting and

    choosing tools, 244–248

    giveaways, 248

    marketing collateral, 248–249

    memorable messaging, 244

    overview, 242

    promotional plan, 243–244

    sponsorships, 180, 247

    virtual trade shows, 247–248

  fees, 173, 177–178, 224

after-action report, 204

agendas, 9, 19

  board of directors meeting, 20

  conference calling and, 203

  planning, 27–28

  sample, 29

agreements

  areas to negotiate, 154–155

  billing errors, 158

  cancellation policies, 119–121, 157, 160

  catering arrangements, 103–107

  checklist, 300–301

  clarifying costs, 62

  cost-cutting tips, 180

  drafting and signing, 156–158

  entertainment, 77

  general rules, 153–154

  liability and insurance, 159–160

  potential pitfalls, 277–280

  requesting perks, 151, 155–156

  RFPs, 148–151

  risk management, 158–159

  safety/security, 158–159

  speaker selection, 119–121

  vendors

    catering, 103–107

    tips for success, 281–284

    vendor list, 152–153

air conditioning (AC), 40, 107, 130

air travel, 107

  airport shuttles, 85–86, 181

  nonstop versus direct flights, 85

  travel arrangements

    booking tickets, 83–84

    online purchase, 84

    ticket classes, 82

  working with travel agents, 85

airport billboards, 246

aisle microphones, 136

alcohol, 72, 100–102

  budget, 182–183

  cost-cutting tips, 182–183

  liability issues and, 61–62, 102

  special events and, 47

allergies, food, 95, 97, 103

ambiance

  décor, 41, 71–74

  preparations, 39–43

American Society of Travel Agents (ASTA), 89

American Speakers Bureau, 119

Americans with Disabilities Act (ADA), 37–38

  compliance checklist, 294

  venue considerations, 67

American-style food service, 105, 295

amusement parks, 125

announcements, 18–19

annual events, 59

annual general meetings

  invitations, 18

  order of business rules, 19–20

  sending announcements, 18–19

annual reports, 19, 20

application sharing, 210

apps, 61, 226, 258

archiving, 211

art galleries, 125

ARTA (Association of Retail Travel Agents), 89

Asana, 275

ASCAP, 139

assistive devices, 37, 296

association newsletters, 246

Association of Retail Travel Agents (ARTA), 89

ASTA (American Society of Travel Agents), 89

ATA Carnet, 287

attention spans, 14

attorneys, 18, 156

attrition, cancellation, termination (ACT) clauses, 157

audience, 13, 70, 94–95, 112

audience response systems, 190–191

audiovisual (AV) presentations

  checklist, 297–298

  cost-cutting tips, 181

  lighting, 42, 130, 139–140, 217

  microphones, 135–136, 137

  outsourcing, 60, 169–170

  projection screens, 136–137

  projectors

    compact LCD, 35, 138, 298

    overview, 138–139, 193–194

  special presentation situations

    Q&A sessions, 9, 142–143

    scripted speeches, 141–142

    team presentations, 140–141

  tips for creating, 214–215

  types of, 110–111

  venue considerations, 61–62

auditory impairments, 37, 87, 296–297

awards recognition functions, 50–51, 69, 98–99, 294–295

B

balloting, 23

banquet event order (BEO), 105–107

banquets, 69, 99–100, 294–296

bartenders, 62, 101–102

Basecamp, 275

bathrooms, 63

BEO (banquet event order), 105–107

beverages

  alcohol

    cost-cutting tips, 182–183

    liability issues, 61–62, 102

    overview, 72, 100–102

    special events, 47

  banquets, 99–100

  breakfast meetings, 96–97

  brunch meetings, 97

  catering

    catering manager, 102–105

    contracts, 103–107

    overview, 36

  checklist, 295, 296

  cost considerations, 9, 94

  dinner events

    checklist, 294–295

    overview, 50–51, 98–99

  lunchtime meetings, 31, 98

  manners, 124

  parties, 99, 100

  receptions, 99

  refreshment breaks, 14, 36, 97–98

  timing, 95–96

  understanding audience, 94–95

  venue considerations, 94

Big Marker, 227

billboards, 246

billing errors, 158

blind participants, 38, 87, 296–297

BMI, 139

board of directors meeting, 20

booking tickets, 82–84

booth sales, 177

boutique lodgings, 64

Braille, 38, 297

brainstorming exercises, 26, 43, 275–276
brand awareness, 47
breakfast meetings, 96–97, 294–295
breakout sessions, 22, 68
breaks, refreshment, 14, 36, 97–98, 103–104
bridgeline, 198
brunch meetings, 97, 294–295
budgets, 9, 171–183
  checklist, 301–303
  cost-cutting tips
    alcohol expenses, 182–183
    contracts/agreements, 180
    economic travel, 181
    meals, 182
    venues, 179
  financial goals, 177–178
  food and beverages, 94, 181, 182
  insurance policies, 174
  potential pitfalls, 280
  preparing
    categorizing, 173–174
    cost control, 174–175
    help, 175–176
    items to include, 172–173
    overview, 172
  revenue, 172–174
  shows, 234, 235, 238
  signage, 174, 177–178
  sponsorships, 100, 173, 177–178, 180
  transportation/travel, 174, 181
buffet-style food service, 94, 105, 181, 182, 295
business class tickets, 82
butler-style food service, 105, 295

C

can lights, 217
cancellation policies, 119–121, 157, 160
Canva software, 36
case studies, 69
cash bars, 101, 182, 295
catering/catering manager (CM), 36, 165–166
  contracts/agreements, 103–107
  food and beverage checklist, 294–296
  guaranteed numbers, 97, 105–106, 158, 166
  overview, 102–103

celebrity speakers, 114, 119
Certified Speaking Professional (CSP), 113
charitable activities, 40, 51
chauffeured vehicles, 86
CheapTickets, 84
cheat sheet, 4
checklists
  accessibility considerations, 296–297
  AV equipment, 297–298
  beverages, 295, 296
  contracts/agreements, 300–301
  evaluation, 43, 261–262, 305–306
  exhibit toolkit, 238–239, 303–305
  food, 294–296
  miscellaneous, 294
  policies, 293
  RFPs, 299–300
  services, 294
  smaller meetings, 43, 291–292
  stage setup, 297, 298–299
  trade show budgeting, 301–302
  transportation, 293
  venues, 67, 292–294, 297–298
children, 46–47
classroom-style seating arrangement, 132
cleanup sessions, 43, 62, 166
clinics, 69
clubs, 8
clutter, 43
CM. See catering/catering manager
CMP (complete meeting package), 103
coach tickets, 82
cocktail parties, 58, 72
collaborative whiteboards, 228
collateral material, 248–249
comedians, 75, 99, 110–111
community leaders, 13
compact liquid crystal display (LCD) projectors, 35, 138, 298
competitors, 267–270
complete meeting package (CMP), 103
compliance checklist, 294
CompuSystems CompuLead app, 258
computers, 36
concurrent sessions, 22, 68

conference calling, 188–189, 197–206
  board of directors meeting, 20
  etiquette, 198, 205–206
  service options, 199–201
  tips, 198, 202–205
conferences, 15, 22, 65
conference-style seating arrangement, 132
conflict management, 21
consumer shows. *See* exhibiting at trade shows
contracts, 147–160
  areas to negotiate, 154–155
  billing errors, 158
  cancellation policies, 119–121, 157, 160
  checklist, 300–301
  clarifying costs, 62
  cost-cutting tips, 180
  drafting and signing, 156–158
  entertainment, 77
  general rules, 153–154
  liability and insurance, 159–160
  potential pitfalls, 277–280
  requesting perks, 151, 155–156
  RFPs, 148–151
  risk management, 158–159
  safety/security, 158–159
  speaker selection, 119–121
  vendors
    catering, 103–107
    tips for success, 281–284
    vendor list, 152–153
Convention and Visitors Bureau (CVB), 64, 65
  budget assistance, 176
  chauffeured vehicles, 86
  hotel visits, 179
  local activities listing, 125
  outsourcing information, 118, 168
convention centers, 65
cooling, 40, 107, 130
copyrights, 139
corded microphones, 35–36, 137, 298
corkage fee, 102, 183
corporate bylaws, 18
corporate retreats, 21, 64, 66

cost-cutting tips
  alcohol expenses, 182–183
  conference calling
    etiquette, 198, 205–206
    overview, 197–198
    service options, 199–201
    tips, 198, 202–205
  economic travel, 181
  meals, 94, 181, 182
  potential pitfalls, 280
  venues, 179
  virtual events
    options, 226–227
    overview, 223–224
    tips, 227–230
    types of, 225–226
  written agreements, 180
Council of Peers Award for Excellence (CPAE), 113
courtesy. *See* etiquette
crescent seating arrangement, 132
cruise meetings, 65, 66
CSP (Certified Speaking Professional), 113
customer relationship management (CRM) system, 259–260
customers, 13
customs, 287
CVB. *See* Convention and Visitors Bureau
Cvent, 64
  Lead Capture app, 258
  outsourcing information, 167, 168
  RFP solutions program, 149
  virtual events via, 227

D

dead stock, 183
deaf participants, 37, 87, 296–297
decision-making meetings, 8, 12, 26
décor, 41, 71–74
demo videos, 113, 118
demonstrations, 69
desktop videoconferencing, 211–212
destination events, 21, 46–47
destination management companies (DMCs), 64, 128, 167–168, 176

destination marketing organization (DMO), 65

Destinations International, 168

dietary restrictions, 36, 94–95, 98, 99, 103, 288

digital balloting, 23

digital deliverables, 228–229

digital light processing (DLP), 138

digital press kit, 48, 246–247

digital replay sales, 178

dinner events, 50–51, 98–99, 294–295

direct costs, 9

direct flights, 85

direct mail marketing, 245

disabled participants, 36–37

  accessibility considerations checklist, 296–297

  ADA compliance and, 37–38, 67, 294

  hard-of-hearing participants, 37, 87

  mobility impairment, 38–39, 87

  transportation, 87

  visual impairment, 38, 87

disc jockeys (DJs), 75, 76, 77, 99

discussion topics, 9

dishware, 166

distractions, 12, 37, 40–41, 130

DLP (digital light processing), 138

DMCs (destination management companies), 64, 128, 167–168, 176

DMO (destination marketing organization), 65

document sharing, 195, 211

dress and grooming, 216, 266, 267

drinks, 72, 100–102

  budget, 182–183

  cost-cutting tips, 182–183

  liability issues and, 61–62, 102

  special events and, 47

Duo app, 226

duration of meetings, 9, 14, 28, 31

E

Eagles Talent Connection, 119

economy tickets, 82

educational speakers, 110

effective communication training, 21

elections, 23

electronic message boards, 246

electronic whiteboards, 191–192, 228

e-mails, 8, 274, 275

emergencies, 41

employee appreciation event, 50–51, 69, 98–99, 294–295

employee's liability insurance, 160

entertainment

  events, 71–72, 75–77

  exhibiting and, 264–265

  music, 139

  nonappearance insurance, 160

  speakers, 110–111

equipment, 34–36, 59–61

  audience response systems, 190–191

  checklist, 297–298

  electronic whiteboards, 191–192

  insurance, 160

  laser pointers, 192, 298

  lighting, 42, 130, 139–140, 217

  microphones

    checklist, 298

    overview, 35–36, 135–136, 137

  projection screens, 136–137

  projectors

    compact LCD, 35, 138, 298

    overview, 138–139, 193–194

etiquette

  conference calling, 198, 205–206

  exhibiting and

    listening, 254

    overview, 266, 267

  food and beverage, 124

  overseas shows, 288

  table, 124

European fairs, 286–289

evaluations, 43, 261–262, 305–306

event management software, 133

events, 1–4, 57–58. See also room setup

  ambiance, 41, 71–74

  AV presentations

    checklist, 297–298

    compact LCD, 35, 138, 298

    cost-cutting tips, 181

    lighting, 42, 130, 139–140, 217

    live presentations, 264–265

    microphones, 135–136, 137

    outsourcing, 60, 169–170

events *(continued)*
  overview, 135
  projection screens, 136–137
  projectors, 138–139, 193–194
  scripted speeches, 141–142
  special presentation situations, 140–143
  tips for creating, 214–215
  types, 110–111
  venue considerations, 61–62
choosing venues
  bathroom considerations, 63
  indoor events, 61–63
  other options, 64–67
  outside events, 60–61
  overview, 59–60
  parking, 60, 61, 63, 67
  virtual tours, 69
cleanup sessions
  outsourcing, 166
  overview, 43
  venue considerations, 62
determining if needed
  audience, 13
  outsourcing, 15
  overview, 7–9
  participants/size, 11–13, 30–31
  purpose of meeting, 9–11
  setting, 15
  timing, 9, 14, 28, 31
entertainment, 71–72, 75–77
extra touches
  exercise/sporting options, 126–127
  finding restaurants, 123–125
  overview, 123
  travel guides, 125–126
  welcoming family members, 127–128
hybrid
  moderators, 222
  overview, 1–4, 226
  stage setup considerations, 134–135, 297, 298–299
meetings versus, 8
photography, 74
potential pitfalls, 215, 277–280
program planning, 68–70
scheduling, 58–59, 277
special events

awards recognition functions, 50–51, 69, 98–99
charitable activities, 40, 51
checklist, 294–295
destination events, 46–47
media events/visits, 47–49
overview, 45, 177
participant families, 46–47
product launches, 51–55
themes, 72–74, 99, 100
understanding audience, 13, 70, 94–95, 112
virtual, 227–230
  hybrid conferences, 226
  options, 226–227
  overview, 223
  understanding, 224
  video calls, 225
  video conferences, 225
  webinars, 225–226
ExecuCar, 86
exercise options, 126–127
exhibiting at trade shows, 233–270
  booth sales, 177
  checklists, 301–303
  dealing with competition, 267–270
  entertainment options, 264–265
  fees, 173
  hospitality suites, 265–266
  insurance, 160
  leads
    follow-up system, 259–260
    listening, 254
    managing, 258–259
    measuring results, 261–262
    qualifying prospects, 255–256, 263–264
    quantifying, 258–259
  overseas, 285–289
  planning
    budget, 238
    checklist, 238–239, 303–305
    choosing right show, 234–235
    determining space and display needs, 239–241
    exhibitor manual/show service kit, 238–239, 303–305
    marketing plan, 235–238
    other details, 241–242
    potential pitfalls, 277–280

promoting
  choosing tools, 244–248
  collateral material, 248–249
  defining plan, 243–244
  giveaways, 248
  memorable messaging, 244
  overview, 242
sponsorships and, 247
staff selection
  creating strong presence, 254–256
  ensuring productive show, 258–260
  hospitality suites, 265–266
  keeping motivated, 256–257
  measuring results, 261–262
  overview, 251–253
  PEOPLE formula, 252
  preparations, 253–254
  qualifying prospects, 255–256
uniforms, 266, 267
EXHIBITOR Magazine, 238
exhibitor manual, 238–239
Expedia, 84
expenses. See also cost-cutting tips
  inclusion in budget, 172–174
  reducing, 180–183
expositions
extra fees, 173
extra touches
  exercise/sporting options, 126–127
  finding restaurants, 123–125
  travel guides, 125–126
  welcoming family members, 127–128
extraordinary general meetings, 18

F

Facetime, 226
facials, 46
facilitation, 9
facility rental, 9, 14, 59–60. See also room setup
  ADA compliance, 37–38, 67, 294
  AV presentations
    checklist, 297–298
    cost-cutting tips, 181
    lighting, 130, 139–140
    live presentations, 264–265

microphones, 135–136, 137
  outsourcing, 60, 169–170
  overview, 135
  projection screens, 136–137
  projectors, 138–139
  scripted speeches, 141–142
  special presentation situations, 140–143
  venue considerations, 61–62
bathroom considerations, 63
checklist, 67
conference centers, 65
contracts/agreements
  overview, 62
  requesting perks, 151, 155–156
convention centers, 65
cost-cutting tips, 179
cruise ships, 66
food and beverage considerations, 94
hotels, 64
indoor events, 61–63
outside events, 60–61
parking, 60, 61, 63, 67
potential pitfalls, 277–280
references, 67, 75–76
resorts, 66
retreat centers, 66
selecting, 292–294
unique environments, 66
virtual tours, 69
visiting, 66–67, 278
families, 8, 13
  destination events and, 46–47
  welcoming, 127–128
FAQs (frequently asked questions), 275
fees
  advertising, 173, 177–178, 224
  corkage, 102, 183
  speakers, 119–121
financial considerations, 9
  budget preparation
    categorizing, 173–174
    cost control, 174–175
    help, 175–176
    items to include, 172–173
    overview, 172

financial considerations *(continued)*
  checklist, 301–303
  cost-cutting tips
    alcohol expenses, 182–183
    contracts/agreements, 180
    economic travel, 181
    meals, 182
    venues, 179
  food and beverages, 94, 181, 182
  goals, 177–178
  insurance policies, 174
  potential pitfalls, 280
  revenue, 172–174
  shows, 234, 235, 238
  signage, 174, 177–178
  sponsorships, 100, 173, 177–178, 180
  transportation/travel, 174, 181
fire alarms, 41
fire insurance, 160
first class tickets, 82
first-tier cities, 65
fixed expenses, 172–174
flip charts, 35, 298
Flitestats, 85
florists, 167
Fodor's guides, 123–124
food, 36, 72
  banquets, 99–100
  breakfast meetings, 96–97
  brunch meetings, 97
  catering
    catering manager, 102–105, 165–166
    contracts/agreements, 103–107
    overview, 36, 94
  checklist, 294–296
  cost considerations, 9, 94, 181, 182
  dietary restrictions, 36, 94–95, 98–99, 103, 288
  dinner events, 50–51, 98–99
  lunchtime meetings, 31, 98
  manners, 124
  parties, 99, 100
  receptions, 99
  refreshment breaks, 14, 36, 97–98
  service styles, 94, 105, 181, 182, 295

  timing, 95–96
  understanding audience, 94–95
food allergies, 95, 97, 103
force majeure clause, 157
formal dinners/events, 58, 59–60
FreeConferenceCall, 198
French-style food service, 105, 295
frequently asked questions (FAQs), 275
Frommer's guides, 123–124

G

gala events, 69, 99–100
games, 43, 75, 193–194, 274
Gameshow Pro software, 193
general liability insurance, 160
general public, 22
general sessions, 21, 68, 139
Giggster, 64, 73
giveaways, 168, 248
glassware, 166
Gold Stars Speakers Bureau, 119
Google Maps app, 61
Google Meet, 189, 198, 226
gourmet dining, 125
governments, 8
grants, 177–178
gratuities, 62, 67
grooming, 216, 266, 267
ground transportation
  airport shuttles, 85–86, 181
  chauffeured vehicles, 86
  contract agreements, 119–121
  cost-cutting tips, 181
  inclusion in budget, 174
  outsourcing, 169
  rental cars, 87–88
  special needs participants, 87
guaranteed numbers, 97, 105–106, 158, 166
guide dogs, 38

H

habitual meetings, 10–11
handheld microphones, 35–36, 136, 137, 298

handicapped participants, 36–37
 accessibility considerations checklist, 296–297
 ADA compliance and, 37–38, 67, 294
 hard-of-hearing participants, 37, 87
 mobility impairment, 38, 87
 transportation, 87
 visual impairment, 38, 87
hard-of-hearing participants, 37, 87, 296–297
Harry Walker Agency, 119
heating, ventilating, and air conditioning (HVAC) system, 40, 107, 130
help. *See* outsourcing
hidden expenses, 172–174
Hilton, 182–183
hired talent, 75–76
historical landmarks, 125
holidays, 59, 179, 277
hollow-square seating arrangement, 132
home-based businesses, 8
hors d'oeuvres, 99
hospitality suites, 265–266, 288
host and liquor liability, 160
hosted bars, 101–102
hotels
 accessibility checklist, 296–297
 ADA compliance, 37–38, 67, 294
 contracts/agreements
  ACT clauses, 157
  areas to negotiate, 154–155
  billing errors, 158
  drafting and signing, 156–158
  general rules, 153–154
  liability and insurance, 159–160
  overview, 147
  potential pitfalls, 277–280
  requesting perks, 151, 155–156
  RFPs, 148–151
  safety/security, 158–159
  vendor list, 152–153
 cost-cutting tips, 179
 luxury hotels, 64
 service demands, 90–92
Hotwire, 84
humorists, 110–111
HVAC (heating, ventilating, and air conditioning) system, 40, 107, 130

Hyatt, 182–183
hybrid events, 1–4, 134–135, 222, 226, 297–299
hybrid meetings, 207–208, 222
 advantages/disadvantages, 208–209
 determining needs, 209–210
hypnotists, 110

I

icons, 3–4
IDEAS promotion, 243–244
IHG, 182–183
impromptu meetings, 24
incentive events, 22
independent contractor liability, 160
independent parking garages, 63
independently owned properties, 64
indirect expenses, 172–174
indirect lighting, 217
indoor events, 61–63
industry/trade publications, 176
informal events, 60
in-kind donations, 13, 177–178
 budget concerns and, 100, 180
 exhibiting and, 247
 inclusion in budget, 173
innovating meetings, 8
in-person events, 1–4
inspirational speakers, 110
insurance policies
 accidents/liability, 61–62, 160
 checklist, 293
 contracts/agreements, 159–160
 inclusion in budget, 174
 nonappearance insurance, 160
interactive chat, 211
International Association of Conference Centers, 65
International Association of Speakers Bureaus, 119
international calls, 198
International Caterers Association, 162
international shows, 234, 285–289
Internet travel sites, 84
interpreting services, 37, 288–289
interviewing, 162–164
invitations, 11–12, 18, 30–31, 244–245

J

jugglers, 75

K

Kahoot! software, 193
Kayak, 84
key customers, 243
key employees, 13
keynote speakers, 21, 34, 110, 139

L

labs, 69
Land's End-Business, 168
lapel microphones, 35–36, 136, 137, 298
laptop computer, 36
larger events, 57–58
laser pointers, 192, 298
lavalier microphones, 35–36, 136, 137, 298
lawyers, 18, 156
LCD (liquid crystal display) projector, 35, 138, 298
leadership development skills, 21
leads
  exhibiting, 263–264
  follow-up system, 259–260
  listening to, 254
  measuring results, 261–262
  qualifying
    managing, 258–259
    overview, 255–256, 263–264
lecterns, 35, 135–136, 137
LED (light emitting diode), 138
LegalShield, 157
length of meetings, 9, 14, 28, 31
liability issues
  alcohol and, 61–62, 102
  contracts/agreements, 159–160
  insurance policies and, 61–62
licensing, 139, 166
light emitting diode (LED), 138
lighting, 42, 130, 139–140
  checklist, 297
  online meetings, 217
limousines, 87

liquid crystal display (LCD) projector, 35, 138, 298
liquor, 72, 100–102
  budget, 182–183
  cost-cutting tips, 182–183
  liability issues and, 61–62, 102
  special events and, 47
listening skills, 254, 283
live marketing, 240
live presentations, 264–265
local dignitaries, 13
local media, 13
local off-site meeting spaces, 32–33
local shows, 235
location/setting, 32–33. See also venues
lodgings, 64
  accessibility checklist, 296–297
  ADA compliance, 37–38, 67, 294
  contracts/agreements
    ACT clauses, 157
    areas to negotiate, 154–155
    billing errors, 158
    drafting and signing, 156–158
    general rules, 153–154
    liability and insurance, 159–160
    overview, 147
    potential pitfalls, 277–280
    requesting perks, 151, 155–156
    RFPs, 148–151
    safety/security, 158–159
    vendor list, 152–153
  cost considerations, 9, 179
  service demands, 90–92
logo merchandise, 74
long meetings, 14
lunchtime meetings, 31, 98, 294–295
luxury hotels, 64. See also hotels

M

magicians, 53, 71, 75, 110
mall shows. See exhibiting at trade shows
manners
  conference calling, 198, 205–206
  exhibiting and, 254, 266, 267
  meals, 124
  overseas shows, 288

maps, 61

marketing. *See also* advertising
- exhibits, 301–303
- failing to do, 278
- live marketing, 246
- potential pitfalls, 277–280
- trade shows, 235–238

marketing collateral, 248–249

Marriott, 182–183

massages, 46

master accounts, 175

master classes, 69

meals, 36, 72
- banquets, 99–100
- breakfast meetings, 96–97
- brunch meetings, 97
- catering
  - catering manager, 102–105, 165–166
  - contracts/agreements, 103–107
  - overview, 36, 94
- checklist, 294–295
- cost considerations, 9, 94, 181, 182
- dietary restrictions, 36, 94–95, 98–99, 103, 288
- dinner events, 50–51, 98–99
- lunchtime meetings, 31, 98
- manners, 124
- parties, 99, 100
- receptions, 99
- refreshment breaks, 14, 36, 97–98
- service styles, 94, 105, 181, 182, 295
- timing, 95–96
- understanding audience, 94–95

media events/visits, 36, 47–49, 245, 246

medical insurance, 160

meetings, 1–4, 8. *See also* room setup; video conferencing
- agenda
  - board of directors meeting, 20
  - conference calling and, 203
  - overview, 9, 19
  - planning, 27–28
  - sample, 29
- alternative to
  - audience response systems, 190–191
  - electronic whiteboards, 191–192
  - laser pointers, 192, 298
  - online conferencing, 189–190, 225–226
  - overview, 187, 273–276
  - selection considerations, 194–195
  - television-style game show elements, 193–194

AV presentations
- checklist, 297–298
- cost-cutting tips, 181
- lighting, 130, 139–140
- live presentations, 264–265
- microphones, 135–136, 137
- outsourcing, 60, 169–170
- overview, 135
- projection screens, 136–137
- projectors, 35, 138–139, 193–194
- scripted speeches, 141–142
- special presentation situations, 140–143
- tips for creating, 214–215
- types, 110–111
- venue considerations, 61–62

cleanup sessions
- outsourcing, 166
- overview, 43
- venue considerations, 62

conference calling
- agenda and, 203
- board of directors meeting, 20
- etiquette, 198, 205–206
- overview, 188–189, 197–198
- service options, 199–201
- tips, 198, 202–205

determining if needed
- audience, 13
- avoiding habitual meetings, 10–11
- effective meetings, 9
- outsourcing, 15
- overview, 7–9
- participants/size, 11–13, 30–31
- purpose of meeting, 9–11
- reasons for holding, 9–10
- setting, 15
- timing, 9, 14, 28, 31

events versus, 8

extra touches
- exercise/sporting options, 126–127
- finding restaurants, 123–125
- overview, 123

meetings *(continued)*
>   travel guides, 125–126
>   welcoming family members, 127–128
>   hybrid
>>   advantages/disadvantages, 208–209
>>   determining needs, 209–210
>>   moderators, 222
>>   overview, 207–208
>   keeping minutes, 43
>   planning
>>   distractions, 12, 37, 40–41, 130
>>   invitations, 11–12, 18, 30–31
>>   lighting, 42
>>   overview, 25–26
>>   performance tips, 42
>>   potential pitfalls, 215, 277–279
>>   purpose of meeting and, 26–27
>>   refreshments, 14, 36, 97–98
>>   setting/location, 32–33
>>   smaller details, 43, 291–292
>>   special needs participants, 36–39
>>   specific materials/equipment, 34–36
>>   temperature, 40, 107, 130
>>   uninvited guests, 40–41
>   small, 43, 291–292
>   understanding audience, 13, 70, 94–95, 112
merchandise, 74, 178
Michelin guides, 124
microphones, 35–36, 135–137, 298
Microsoft Teams, 275
mimes, 75, 110
mimio whiteboard software, 192
minutes, keeping, 43
mobile phones, 40
mobility-impaired participants, 38–39, 87, 296–297
moderators, 69, 143, 222
monitors, 217
monthly meetings, 14
Most Valued Booth Staff Person (MVBSP) award, 257
motels, 38, 90–92
motivational meetings, 22–23
motivational speakers, 110
MOV software, 36
museums, 66, 126
music/musicians, 71, 75, 99, 110, 139
MVBSP (Most Valued Booth Staff Person) award, 257

N

name cards, 43
napkins, 166
National Association of Catering Executives, 162
National Association of the Deaf, 37
National Federation for the Blind, 38
National Park Service, 125
national shows, 234
National Speakers Association, 113, 119, 162
nature preserves, 126
negotiations. *See also* contracts
>   areas to negotiate, 154–155
>   billing errors, 158
>   cost-cutting tips, 180
>   drafting and signing contracts, 156–158
>   general rules, 153–154
>   liability and insurance, 159–160
>   potential pitfalls, 277–280
>   requesting perks, 151, 155–156
>   RFPs, 148–151
>   safety and security, 158–159
>   tips for success, 281–284
>   vendor list, 152–153
networking sessions, 69
newsletters, 246
noise, 37, 40–41
nonappearance insurance, 160
nonstop flights, 85
Nxt Event, 167

O

office supplies, 304
off-site meeting spaces, 32, 33
online airline tickets, 84
online conferencing, 189–190, 225–226
online meetings
>   advantages/disadvantages, 208–209
>   choosing format, 210–212
>   determining needs, 209–210
>   hybrid, 209–210
>>   advantages/disadvantages, 208–209
>>   moderators, 222
>>   overview, 207–208
>   moderators, 222

promoting, 219–220

scripted speeches, 141–142

site facilitators, 210

special considerations, 220–222

tips for success

  connection speed, 215–216

  creating presentation, 214–215

  dress and grooming, 216

  early planning, 212–213

  final preparations, 213–214

  potential pitfalls, 215, 277–280

  room setup, 216–217

  running meeting, 217–219

  troubleshooting, 210, 215, 219–220

on-site catering, 36, 94

on-site meeting spaces, 32

on-site office insurance, 160

open bars, 101, 295

order of business rules, 19–20

out-of-town meeting space, 33

outside distractions, 41

outside events, 60–61

outsourcing, 15

  AV companies, 60, 169–170

  caterers, 165–166

  catering

    contracts/agreements, 103–107

    food and beverage checklist, 294–296

    guaranteed numbers, 97, 105–106, 158, 166

    licensing, 162, 166

    overview, 102–105, 165–166

    on-site, 36, 94

  corporate retreats, 21, 64, 66

  destination management companies, 167–168

  entertainment, 75–76

  florists, 167

  giveaways, 168

  ground transportation providers, 169

  negotiations

    areas to negotiate, 154–155

    billing errors, 158

    cost-cutting tips, 180

    drafting and signing, 156–158

    general rules, 153–154

    liability and insurance, 159–160

    overview, 147

    potential pitfalls, 277–280

    requesting perks, 151, 155–156

    RFPs, 148–151

    safety/security, 158–159

    tips for success, 281–284

    vendor list, 152–153

  overview, 162–165

  product launches, 53

  professional planners, 168–169

  promotional items, 168

  references

    overview, 162, 163–164, 294

    speakers, 112–113, 115–116

    venues, 67, 75–76

  searching for, 162–165

Ovation, 167

P

packing tips, 90

panel discussions, 31, 69

parking, 34, 60, 61, 63, 67

parks, 126

participants

  determining right number, 11–13, 30–31

  extra touches for

    exercise/sporting options, 126–127

    finding restaurants, 123–125

    overview, 123

    travel guides, 125–126

    welcoming family members, 127–128

  special needs

    auditory impairments, 37, 87

    checklist, 296–297

    mobility impairments, 38–39, 87

    overview, 36–37

    visual impairments, 38, 87

parties

  cocktail parties, 58, 72

  food and beverage considerations, 99, 294–296

  themes, 99, 100

passive participation, 58

passwords, 41

PEOPLE formula, 252

per diem expenses, 181

performance tips, 42

perks, 151, 155–156

personal growth, 21

personal invitations, 244–245

phone calls, 8, 274

  conference calling

    board of directors meeting, 20

    etiquette, 198, 205–206

    overview, 188–189, 197

    service options, 199–201

    tips, 198, 202–205

photography, 74

pitfalls, 215, 277–280

plenary sessions, 21

podiums, 35, 135–136, 137

policies

  cancellations, 119–121, 157, 160

  checklist, 293

  insurance

    accidents/liability, 61–62, 160

    inclusion in budget, 174

    nonappearance insurance, 160

    overview, 159–160

polling, 201, 211

portable bathrooms, 63

positivity, 12, 47, 203, 266, 283

poster sessions, 69

PowerPoint software, 35, 36, 214–215

PRA Nashville, 168

Preferred Group, 64

presentations

  AV needs

    compact LCD, 35, 138, 298

    cost-cutting tips, 181

    lighting, 130, 139–140

    microphones, 135–136, 137

    outsourcing, 60, 169–170

    overview, 135

    projection screens, 136–137

    projectors, 138–139, 193–194

    venue considerations, 61–62

  checklist, 297–298

  live, 264–265

  special situations

    Q&A sessions, 9, 142–143

    scripted speeches, 141–142

  team presentations, 140–141

  tips for creating, 214–215

  types of, 110–111

press release kits, 48, 246–247

Prezi software, 36

Priceline, 84

print marketing, 245, 246

private limousines, 87

product launches, 22, 51–55

productivity, 14, 275

professional planners, 168–169

professional speakers, 109

  scripted speeches, 141–142

  selecting

    asking/providing information, 115–116

    cautions, 114

    celebrity speakers, 114, 119

    contracts/agreements, 119–121

    fees, 119–121

    help for finding, 117–119

    maximizing opportunities, 116–117

    program objectives, 111

    speaker reputation, 112–113

    understanding audience, 112

    types of presentations, 110–111

program planning, 68–70, 246

projection screens, 136–137

projectors, 35, 138–139, 193–194, 298

promotional materials, 74, 168, 301–303

prospects

  exhibiting and, 263–264

  follow-up system, 259–260

  listening to, 254

  measuring results, 261–262

  promoting exhibit, 243

  qualifying

    managing, 258–259

    overview, 255–256, 263–264

proxies, 18

public meetings, 22

public relations, 245

publications, 246

Puck, Wolfgang, 125

Q

Q&A sessions, 9, 142–143
quarterly meetings, 14
QuizXpress software, 193
quorum rules, 18

R

rack rates, 179
radio advertising, 245, 246
real-time polling, 201, 211
receptions, 69, 99, 294–296
record locators, 83
recorded messages, 274
recording/rebroadcast, 201, 211
references
 pitfalls, 279
 RFPs, 148–149, 151
 vendors
  overview, 162, 163–164, 294
  speakers, 112–113, 115–116
  venues, 67, 75–76
refreshment breaks, 14, 36, 97–98, 103–104
regional shows, 234
registration fees, 173, 177
The Registry of Interpreters for the Deaf website, 37
religious holidays, 59, 277
rental cars, 87–88, 90–92
reports, 19, 20, 43, 204, 261–262, 305–306
request for proposals (RFPs), 162–164
 checklist, 299–300
 contract negotiations, 148–151
 references, 148–149, 151
 Wi-Fi connection, 150
resorts, 38, 64, 66
Resorts Online, 66
restaurants, 123–125
retreat centers, 21, 64, 66
revenues
 financial goals and, 177–178
 inclusion in budget, 172–174
RFPs. See request for proposals
ride-share services, 88
risk management, 158–159
Robert's Rules of Order (Robert), 19

Rocketlawyer, 18
room blocks, 179
room setup
 seating arrangements
  cost-cutting tips, 180
  events, 39–40
  food and beverage considerations, 106–107
  meetings, 130, 132–134
  online meetings, 216–217
 stage setup, 134–135, 297, 298–299
room-based videoconferencing, 211–212
roundtable discussions, 69, 117
Russian-style food service, 105, 295

S

safety, 158–159
sales, 8, 22–23
 handling leads, 263–264
  follow-up system, 259–260
  listening, 254
  measuring results, 261–262
  qualifying and managing, 255–256, 258–259, 263–264
salty foods, 182
scheduling, 58–59, 277
schools, 8
screens, 136–137
scripted speeches, 141–142
seating arrangements
 cost-cutting tips, 180
 events, 130, 132–134, 216–217
 food and beverage considerations, 106–107
 meetings, 39–40, 130, 132–134
second-tier cities, 65
secured phone lines, 201
security, 158–159
seminars, 22, 31, 110
service animals, 38
service demands, 90–92
services checklist, 294
setting/location. See venues
shareholders meetings, 17–18
 invitations, 18
 order of business rules, 19–20
 sending announcements, 18–19
shipping/freight charges, 173, 174

show programs, 246
show service kit, 238–239, 303–305
shuttles, 85–86, 181
sight lines, 130
sightseeing tours, 46, 126
Sign Language Associates, Inc, 37
signage
  cost-cutting tips, 181
  inclusion in budget, 174, 177–178
  outside events, 61
Silberstein, Diane T., 67, 292
silverware, 166
site facilitators, 210
size of meeting/event, 11–13, 30–31
slide shows, 75
smaller meetings, 43, 291–292
snacks, 14, 97–98
social media, 13, 22, 74, 245
SocialTables, 73
sound system, 298. See also equipment
souvenirs, 168, 248
spas, 46
speakers
  keynote, 21, 34, 110, 139
  nonappearance insurance, 160
  references, 112–113, 115–116
  scripted speeches, 141–142
  selecting
    asking/providing information, 115–116
    cautions, 114
    celebrity speakers, 114, 119
    contracts/agreements, 119–121
    fees, 119–121
    help for finding, 117–119
    maximizing opportunities, 116–117
    program objectives, 111
    speaker reputation, 112–113
    understanding audience, 112
  types of presentations, 110–111
Speakers Unlimited, 119
special board meetings, 20
special events, 45, 177
  awards recognition functions, 50–51, 69, 98–99
  charitable activities, 40, 51
  checklist, 294–295
  destination events, 46–47

media events/visits, 47–49
participant families and, 46–47
product launches, 51–55
special needs participants, 36–39, 87, 296–297
special presentation situations
  Q&A sessions, 9, 142–143
  scripted speeches, 141–142
  team presentations, 140–141
special shareholders meetings, 18
spectacles, 75
speeches
  scripted, 141–142
  venues and, 60
sponsorships, 13, 177–178
  exhibiting and, 247
  inclusion in budget, 100, 173, 180
sporting events, 59, 126–127, 273
spur-of-the-moment meetings, 24
staffing
  exhibiting at trade shows
    creating strong presence, 254–256
    ensuring productive, 258–260
    hospitality suites, 265–266
    keeping motivated, 256–257
    measuring results, 261–262
    overview, 251–253
    PEOPLE formula, 252
    preparations, 253–254
    qualifying and managing leads, 255–256, 258–259, 263–264
  wait staff
    cost-cutting tips, 182–183
    drinks, 100–102
    outsourcing, 164–166
    overview, 62, 295
stage setup, 134–135, 297, 298–299
standing microphones, 136
stands, 286–289
state laws, 18
state shows, 234
state-of-the-business address, 20
stockholders, 13
subconferencing, 200
Super Shuttle Express, 86
suppliers, 53, 148–151
surveys, 276

T

table linens, 166

table microphones, 136, 137

talent, 75–76

taxis, 88, 181

TDD machines (Telecommunications Devices for the Deaf), 37, 296

team building, 21

team presentations, 140–141

technology. *See also* conference calling; video conferencing

  audience response systems, 190–191

  board of directors meeting, 20

  electronic whiteboards, 191–192

  laser pointers, 192, 298

  online conferencing, 189–190, 225–226

  projectors

    compact LCD, 35, 138, 298

    overview, 138–139, 193–194

  selection considerations, 194–195

  television-style game show elements, 193–194

  virtual meetings, 188

Telecommunications Devices for the Deaf (TDD) machines, 37, 296

telecommuting, 8

teleconferencing, 188–189

  board of directors meeting, 20

  etiquette, 198, 205–206

  service options, 199–201

  tips, 198, 202–205

telemarketing, 245

telephone calls, 8, 274

  conference calling

    board of directors meeting, 20

    etiquette, 198, 205–206

    overview, 188–189, 197

    service options, 199–201

    tips, 198, 202–205

television advertising, 245, 246

television-style game show elements, 193–194

temperature, 40, 107, 130

termination clauses, 157

theaters, 58, 61, 66, 75

theater-style seating arrangement, 132

theme-logo merchandise, 74

themes, 72–74, 99, 100

ticket classes, 82

time poverty, 9

time-wasting activities, 8

timing

  events/meetings, 9, 14, 28, 31

  meals, 95–96

tipping, 62, 67

Toastmasters International, 119

trade shows

  booth sales, 177

  checklists, 301–303

  dealing with competition, 267–270

  entertainment options, 264–265

  fees, 173

  hospitality suites, 265–266

  insurance, 160

  leads

    follow-up system, 259–260

    listening, 254

    managing, 258–259

    measuring results, 261–262

    qualifying prospects, 255–256, 263–264

    quantifying, 258–259

  overseas, 285–289

  planning

    budget, 238

    checklist, 238–239, 303–305

    choosing right show, 234–235

    determining space and display needs, 239–241

    exhibitor manual/show service kit, 238–239, 303–305

    marketing plan, 235–238

    other details, 241–242

    potential pitfalls, 277–280

  promoting

    choosing tools, 244–248

    collateral material, 248–249

    defining plan, 243–244

    giveaways, 248

    memorable messaging, 244

    overview, 242

  sponsorships and, 247

  staff selection

    creating strong presence, 254–256

    ensuring productive show, 258–260

    hospitality suites, 265–266

trade shows *(continued)*
  keeping motivated, 256–257
  measuring results, 261–262
  overview, 251–253
  PEOPLE formula, 252
  preparations, 253–254
  qualifying prospects, 255–256
  uniforms, 266, 267
  websites, 246
trade/industry publications, 176, 246
trademarks, 139
traditional media, 245, 246
training meetings, 8
transit advertising, 246
translation services, 37, 288–289
Transportation Security Administration (TSA), 90
transport/travel arrangements, 9, 34, 81
  air travel
    booking tickets, 83–84
    nonstop versus direct flights, 85
    online purchase, 84
    ticket classes, 82
    travel agents, 85, 88–90
  checklist, 293
  considering service demands, 90–92
  contracts/agreements, 119–121
  corporate retreats and, 21
  cost-cutting tips, 181
  ground transportation
    airport shuttles, 85–86, 181
    chauffeured vehicles, 86
    outsourcing, 169
    rental cars, 87–88
    special needs participants, 87
  inclusion in budget, 174
  insurance, 61–62, 160
  packing tips, 90
  venue considerations, 67
travel agents, 85, 88–90
travel guides, 123–124, 125–126
Travelocity, 84
Trello, 275
TripAdvisor, 64, 124
troubleshooting, 210, 215, 219–220. *See also* pitfalls
TSA (Transportation Security Administration), 90

U

uniforms, 266, 267
uninvited guests, 40–41
unique environments, 65
upper management, 13
U.S. Congress, 21, 23
U.S. Council for International Business, 287
U.S. Department of Commerce International Trade Administration (USDC-ITA), 286
U.S. Securities and Exchange Commission, 18
U-shaped seating arrangement, 39, 132, 216–217

V

Validar vCapture app, 258
variable expenses, 172–174
vendors, 13
  catering
    contracts/agreements, 103–107
    food and beverages, 36, 294–296
    guaranteed numbers, 97, 105–106, 158, 166
    overview, 102–105, 165–166
    on-site, 36, 94
  interviewing, 162–164
  negotiations
    areas to negotiate, 154–155
    billing errors, 158
    cost-cutting tips, 180
    drafting and signing, 156–158
    general rules, 153–154
    liability and insurance, 159–160
    overview, 147
    potential pitfalls, 277–280
    requesting perks, 151, 155–156
    RFPs, 148–151
    safety/security, 158–159
    tips for success, 281–284
    vendor list, 152–153
  product launches, 53
  references
    overview, 162, 163–164, 294
    speakers, 112–113, 115–116
    venues, 67, 75–76
  RFPs, 148–151
  searching for, 162–165

types of
  AV companies, 60, 169–170
  destination management companies, 167–168
  florists, 167
  ground transportation providers, 169
  overview, 165
  professional planners, 168–169
  promotional items for, 168
  speakers, 112–113, 115–116
ventilation, 40, 107, 130
venues, 9, 14, 59–60. See also room setup
  ADA compliance, 37–38, 67, 294
  AV presentations
    checklist, 297–298
    cost-cutting tips, 181
    lighting, 130, 139–140
    live presentations, 264–265
    microphones, 135–136, 137
    outsourcing, 60, 169–170
    overview, 135
    projection screens, 136–137
    projectors, 138–139
    scripted speeches, 141–142
    special presentation situations, 140–143
    venue considerations, 61–62
  bathroom considerations, 63
  checklist, 67
  contracts/agreements
    overview, 62
    requesting perks, 151, 155–156
  cost-cutting tips, 179
  food and beverage considerations, 94
  indoor events, 61–63
  other options, 64–67
  outside events, 60–61
  parking, 60, 61, 63, 67
  potential pitfalls, 277–280
  references, 67, 75–76
  selecting, 292–294
  virtual tours, 69
  visiting, 66–67, 278
verbal agreements, 180. See also contracts
video conferencing, 20, 189, 207–208, 225
  advantages/disadvantages, 208–209
  board of directors meeting, 20
  determining needs, 209–210
  tips for success
    connection speed, 215–216
    creating presentation, 214–215
    dress and grooming, 216
    early planning, 212–213
    final preparations, 213–214
    potential pitfalls, 215, 277–280
    room control, 216–217
    running meeting, 217–219
    troubleshooting, 210, 215, 219–220
videos, 75
virtual events
  options, 226–227
  tips, 227–230
  types of, 225–226
  understanding, 224
virtual meetings. See also video conferencing
  audience response systems, 190–191
  conference calling, 188–189
  electronic whiteboards, 191–192
  laser pointers, 192
  online conferencing, 189–190, 225–226
  projectors, 138–139, 193–194
  selection considerations, 194–195
  television-style game show elements, 193–194
Virtual Private Network (VPN), 211
virtual summits, 224, 226
virtual tours, 69
virtual trade shows, 247–248
Vispronet, 238
Vistaprint, 168
visually-impaired participants, 38, 87, 296–297
viva voce, 23
voting, 20, 23
VPN (Virtual Private Network), 211
V-shaped seating arrangement, 132, 216–217

W

wait staff, 62, 295
  cost-cutting tips, 182–183
  drinks, 100–102
  outsourcing, 164–166
Washington Speakers Bureau, 119
web browser sharing, 211

web-based surveys, 43
web-conferencing, 20, 41
webinars, 189–190, 207–208, 225–226
  moderators, 222
  special considerations, 220–222
weekly meetings, 14
What3Words app, 61
wheelchair-accessibility, 38, 87, 296–297
whiteboards
  as alternative to meetings, 275–276
  collaborative, 228
  electronic, 191–192
Wi-Fi connection
  checklist, 294, 298, 300
  connection speed, 215–216
  exhibiting and, 241, 247
  RFPs, 150
Windows Media Video software, 36
wireless lavaliere microphones, 35–36, 136, 137, 298
worker's compensation, 160
workshops, 22, 69, 110
workshop-style seating arrangement, 132
Worldly, 198
written agreements, 180
  areas to negotiate, 154–155
  billing errors, 158
  cancellation policies, 119–121, 157, 160

catering arrangements, 103–107
checklist, 300–301
clarifying costs, 62
cost-cutting tips, 180
drafting and signing, 156–158
entertainment, 77
general rules, 153–154
liability and insurance, 159–160
potential pitfalls, 277–280
requesting perks, 151, 155–156
RFPs, 148–151
risk management, 158–159
safety/security, 158–159
speaker selection, 119–121
vendors
  catering, 103–107
  tips for success, 281–284
  vendor list, 152–153

Y

Yelp, 124
YouTube, 36

Z

Zoom, 189, 198, 226

About the Author

Susan Friedmann, CSP (Certified Speaking Professional), is a well-respected niche marketer on a mission to wipe out sameness and add vitality and differentiation to entrepreneurial marketing.

For over 30 years, she's traveled the world training and coaching small business owners on how to become a recognized trusted authority in their niche market. One of her tools for captivating a market is through well-executed events, in person and online. She's trained and coached over 10,000 people on four continents.

A prolific author, Susan is an international bestselling author of 18 books, many of which appear in multiple languages. She's frequently a guest expert on a variety of radio and TV talk shows and hosts the award-winning podcast Book Marketing Mentors. Her passion is working with non-fiction authors who want to share their message and value around the globe.

From being chased by an elephant to hugging a tiger, from teaching yoga to being rescued by the National Guard, enjoying three grandchildren, and traveling with her life partner of 52 years, she leads a full and exciting life.

Author's Acknowledgments

It is impossible to write a book without the help and support of so many people. I am deeply grateful to all my wonderful colleagues, friends, and helpful readers for your encouragement that inspired the tweaks and new material, which allowed me to expand on ideas even more in this new book!

However, there are a few extra special people whom I want to take the time to acknowledge. First, the amazing For Dummies team at Wiley allowed me the opportunity to revise and improve the material in this book after 20 years of successful sales. In particular, my thanks go to Elizabeth Stilwell, Acquisitions Editor, who helped make many changes possible. To Daniel Mersey and Vicki Adang, editors extraordinaire. Every author should have the privilege and luck to work with such talented individuals who know exactly how to make language zing.

When you write a book such as this, you need plenty of technical advice, which in my case came from Corbin Ball, CMP, a true legend and expert in the meetings industry. Thank you, Corbin for the exceptional job you did verifying the technical details.

An extra special thanks go to my excellent and extremely talented assistant, Jane Maulucci, who worked long and hard on this project. She never tired of me requesting more and more material to find just the right information to include. And most importantly, she kept me sane with her quirky humor and on track with her attention to detail. Jane, you're my lifesaver!

And finally, to my life partner of 52 years. Alec, you're my rock, cheerleader, and constant companion. I truly value your unending love and support in all my various ventures.

Publisher's Acknowledgments

Acquisitions Editor: Elizabeth Stilwell
Development Editor: Dan Mersey
Technical Editor: Corbin Ball

Managing Editor: Kelsey Baird
Production Editor: Saikarthick Kumarasamy
Cover Image: © Andrey_Popov/Shutterstock

Leverage the powe

Dummies is the global leader in the reference category and one of the most trusted and highly regarded brands in the world. No longer just focused on books, customers now have access to the dummies content they need in the format they want. Together we'll craft a solution that engages your customers, stands out from the competition, and helps you meet your goals.

Advertising & Sponsorships

Connect with an engaged audience on a powerful multimedia site, and position your message alongside expert how-to content. Dummies.com is a one-stop shop for free, online information and know-how curated by a team of experts.

- Targeted ads
- Video
- Email Marketing

- Microsites
- Sweepstakes sponsorship

20 MILLION PAGE VIEWS EVERY SINGLE MONTH

15 MILLION UNIQUE VISITORS PER MONTH

43% OF ALL VISITORS ACCESS THE SITE VIA THEIR MOBILE DEVICES

700,000 NEWSLETT SUBSCRIPTIO TO THE INBOXES OF *300,000* UNIQUE INDIVIDUALS EVERY WEEK

# of dummies

Custom Publishing

Reach a global audience in any language by creating a solution that will differentiate you from competitors, amplify your message, and encourage customers to make a buying decision.

- Apps
- Books
- eBooks
- Video
- Audio
- Webinars

Brand Licensing & Content

Leverage the strength of the world's most popular reference brand to reach new audiences and channels of distribution.

For more information, visit **dummies.com/biz**

 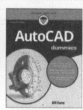 

Learning Made Easy

ACADEMIC

Algebra I *dummies*

Mary Jane Sterling

9781119293576
USA $19.99
CAN $23.99
UK £15.99

Basic Math & Pre-Algebra *dummies*

Mark Zegarelli

9781119293637
USA $19.99
CAN $23.99
UK £15.99

Calculus *dummies*

Mark Ryan

9781119293491
USA $19.99
CAN $23.99
UK £15.99

Chemistry *dummies*

John T. Moore, EdD

9781119293460
USA $19.99
CAN $23.99
UK £15.99

Physics I *dummies*

Steven Holzner, PhD

9781119293590
USA $19.99
CAN $23.99
UK £15.99

1,001 Practice Questions SAT *dummies*

Ron Woldoff

9781119215844
USA $26.99
CAN $31.99
UK £19.99

Organic Chemistry I *dummies*

Arthur Winter

9781119293378
USA $22.99
CAN $27.99
UK £16.99

Statistics *dummies*

Deborah J. Rumsey, PhD

9781119293521
USA $19.99
CAN $23.99
UK £15.99

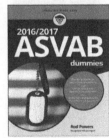

2016/2017 ASVAB *dummies*

Rod Powers

9781119239178
USA $18.99
CAN $22.99
UK £14.99

1,001 Practice Questions Praxis Core *dummies*

Carla Kirkland Chan Cleveland

9781119263883
USA $26.99
CAN $31.99
UK £19.99

Available Everywhere Books Are Sold

dummies.com

Small books for big imaginations

9781119177173
USA $9.99
CAN $9.99
UK £8.99

9781119177272
USA $9.99
CAN $9.99
UK £8.99

9781119177241
USA $9.99
CAN $9.99
UK £8.99

9781119177210
USA $9.99
CAN $9.99
UK £8.99

9781119262657
USA $9.99
CAN $9.99
UK £6.99

9781119291336
USA $9.99
CAN $9.99
UK £6.99

9781119233527
USA $9.99
CAN $9.99
UK £6.99

9781119291220
USA $9.99
CAN $9.99
UK £6.99

9781119177302
USA $9.99
CAN $9.99
UK £8.99

Unleash Their Creativity

dummies.com

dummies
A Wiley Brand